How the Computer Went to School

How the Computer Went to School

Australian Government Policies for Computers in Schools, 1983–2013

Denise Beale

MONASH University Publishing

Monash University Publishing
Building 4, Monash University
Clayton, Victoria 3800, Australia
www.publishing.monash.edu

Monash University Publishing brings to the world publications which advance the best traditions of humane and enlightened thought.

This title has been peer reviewed. Monash University Publishing titles pass through a rigorous process of independent peer review.

www.publishing.monash.edu/books/hcws-9781922235169.html

Series: Education

Design: Les Thomas

National Library of Australia Cataloguing-in-Publication entry:

Author:	Beale, Denise, author.
Title:	How the computer went to school: Australian government policies for computers in schools, 1983–2013 / Denise Beale.
ISBN:	9781922235169
Subjects:	Education and state--Australia.
	Computer literacy--Government policy--Australia.
	Computer assisted instruction--Government policy--Australia.
	Computers and literacy--Australia.
	Education--Data processing.
	Students--Effects of technological innovations on--Australia.
Dewey Number:	379.94

Printed in the United States of America

Contents

List of Abbreviations and Terms

AACRDE	Australian Advisory Committee on Research and Development in Education
ABC	Australian Broadcasting Commission
ABS	Australian Bureau of Statistics
ACARA	Australian Curriculum, Assessment and Reporting Authority
ACER	Australian Council for Educational Research
ACMA	Australian Communications and Media Authority
AEC	Australian Education Council
AGPS	Australian Government Publishing Service
AICTEC	Australian Information and Communications Technology in Education Committee
ALP	Australian Labor Party
ARPA	Advanced Projects Research Agency
ARPANET	Advanced Projects Research Agency Network
ASX	Australian Stock Exchange
BBN	Bolt Beranek and Newman
BCA	Business Council of Australia
BER	Building the Education Revolution
COAG	Council of Australian Governments
CSC	Commonwealth Schools Commission
CSIRAC	Commonwealth Scientific and Industrial Research Automatic Computer
CSIRO	Commonwealth Scientific and Industrial Research Organisation
CSTB	Computer Science and Telecommunications Board
DBCDE	Department of Broadband, Communications and the Digital Economy
DCITA	Department of Communications, Information Technology and the Arts
DEECD	Department of Education and Early Childhood Development (Vic)
DEET	Department of Employment, Education and Training

DEEWR	Department of Education, Employment and Workplace Relations
DER	Digital Education Revolution
DEST	Department of Education, Science and Training
DET	Department of Education and Training (NSW)
DETYA	Department of Education, Training and Youth Affairs
DPMC	Department of Prime Minister and Cabinet
EdNA	Education Network Australia
ENIAC	Electronic Numerical Integrator and Computer
ERC	Education Network Australia Reference Committee
ICT	Information and Communications Technology
JCPAA	Joint Committee of Public Accounts and Audit
LNP	Liberal–National Party
MCEETYA	Ministerial Council on Education, Employment, Training and Youth Affairs
MLC	Methodist Ladies' College
MOVEET	Ministerial Council for Vocational and Technical Education
NAA	National Archives of Australia
NACCS	National Advisory Committee on Computers in Schools
NAPLAN	National Assessment Program – Literacy and Numeracy
NBEET	National Board of Employment, Education and Training
NBN	National Broadband Network
NCA	National Commission of Audit
NCLB	No Child Left Behind
NOIE	National Office for the Information Economy
NSF	National Science Foundation
NSFNET	National Science Foundation Network
NSSCF	National Secondary School Computer Fund
NSW	New South Wales
NTIA	National Telecommunications and Information Administration
OECD	Organisation for Economic Co-operation and Development
OECD. CERI	Organisation for Economic Co-operation and Development. Centre for Educational Research and Innovation

OTA	Office of Technology Assessment
PAWG	Productivity Agenda Working Group
PC	Productivity Commission
PISA	Program for International Student Assessment
SOCCI	Schools Online Curriculum Content Initiative
STEM	Science, Technology, Engineering and Mathematics
UN	United Nations
UNESCO	United Nations Educational, Scientific and Cultural Organization
UK	United Kingdom
US	United States
Vic	Victoria
VOIP	Voice Over Internet Protocol
WCCIPAS	Working Conference on Computing and Information Processing in Australian Schools

Acknowledgements

This book is based on my doctoral thesis which was completed in 2009. I owe Sue Webb thanks for suggesting that I adapt the thesis into a book and for her encouragement of the project. During my PhD candidature, I was fortunate indeed to have an outstanding supervisor in Ilana Snyder. She was always rigorous but generous, provocative but supportive, and with powerful insights which enabled me to move forward. Our later work together as colleagues was invaluable and I appreciated her advice in the early stages of the book's preparation. I will always be grateful to her. I thank also my associate supervisor, Lesley Farrell. At a time of deep personal loss, her empathy and gentle encouragement gave me the motivation to continue candidature. My examiners, Chris Bigum and Bob Lingard, gave me valuable suggestions to improve the work, some of which I hope I have incorporated, however imperfectly. The Faculty of Education Editorial Board also provided essential support.

My daughter, Shoshanna Beale, read the draft carefully in its late stages, offering thoughtful and constructive suggestions which I have tried to adopt. At the same time, she corrected the many mistakes which I had overlooked and I valued her substantial role in bringing the work to completion. Lidia Green was also an interested and attentive reader whose comments contributed to shaping the work in its final form. I was also sustained by the interest in the project from my son Morgan and his wife Renee, my parents Jim and Clarice, and friend John Green. Above all I wish to thank my husband Gary for his crucial support over the years of candidature and writing. While he often used his considerable technical knowledge as well as his mathematical skills to assist me, even more helpful were the on-going discussions as the work of both thesis and book progressed. My thanks go also to Nathan Hollier and the team at Monash University Publishing.

Permission to reproduce excerpts from the following works is gratefully acknowledged: *Education and Technology Convergence: A Survey of Techno-logical Infrastructure in Education and the Professional Development and Support of Educators and Trainers in Information and Communications Technologies*, Commissioned Report no 43 for the National Board of Employment, Education and Training, Employment and Skills Council (Tinkler, Lepani and Mitchell 1996); 'Learning in an online world', included in *Learning for the Knowledge Society: An Education and Training Action Plan for the Information*

Economy (DETYA 2000); *Recommendations for 1984* (Commonwealth Schools Commission 1983); *Teaching, Learning and Computers: Report of the National Advisory Committee on Computers in Schools* (Commonwealth Schools Commission. National Advisory Committee on Computers in Schools 1983). Copyright Commonwealth of Australia reproduced by permission. The Australian Labor Party granted permission to reproduce excerpts from: *A Digital Education Revolution* (Rudd, Smith and Conroy 2007); *Campaign Launch 2007* (Rudd 2007); and *The Australian Economy Needs an Education Revolution* (Rudd and Smith 2007).

For Gary

Introduction

The Toolbox of the 21st Century?

At a press conference in October in the run up to the 2007 federal election campaign, Australian Labor Party Opposition Leader, Kevin Rudd, held up an open laptop computer and proclaimed it to be the 'toolbox of the 21st century'. Designed to capture attention, the computer symbolised the new policy he announced: a tax rebate to encourage parents to buy computers for their school-age children. Once the election campaign was underway, Rudd pledged to bring about a 'Digital Education Revolution' by putting a computer on every senior school student's desk if the ALP were elected (Rudd, Smith and Conroy 2007). The Digital Education Revolution, in turn, was linked to the construction of a high-speed National Broadband Network (NBN), the infrastructure on which the Digital Education Revolution would be built. Throughout 2007, Rudd had argued that high-speed broadband was critical, describing the broadband network as a 'nation-building investment' (Rudd, Conroy and Tanner 2007, n.p.). The provision of computers to school students via the planned National Secondary School Computer Fund (NSSCF) would enable young people to connect to the NBN through their schools to 'turbo-charge' their learning, because, Mr Rudd explained, 'Labor understands that in the 21st century, information technology is not just a key subject to learn, it is now the key to learning all subjects'. Education, he declared, was 'the engine room of the economy' (Rudd 2007, n.p.).

The Digital Education Revolution policy drew praise from educators. Immediately following the election of the Rudd Government in December 2007, the implications of the policy were explored in a segment on the national broadcaster's flagship current affairs program, *The 7.30 Report* (ABC 2007). Presenter Kerry O'Brien noted that the new government's education program was a 'billion dollar promise'. However, several principals who appeared on the show to discuss the policy were enthusiastic about the promise of greater numbers of computers for students and improved access to broadband. 'I thought it was fantastic. I mean it was a real vision for what education might be in the future,' said Julie Williams, the principal of Kealba Secondary College, while Rick Tudor, the principal of Trinity Grammar in Kew, spoke of it as a 'wonderful initiative'. Concerns were raised by one education academic about the focus on laptop computers while another pointed out the extra training teachers would require, but there was no hint within the segment that computers were anything other than a positive for learning in both the classroom and at home.

The policy's adoption as part of the ALP's platform suggested a perceived electoral advantage in the pledge to provide senior school students with an individual computer. But what was the appeal of such a pitch? Why was it seen to be a potential vote-winner? What meanings did Rudd and the ALP invest in the computer? How did these gain purchase? In 2007, putting computers in schools was hardly a new idea. For years, governments around the world have advocated the use of computers in schools as an essential learning technology. Over time, the view that computers can enhance student learning has gained broad acceptance. When Australian schools promote the use in their classrooms of the latest computing technology, now iPads, they signal their technological sophistication and the promise of academic success. However, the association of computers with success in school was not inevitable. Computers did not simply appear overnight on students' desks. Over more than 30 years, individuals and organisations actively promoted computers as learning technologies. Enormous amounts of money and time have been, and continue to be, devoted to educational computing with the inevitable inequities which are intrinsically associated with the dispensation of funds.

Powerful actors contribute to the formation of views in the public mind, including conceptions of new technologies and of the purposes for which they are to be used. Since 1983, one such powerful actor, the Australian federal government, has promoted computers as essential for school students and for the future of the nation. Until the ALP's institution of the Digital Education Revolution, state and territory governments have been considered more often as the locus of educational computing policies (but see Lankshear, Snyder and Green 2000; Moyle 2002; Zammit 1989). However, the federal government has had a longer involvement in the promotion of computers for schools than is commonly assumed, consistent with its more prominent role in policy direction, particularly since the 1980s. The first national policy on computing in schools was produced during the election campaign of 1983. Between 1983 and 2007, other federal government policy texts represented computers as an essential component of a modern school education.

Federal government policy texts have shaped public conceptualisations of computers and their perceived benefits for school students, leading to increased emphasis on computers as an indispensable element of a good school and vital for academic success. Schools have reorganised and in some cases restructured buildings, curricula and timetables to accommodate computers. Teachers have been placed under considerable pressure to use computers, whatever their educational philosophy, and have been labelled as reluctant to accept change if they argued a contrary case. Not all students, despite beliefs to the contrary, have enjoyed using computers in their learning. Nor can it be argued unambiguously that computers have markedly improved learning, let alone transformed it, despite expectations to the contrary. Nevertheless, the substantive and increasingly expensive nature of this enterprise has become accepted by the public.

This book presents an account of how and why the computer came to be considered as a powerful learning technology which was essential for schooling. It argues that a historical perspective is crucial and illuminates how conceptualisations of computers emerged from their early history and the purposes for which they were used. An important backdrop to understanding the production of policies for educational computing in Australia is the development of computers and their patterns of use in the US. Accordingly this book explains how computers were developed and introduced into American workplaces and schools. The US federal government was intimately involved in these aspects and was prominent in framing the computer as a suitable technology for schools.

For Australia, strongly influenced by its close relationship with the US, computers represented both a threat and a promise: a threat of marginalisation as other countries adopted computing technologies; and a promise of economic benefit should they be adopted for use in Australia. In the very different Australian environment, computers came into use much later than in the US. Initially regarded as an instrument to achieve greater efficiency in government and large organisations, as they were deployed more widely in Australian society the impact of new computing technologies raised concerns amongst policymakers. The dual positioning of threat and promise is central to understanding the uses imagined for computers in Australian schools and the beliefs which animated their proposed purposes in education. Around the world, at different times, other countries developed policies to introduce computers into school education or chose to prioritise goals for schooling which did not involve computers (Bakia, Murphy, Anderson and Trinidad 2011; UNESCO 2011). Some of these countries also exercised influence over policy in Australia, particularly the UK. However, rather than explore these, I have focused on the Australian experience and the way in which it contrasted with that of the US, the global leader in computing technologies.

About this book

How the Computer Went to School is based on doctoral research which had its genesis in my professional practice. In the late 1990s, I taught in a small Victorian independent school which introduced a program to mandate a personal laptop computer for all Year 8 students. Rather than the smooth transition to more effective learning which had been anticipated, the sheer disorder in the classroom which resulted was striking. Power cords snaked across the room, books did not fit on tables, computer bags cluttered the aisles. Lesson time was consumed by the practical difficulties of negotiating the hardware and the students' need for constant troubleshooting. The messiness of these early experiences contrasted forcibly with the trans-formative vision projected in the school's carefully crafted technology plan. A constant drumbeat in the background to the adoption of the computer program was the media refrain of the 'new economy' and its driver, the Internet. Both inside and outside the school, professional development was concentrated on the computer, its potential applications and ways to incorporate the technology into the curriculum. Policy statements from the state government promoted 'e-learning'. Similar statements from the federal government were fewer but funding was provided by the Howard Coalition Government for professional development to integrate computing technologies into teaching and learning in schools, a powerful signal of priorities.

The rhetoric of the coming transformation of learning enabled by the computer was far distant from the reality of my classroom and those of my colleagues. This dissonance led me to wonder how, and by whom, the computer could ever have been considered as necessary in schools. Like many Australians, I had long held a belief that federal government actions profoundly influenced lives, a belief which led to me to situate my doctoral research at the federal government level and to investigate its role in the promotion of computing in schools. What had initially seemed a straightforward undertaking proved to be more complex and with deeper roots than I had imagined. To trace these roots, I turned to policy texts, the medium through which governments present plans for change and map paths for action. My focus was on the use of language in specific texts:

the values and beliefs about computers and education which were preserved within them; and how language was used persuasively to mould public views towards the acceptance of prescriptions for particular courses of action. Using the tool of language analysis applied to four important policy texts, I examined the nature of the claims made for computers in schools and the purposes projected for their use by the federal government.

Kevin Rudd's metaphor of the computer as the 'toolbox of the 21st century' and his announcement of the Digital Education Revolution during the election campaign of 2007 caught my attention. My doctoral research was nearly complete and I knew that this was not the first time that a policy on computers in education had featured in an election campaign, although it was the most prominent. However, the metaphor of the 'toolbox' signalled a shift in understandings of the computer and an attempt to recast its meaning for the electorate. At the same time, the metaphor also built on and reprised key framings of computers as an educational technology which have a long, but largely forgotten, history. Rudd's use of the metaphor of the computer as a 'toolbox' was a political ploy on one level but on another, it expressed a sense of mastery over the technology which had been absent from earlier projections. Metaphor was a key focus in the language analysis I employed in my research and the shift in understanding of the computer, from 'tool' to 'toolbox', neatly captured the changing views of the computer and its purposes in education over the period of my study.

This book explores when and why the federal government acted to advocate the use of computers into schools. I argue that in policy texts from 1983 to 2007, federal government policymakers attempted to fix the nature of computing technologies and to map practices for their use in schools in ways that promoted, prescribed and proscribed, inevitably valorising some purposes, particularly economic ones, over others. These findings were built on detailed language analysis which is synthesised here in order to be accessible for a wider readership. Accordingly, the presentation of the language analysis here covers only two aspects of the textual analysis contained within the thesis. These are the different discourses within each policy text and the use of metaphor. I use the term 'discourses' to mean the divergent world views which derive from differing sets of values. Tracing world views and the interests with which they are associated sheds light on those involved in policy construction and the purposes they envisage. The linguistic device of metaphor, which conjures particular meanings, is used by policymakers to depict new technologies such as that of the computer and to shape conceptualisations that privilege some practices over others.

The book includes a new chapter which examines the ALP's Digital Education Revolution policy text and the implementation of the policy during its term in government. Policy shifts and new technological developments between 2009 and 2013 are also brought up to date. A critical approach is intrinsic to this book. It underlies the discussion of changing perceptions of computers over time, how later concepts built on and obscured earlier ideas and the relationship of these to the political, economic and social circumstances within each policy was produced. Drawing attention to which purposes were prioritised for computing technologies in education offers the potential to add a new dimension to the understandings of the computer and its possibilities to those which have been advanced by successive federal governments since 1983.

Key understandings: technology, policy and education

This book is underpinned by several key theoretical understandings, of technology, policy and education. An outline of how they have informed my research and hence this book follows in summary form, as does a short explanation of the critical discourse analytic approach I employed to undertake the language analysis.

Technology

Technology is commonly thought of as a set of tools requiring some degree of technical skill to operate. Instead, I have conceptualised it, as with other technologies, as part of the social world, that is, as 'social practice' (Lankshear et al. 2000, 32). Computing and communications technologies, as with other technologies, are produced by people who have particular ends in mind. As the product of the social world, they cannot be conceived of as value-free, that is, standing apart from the world in which they are developed and utilised. Computing technologies are produced within a commercial system and are subject to the regulation which applies to those activities. The operation of computing and communications technologies involves other regulations instituted by government as communications technologies in particular have long been subject to stringent controls (Sussman 1997). The process of developing and applying regulation is a political one in which proponents of a particular technology will seek to advance their interests (Galperin 2004a). Institutional frameworks channel the representation of interests in ways which privilege some over others. Examination of these institutional frameworks, their constitution and reconstitution, and the way these contribute to the formation of meaning, sheds light on the relationship between the interests involved and the political construction of regulation.

State and territory governments constitute powerful interests with which federal government policymakers must contend. With education the constitutional responsibility of the states and territories in Australia, the federal government's intervention can be welcomed or fiercely contested. Federal and state relations are a constant undercurrent in education policy-making at both the state and the national level (Lingard 2000) and evidence of the often fractious nature of federal and state policymaking in education is embedded in the policy texts examined in this book. The negotiation of these tensions between the federal and state and territory governments illuminates the ambitions of successive federal governments, but also demonstrates some of the limits on their power in a federal system of government.

Governments were early users of computing technologies, investing them with the weight of their authority, but they also opened a new space for contestation. The introduction of the new technology of the microcomputer in the late 1970s and early 1980s, for instance, created struggles over the existing terrain of school education which led to pressure on governments to act to introduce computers into schools. The ways in which people used the new computing and communications technologies led to changing social practices and aroused public anxiety. Media coverage emphasised and amplified the disruption, disjuncture and the potential future benefit of such technologies, informing views as to their nature and possible further uses. Governments at both the state and national level reacted to these challenges and employed policy as one part of a process of bringing about change (Bell and Stevenson 2006).

Policy

To frame my research, I adopted a view of policy at the governmental level as about change: governments responding to change or the perceptions of change, instigating change, seeking to manage and direct change to achieve specific purposes (Bell and Stevenson 2006). Rather than thinking of policy as the methodical construction of a technical plan, I have taken a critical approach which considers policy to be the outcome of a development process in which particular interests, values and beliefs are prioritised over others. This process is inherently political and contested at every level (Bell and Stevenson 2006; Taylor, Rizvi, Lingard and Henry 1997). Within the language of the policy texts that are the outcome of the process, these conflicts are preserved (Taylor et al. 1997).

A vivid illustration of this contestation over meaning was given by Western Australian Premier, Colin Barnett, following the April 2013 Council of Australian Governments (COAG) meeting over the federal government's proposed reform to school funding. Asked on the ABC's (2013) *Capital Hill* program to describe the COAG process, he replied testily that 'we've just spent two hours arguing about the choice of individual words in a communique'. In the research, I aimed to uncover the imprint of the political struggles of the day of the kind Barnett drew attention to, the beliefs and values which animated them and importantly, the competing interests involved in policies which promoted computing for schools. At the same time, I was interested in the window the texts could open into moments of instability when new meanings were being formed, before they became accepted as settled.

Policy visions delineated for the future of schooling must appeal to, and aim to attract, differing groups with divergent views. To provide plausible grounds for change, the vision of the future delivered within policy texts must be persuasive. In the case of computers, these technologies were not always considered to be an integral component of education. The project to promote the adoption and use of computers in schools has required discursive work, which has formed meanings and preferred practices for the use of computers in schools. Policy texts contributed to describing, shaping and circumscribing the field of educational computing (Rose 1999). The computer was represented in ways that attempted to naturalise it as an integral component of a modern education through the projection of an 'imaginary', that is, a vision for the future, which was contrasted to a less than satisfactory present (Fairclough 2001, 3). Values and beliefs about education and its purposes are contained within these representations (Taylor et al. 1997).

Education

While education is regarded universally as vital, views on the purposes and content of education differ markedly. Indeed, conflict over education, its purposes and the values prioritised within it, is endemic as education 'touches the lives of every citizen' (Marginson 1997a, 4). Historically situated, purposes for education change over time. For governments, vocational purposes have co-existed with nation-building and citizenship purposes, often uneasily (Marginson 1997a). For others in the community, education has different purposes, depending on their perspective. Some important purposes include the development of individual potential and the

transmission of valued cultural knowledge (Marginson 1997a). But critically, education certifies and credentials students, fundamentally affecting
their future lives and their access to valued social goods (Marginson 1997a).
Policymakers have sought to improve access to higher levels of education
for the disadvantaged and thereby to enhance their prospects, but the move
to mass education has not resulted in the elimination of social inequality
as had been hoped. Instead, the inequalities that exist in society are not
just reproduced, but reinforced and intensified in the educational process,
as those with social power are able to use the system to their advantage
(Teese and Polesol 2003). In my view, one important goal for education is
to achieve greater equality for all students, particularly for those who are
disadvantaged.

Policies for computing technologies in education, as with others, can
contribute to or detract from greater equality in education. Judgements were
made by policymakers on computing technologies and their place in school
education which involved values and assumptions as to who should use
them, how, and for what purposes. Particular practices were privileged, with
certain ends in mind. Seldom are these explicitly stated within educational
policies. In the research I set out to trace the values and beliefs within
selected policy texts through a critical discourse analysis approach.

A critical discourse analysis approach

The conceptual basis of critical discourse analysis draws from a range
of sources but I have adopted and adapted the approaches of Norman
Fairclough and Ruth Wodak who have studied political discourse exten-
sively (eg, Fairclough 2000a, 2000b; Reisigl and Wodak 2001; Wodak
2001a, 2001b). Central to critical discourse analysis is the concept of
discourse, or language and its use in society. It is through language that
people make sense of the world, communicate that meaning to others, and
these meanings in turn shape society (Fairclough and Wodak 1997). Because
of its social location, language is imbued with power relations. Expressed in
language, these shape people's perceptions of the world. People's world views
are expressed and consolidated in language, including where people belong
and how they should be categorised (Fairclough 2000a). These differing
world views are known as discourses. As there are many differing world
views, so too are there many different discourses, each of which embodies
different value systems (Fairclough 2003). These contend against each other
for dominance within texts, with a text considered to be 'any actual instance
of language in use' (Fairclough 2003, 4). The discourses that dominate

are critical in signalling, authorising and legitimising practices such as, for instance, the allocation of resources for some purposes and not for others. In this way discourses contribute to, or challenge, the constitution and maintenance of social inequalities (Fairclough 2003).

It is this concept of different discourses and the value systems embedded within them that enables their disentanglement through analysis of a text. Each text can incorporate numbers of different discourses, particularly policy texts, as they often have multiple authors (Taylor 2004). Negotiation of meaning and struggles over different ways of understanding and representing the world are thus traceable in these different discourses. Over time, meanings become accepted as common sense and their initial circumstances are forgotten (Fairclough 2003). Detailed textual analysis elucidates the linguistic mechanisms and manoeuvres by which constructions of the world are realised (Fairclough 2003). The application of critical discourse analysis to policy texts enabled me to denaturalise and destabilise the existing 'common sense' (Apple 1993, 53) meanings that were attributed to computers and their role in education and, instead, to suggest that they should be considered as 'truth claims' which have been made by particular interests for particular purposes (Fairclough 2003, 167). Considered as claims rather than as truths, apparently common sense meanings can be subjected to scrutiny on those terms.

The shifting terminology of the computer

From its earliest history until the present, there have been a number of terms, often used interchangeably, to designate a computer and its associated technology. The difficulty of definition in itself reveals the shifting nature of the technology and its use, but it also suggests the multiple meanings attached to the object. Technical changes over the last 50 years mean that the word 'computer' describes something that is very different now from the earliest machines and from what will exist in the future (Schnaars and Carvalho 2004). Originally, the term 'computer' was applied to a human who performed computations (Campbell-Kelly and Aspray 1996; Ceruzzi 2003). One of the earliest electronic computers, the Electronic Numerical Integrator and Computer (ENIAC), was designated a 'computer' to associate the new machine with people trained for computation and to confer on it those professional attributes (Pugh and Aspray 1996).

While the term 'computer' remains in use, continuing technological change has seen different descriptors used to distinguish amongst newer types of computers: thus the 'minicomputer', the 'microcomputer', the 'personal computer', the 'laptop' computer. More recently, with smart phones and tablets, the word 'computer' has begun to disappear. At the same time, new terms that attempted to encompass the range of computers and peripherals came into use. The most widely used of these is 'information technology', which was expanded to 'information and communications technologies' (ICT) when computing devices also enabled communication.

In this book, I use the term 'computer' to focus on the object, its development and application, and the phrase 'computing technologies', following Moyle (2005), or 'computing and communications technologies', to denote the broader range of technologies. Rather than attribute human characteristics to these technologies, I view these terms as directing attention to technology as the product of people's interactions.

A note on method

A review of the literature on computers in education from the 1960s till 2007 formed the basis for the selection of policy texts examined in this book. This literature comprised academic journals, books, conference proceedings, PhD and Masters theses, both published and unpublished, and reports to and policies of the Victorian and the federal governments. To establish the wider context, I also reviewed selected literature from the same sources across the disciplines of economics, politics, history, education and technology studies dating back to 1945. I selected four policy texts for close analysis. These are:

> *Teaching, Learning and Computers* (CSC. NACCS 1983) (see Chapter 3);
>
> *Education and Technology Convergence* (Tinkler, Lepani and Mitchell 1996) (see Chapter 4);
>
> 'Learning in an online world' (DETYA 2000b) (see Chapter 5);
>
> *A Digital Education Revolution* (Rudd, Smith and Conroy 2007) (see Chapter 6).

In this book I present a personal reading of the texts and their historical situation which is built on textual analysis. Inevitably I have made choices as to which elements appeared to be relevant, interesting or worthy of investigation. I have aimed to present a nuanced account of specific texts and the discourses within them through tracing their origins and considering how these foundational ideas may continue nevertheless to exert influence into the present. My focus is different from that of the historian. It is on the claims made for computers over time, by whom, and on how those claims have been legitimised.

Outline of the book

Chapter One presents aspects of the computer's development in the US between 1946 and 2012. It explores the role of the US federal government, the academy, business and industry in this development and how computers came to be considered as worthwhile for school education. In Chapter Two, the diffusion of the computer into Australian society is compared with that in the US and linked to the Australian federal government's promotion of computers in schools between 1983 and 2007. Chapters One and Two form the backdrop to a close analysis of specific policies produced in 1983, 1996, 2000 and 2007 which are the subjects of Chapters Three to Six.

Chapter Three is concerned with the first national policy statement on computers in Australian schools, *Teaching, Learning and Computers* (CSC. NACCS 1983). The chapter examines the specific factors that influenced the production of the policy, the claims made about the benefits of computers for students in schools and the relationship between these. The Keating ALP Government's policy document, *Education and Technology Convergence* (Tinkler et al. 1996) is the subject of Chapter Four. New meanings for computing technologies in education were being advanced and new purposes imagined. In Chapter Five, the first Howard Coalition Government policy, 'Learning in an Online World' of 2000, is detailed. The chapter also considers changing policymaking structures and the shifting terrain of federal and state and territory responsibilities in education. The foundational text, *A Digital Education Revolution* (Rudd, Smith and Conroy 2007), and its relationship to the NBN is the subject of Chapter Six. The implementation of the policy during the ALP's term in government is explained in detail and consideration is given to the imprint of the implementation process in the construction of meanings for the computer in school education.

Chapter Seven compares the discourses of each of the four policies examined in this book, exploring the continuities amongst them but also the disjunctures. It draws conclusions as to the values and beliefs about computing and education which are represented in the policies, the meanings proposed for educational computing and the practices which were preferred. It also considers which meanings were foreclosed and the voices within the policy process which were silenced or ignored. Chapter Eight concludes with an argument for a renewed scrutiny of the attributes ascribed to the computer to contribute to a more informed debate as to future directions for educational computing.

Chapter One

From Laboratory to Classroom

Early in 1946, the American War Department unveiled a closely guarded wartime secret to the American public: the first electronic computer, the Electronic Numerical Integrator and Computer (ENIAC), which was developed to perform time-consuming and labour-intensive calculations of weapons trajectories during the Second World War. After the war, the machine's inventors, Dr John Mauchly and J. Presper Eckert Jr, provided a demonstration of the machine and its problem-solving capacities to an attentive press audience. On its front page, *The New York Times* celebrated the achievement of scientists and the military under the banner heading, 'Electronic computer flashes answers, may speed engineering' (Kennedy 1946).

New purposes had to be found for the machine in peacetime. Scientists believed the new machine 'could revolutionize modern engineering', reported T R Kennedy (1946, 1), journalist for *The New York Times*. It was an 'electronic speed marvel', able to complete mathematical calculations which had until then been difficult to solve. How to explain the complex new technology to a general audience presented Kennedy with a challenge. The picture of the huge machine, descriptions of its size, its construction and its performance of abstruse calculations could not capture its uniqueness. Metaphor was the device Kennedy used to enable his audience to imagine the technology and to picture its capacities. 'It has the human faculty of "memory"' he wrote (Kennedy 1946, 3). Eckert, one of the ENIAC's inventors, predicted the machine's potential impact: 'the old era is going, the new one of electronic speed is on the way' (Kennedy 1946, 3).

Since that moment in 1946 when the ENIAC was unveiled, aspects of computer development have been considered newsworthy and also attracted political and scholarly attention. Contemporary accounts of computers and debates over their deployment provide a window into the past at moments of inflection as the terrain of a new technology was being mapped discursively. These accounts open to view people's perceptions that existing practices were changing because of the computer but also before new practices had become accepted as normal and the disjunctures with the old were forgotten (Reed 2000). As the nature of the new technology and its potential was explored, it was also explained in ways which suggested how the public should view it and respond to it (Stahl 1995). Accounts such as Kennedy's description of the ENIAC reveal the attributes and capacities ascribed to the computer, but also the purposes for which it was used and by whom. In addition, these accounts illuminate too the range of imagined futures: what people believed were possible, likely or even desirable outcomes of computer use.

When the computer was new

When the computer was new it was impossible to imagine its trajectory and the multiple uses which would be found for this protean machine. Its origins and the course of its early development are disputed, but scholars agree that the period of the Second World War was critical (Campbell-Kelly and Aspray 1996). The US federal government was crucial to the development of the computer and later, to its support of the computer as an educational technology. The Second World War provided the vital imperative for the US government to undertake the hugely expensive task of constructing a working electronic computer (CSTB 1999). After the end of the Second World War, the Cold War ensured that substantial military funding for on-going work on computing technologies continued. The US federal government, primarily through the Department of Defense, created demand for computers through the award of contracts for their design and construction, essential elements in the establishment of the early commercial foundations of the computer industry (CSTB 1999).

The beginning of the Korean War in 1950, however, was the catalyst for dramatically expanded military spending, including support of further research and development on the computer (Johnson 1983). Much of this was carried out in private firms and in the academy, particularly Harvard University, Princeton University and later, Stanford University and the Massachusetts Institute of Technology (CSTB 1999; Richtmyer 1965). Such funding for computer technology signified the commitment at the highest levels of the American political elite to gain global hegemony through advanced weapons technology during the Second World War and then later, in the succeeding Cold War. The authority of the military and the government funding that supported the development of the computer associated it with the national interest and the defence of the US, thus powerfully legitimising the computer from its inception.

The on-going military basis of the computer was represented in 1950 in a *Time* cover picture which portrayed the Navy's newest computer, the Harvard Mark III, as part Navy commander and part machine (*Time* 1950a). Importantly, *Time*'s cover picture positioned the computer squarely within the social and political context of its construction. The Navy was fundamental to the continuing development of the computer (Boslaugh 1999). The caption for *Time*'s cover, *Can Man Build a Superman?* suggested other possibilities for the machine: the computer as the creation of humankind but also as a potential creator, a question that continues to resonate today. *Time*'s cover story on the Harvard Mark III explained the highly complex machine to a general audience through personification. It was 'the thinking machine' (*Time* 1950b). Only a year before, a popular book, *Giant Brains: or, Machines That Think*, publicised computers through likening them to people (Berkeley 1949). As Kennedy in 1946 employed metaphor to characterise the new technology, so too Berkeley and the unnamed *Time* writer used metaphor to expand the notion of the computer as human-like and therefore more than a machine. Metaphor could denote the attributes of the computer and create an understanding of the technology when no commonly accepted terms then existed for it (Goatly 1997).

By the early 1950s, private businesses and the academy were collaborating on the design, construction and marketing of computers, producing new general purpose computers which were employed for information processing and systems control purposes in business, industry and governmental organisations. Companies such as IBM leveraged their research base to target a limited range of less sophisticated computers to business (Usselman 1996). The links between companies and government were exploited for marketing purposes, with IBM and Remington Rand using public demonstrations of the computer to associate these companies with the new device, enhancing their public image and credibility (Campbell-Kelly and Aspray 1996). At the same time, these companies helped to create an image of a new technology which was still mysterious for the wider public. In a publicity stunt in 1952, Remington Rand arranged for one of its computers to call the results of the presidential election on television. The successful call cemented the belief in the public's mind that the computer had human capacities – a brain and memory – giving force to the earlier metaphor of the computer as a disembodied but thinking brain (Campbell-Kelly and Aspray 1996). Public understandings were shaped by this foundational portrayal.

Companies associated with the government and the military not only gained legitimacy through these interactions but also gained new opportunities to maximise profits. Numerous firms jockeyed for position in the emerging marketplace, but IBM's existing relationships with the government and its established sales and technical facilities meant that it quickly dominated the nascent industry. The successful adoption of IBM's new 650 model in 1953 by more businesses than anticipated was pivotal in the development of the computer industry. IBM's dominance in the field was confirmed and other firms with an eye to the business market were attracted (Usselman 1996). Very significant funding had supported private research and development as well as the risks inherent in the commercialisation and development of the new technologies that had emerged from military and academic institutions (Noble 1984). The returns, however, went into private hands.

Private sector firms flourished in this environment and increasingly used research and development to meet business and industry demand for data processing and systems control. During the late 1950s and 1960s, while the computer continued to be employed by the military, it became a prominent tool for businesses, large government organisations and in industry to manage information and to control automation processes. This use was not without impact. Automation and its effects on work processes began to be felt in American society (Philipson 1962).

The computer in the office

The most significant moment in the development of the computer was its adoption by the business community, particularly in offices, as a general purpose machine (Ceruzzi 2003). Its introduction into white collar work-places had a profound impact. The employment of the computer to automate data processing in offices and organisations meant a loss of status, relocation and shift work for many workers. Importantly, jobs were eliminated altogether (Hoos 1960). Computer manufacturers, with an eye to substantial new markets, promoted the computer as 'the thinking machine', one which could work faster and with fewer workers, thus generating higher profits for business. Such potential gains in turn led new businesses to install computers (Solo 1963). Businesses were attracted to the computer's speed and lower cost in comparison to that of a human worker. While automation had been introduced earlier into manufacturing processes with consequent effects on blue collar workers, the replacement of white collar workers aroused considerable fear in the middle class. The job loss that had accompanied the deployment of computer-controlled systems in heavy industry was projected into the office environment (Philipson 1962).

By 1965, the penetration of the computer into workplaces meant that predictions of a second industrial revolution had become commonplace (eg, Diebold 1962). At the same time, the computer industry had been created so successfully in the US, supported by early and continuing federal government funding, that it rapidly displaced the evolving computer industries in several other countries, for instance, in Britain (Usselman 1996). The success of the computer as a business machine and its diffusion into workplaces was pivotal to its later use in education. The belief that business and industry would require a skilled labour force to work with the new technologies at all levels, from data processing to programming to manufacturing, led to suggestions that the computer should be introduced into schools (Diebold 1962). Both government and business were concerned to maintain American supremacy through technological superiority in the military and commercial domains, as the second depended on the first. Increasingly, education came to be viewed as part of the enterprise to retain American pre-eminence.

The general public viewed the increasing use of computers with growing anxiety, particularly the perceived association between computers and un-employment (Schnaars and Carvalho 2004). Film and television presented images of the future that were enticing but terrifying at the same time, attrib-uting a wide range of possible scenarios to computers. In reality, however, the use of computers in workplaces was limited to large organisations and agencies. Newer and smaller computers became more affordable for other businesses and organisations through the 1960s and 1970s, but it was the invention and commercialisation of the personal computer that finally made them accessible to many more firms, including small businesses.

The computer and small business

The hobbyist origins of the personal computer, or microcomputer, could not have been more different from the interconnected governmental, academic and business foundations of the mainstream computer industry. The first microcomputer, the Altair, was a machine based on the microprocessor and sold in kitform to enthusiasts, often computer science graduates from tertiary institutions (Brock 2003). The Altair, however, stimulated other hobbyists to develop hardware and software applications which aimed to refine and develop new personal computers and programs. Ultimately, these led to the founding of firms such as Microsoft and Apple (Brock 2003). The first Apple II computer was released in 1976 (Usselman 1996).

Initially, large computer manufacturers ignored the microcomputer. However, threatened by its remarkable success, IBM developed a micro-computer which it released in August 1981 and designated the 'Personal

Computer'. The name served to publicise IBM's computer and also widened its appeal. The backing of IBM, with its established place as a marketer to business, legitimised the new computer for business use (Falk 1981). For small businesses, the personal computer was affordable, unlike the larger mainframes. Initially, companies had focused on personal computers as an entertainment device to deliver games for the home market, but newer machines and rapid technological development enabled a wider range of applications, such as word processing, accounting programs and databases which appealed to business (Gatty 1983). Competition amongst manufacturers was intense, with the affluent home consumer first targeted, followed by the small business sector (US Congress. OTA 1981).

An extraordinary explosion in the number of personal computers acquired for home use began. From around 70,000 in 1979, the number swelled to over four million in 1983. In addition, more than two million personal computers in 1983 had been bought by big business in a market estimated to be worth US$9 billion (Gatty 1983). At the same time, new networked computers were able to enhance the range of applications and uses for businesses (Brock 2003). Substantially funded by the federal government, network technologies offered considerable advantages for larger businesses. The computer was promoted as the ultimate business tool for the busy professional or manager, offering control, flexibility and rapid access, not just to data but also to information. From its hobbyist origins, the personal computer became a signifier of social status, acquired by managers and affluent households (Gatty 1983).

The proliferation of computers was accompanied by a sense of profound change, reflected in the January edition of *Time* 1983 which named the personal computer 'the Machine of the Year', instead of its usual nomination of 'Person of the Year' (*Time* 1983a). Popular media lauded the personal computer as revolutionary, a mysterious and magical force which was impossible to resist. These views partly echoed but also helped to shape the views of the public at large as they were coming into contact with the new technology (Stahl 1995). To learn to use the new machines that would become increasingly important in society was presented as a necessity but also as liberating (*Time* 1983b).

Yet there was also ambivalence amongst the public. In contrast to the 1960s, the rapid deployment of personal computers and workstations in many more businesses and organisations confronted the workforce with computers more directly than had the previous mainframes, arousing anxiety about the technology and the necessity to use an unfamiliar and complex machine on a routine basis in daily life (Reed 2000). While the home market for computers was important, its use in the workplace was critical. As more and more computers were installed, work practices underwent significant changes on a daily basis. Employees who were reluctant to use computers had no choice. They were placed under pressure to understand the computer through using it and to develop computer literacy, now argued to be the new prerequisite for the workplace (Gatty 1983). Ongoing changes in roles, status, salary, training and daily practices became the norm.

International competitors, particularly Japan, had begun to use the microprocessor technology developed in the US to produce computers and other electronic equipment (Falk 1981). In the mid 1980s, this competition in an already competitive marketplace aroused concern over challenges to US economic supremacy (US Congress. OTA 1988b). The Reagan administration's deregulation agenda led to large-scale labour shedding as smaller firms were amalgamated into much larger ones. At the same time, a sharp recession also produced significant job losses. Upgraded workforce skills, particularly in computing, were viewed as enabling workers to adjust more quickly, but these were skills which the American education system was seen as failing to provide (US Congress. OTA 1988b). Computing technologies were positioned as tools for revitalising an ailing American economy.

The coming of cyberspace

Alongside the development of the computer, dependent on it but different in purpose and trajectory, scientists worked on the construction of what became the Internet. Only after the creation and commercialisation of the World Wide Web did this technology become newsworthy. However, the development of the Internet reflected similar elements to those of the early years of computing, that is, the interconnected roles of the federal government, the academy and business (Kahn et al. 1997). The World Wide Web was built on the Internet which originated in the late 1950s with the establishment of the Advanced Projects Research Agency (ARPA) following the launch of Sputnik by the Soviet Union in 1957. Formed as an agency of the Department of Defense, ARPA's role was to sponsor research into ways in which communications within the Department could be strengthened and protected in the atmosphere of the Cold War (Rosenzweig 1998).

ARPA funded academic researchers to investigate methods of communication. The foundation of this was packet-switching technology, which enabled communications between computers via telephone lines (Kahn et al. 1997). In 1968, ARPA began a project to build a network of computers for communications purposes, using packet-switching, and commissioned Bolt Beranek and Newman (BBN) to construct it (Kahn et al. 1997). Small experimental networks were established to allow scientists to communicate with each other and in 1972 the network that had become known as the ARPANET was presented at an international conference (CSTB 1999). Networks of computers were established for academic users and funded through federal government departments. Users transmitted messages via electronic mail, with the first sent in 1972 from a program developed at BBN (CSTB 1999). During the 1970s, important technical advances were made that improved the functioning of these networks and laid the foundations for the Internet. These included the adoption of an open architecture system and the development of protocols for file transfer, routing and the operating system (Kahn et al. 1997). By 1981, the existing networks were already being described as the 'Internet' (US Congress. OTA 1981, 15), with a growing recognition that 'computer and communication technologies are increasingly interdependent' (US Congress. OTA 1981, 4).

Networks built for academic communities were linked to the ARPANET in the early 1980s (US Congress. House of Representatives 1992). The initial purpose of networked computers had been to provide for communication between groups of scientists. The growth of these networks, which was both enabled and extended by rapid advances in computer technology, allowed for greater storage and processing capacities at the same time as improvements in the transmission of data made for more efficient and effective information processing. Where previously the computer had been envisaged as a machine for calculation, for graphing and simulation, when connected to a network it became a means to communicate across distances and to transmit data much more quickly and cheaply than had been the case before (US Congress. OTA 1981). These features made networked technology attractive, particularly to small businesses which had not previously been able to afford larger mainframe computers.

The growth of further networks was fostered by the federal government, particularly through the development of the NSFNET by the National Science Foundation in the period between 1985 and 1990. The network was built as the foundation of an expanded Internet, with the construction, funded by government, of several supercomputing centres to link together educational and research institutions. Built and operated through private sector contracts, it also promoted the establishment of commercial networks with the intention of later moving to full privatisation of the Internet (US Congress. House of Representatives 1992). Its civilian and non-commercial use was primarily for communication amongst researchers and members of the educational community. By 1992, the NSFNET was substantial in size, with over 5000 networks, numbers of them international. It linked together hundreds of colleges and libraries and over 1000 schools (US Congress. House of Representatives 1992). It also paved the way for commercial services. In the years immediately prior to the full privatisation of the Internet, numerous commercial providers offered internet services to growing numbers of users. In 1992, the value of these was already more than US$4 billion (US Congress. House of Representatives 1992).

The shift to privatisation of the Internet began in 1990. The belief in the private sector as the engine of innovation and growth is a central value within the American political system. The Internet was envisioned as a critical technology for the new information age (US Congress. House of Representatives 1992). As important was the belief that computing technology was vital to the nation, enshrined by Congress in the legislation to establish the National Research and Education Network in 1991 which built on the NSFNET. Advanced computing technology was designated as 'vital to the Nation's prosperity, national and economic security, industrial production, engineering, and scientific advancement', the supremacy of which was 'being challenged by foreign competitors' (US Congress 1991, n.p.). Communications, computing and education were thus linked with the national interest. While the Internet had been used as a medium for research communication and for accessing information in numbers of educational institutions including schools across the US, government interest was more focused on the privatisation and development of a commercial service as a means of assuring American technological and business dominance.

An important element of the original architecture of the Internet had been its ability to support multiple applications which encouraged the collaboration of researchers and private sector developers. One of these applications was the World Wide Web which enabled the storage and retrieval of information through the use of hypertext, expanding useability (CSTB 1999). In 1993, the invention of the browser, Mosaic, enabled better use of the World Wide Web through the ability to incorporate features other than text, such as images and sound. The capacity for individual users to search and retrieve information greatly expanded the reach of the Internet to home users of computers who could link to the Internet through the telephone cable (CSTB 1999).

The National Science Foundation had provided funding to establish the supercomputer centres in the High Performance Computing Act of 1991, which had been sponsored by Al Gore, and it was this funding that supported the production of Mosaic (CSTB 1999). As with the development of the computer, research and development had been underwritten by the federal government, but private firms profited. The commercialisation of Mosaic by Netscape enabled both more diverse content and easier access to that content on computers networked to each other across the world, resulting in an extraordinary increase of users over a short period (CSTB 1999). This rapid adoption of internet technology after its commercialisation spurred interest in its potential use in education.

In 1994, Al Gore, then Vice President in the Clinton administration, promoted the concept of the National Information Infrastructure centred on the Internet and its creation in part as a function of competitive markets in communications. The analogy of the 'national information infrastructure' as a key economic element, likened to railways and highways (Gore 1994, n.p.), was a rhetorical device to introduce reforms to the telecommunications sector that aimed at making the regulated utilities sector more like the less regulated and market-oriented computer sector (Brock 2003). The distinction between them mattered, as telecommunications regulations were based on a principle of public utility, whereas computers were a product sold competitively within the marketplace (Brock 2003).

When computers and communications began to blur, greater pressure was placed on the notion of public utility and the public provision of information and information services. The Internet was at once 'the information superhighway' able to 'transcend international boundaries' with the promise of 'lower prices and better services', but also the preserve of private business (Gore 1994, n.p.). A goal of the federal government was to provide internet access for all schools in the US, but despite its insistence that computing technologies were essential, the new service was to be provided by private firms in the pursuit of profit rather than by government. In 1995, the commitment to commercialise the NSFNET was achieved when the network was fully privatised and regional networks, which hosted academic and educational services, were instead subsidised to buy services from private internet providers rather than directly funded by the National Science Foundation (Kahn et al. 1997). Access to the Internet for educational institutions, including schools, was no longer through public provision, but on a user-pays basis.

The computer as portal

New internet services, commonly referred to as Web 2.0, began in the years immediately following 2000 and the crash of the technology boom. With the decline in technology stocks, investment in new applications for business disappeared. Instead, already large firms such as Google and Amazon became the innovators, offering consumers customised services which have been extended over the intervening years (Allard 2008). Notably, as with the development of the personal computer, private companies rather than government were behind these applications.

Social media platforms were also developed and enable users to post their own content, communicate that content to others and receive feedback on it on sites such as Twitter, Facebook and YouTube, amongst others. New gaming platforms have been enabled. Importantly, the distinction between communication and computing, already blurred, has become more so. Web technology on smart phones, handheld devices such as tablets and telephone services via VOIP now further stretch the boundaries. For many, the computer that they use to connect to the World Wide Web has become the taken for granted point of access, rather than the focus of attention. Applications and data have moved to the Web rather than remaining on individual computers. Web-based services have become indispensable for governments, businesses and for many millions of people for a variety of different purposes.

Web technologies open new communicative possibilities, particularly for individuals to interact with others across the world in real time at relatively little cost. They offer new opportunities for businesses to reduce costs through more direct contact with customers. For governments, too, they offer similar opportunities. More technologically oriented politicians have been quick to utilise newer web technologies to address the electorate. In Australia, Kevin Rudd used the Kevin07 website during the 2007 election campaign to communicate with the electorate. In the US, Barack Obama's 2008 and 2012 presidential campaigns made sophisticated use of web technologies to engage, mobilise and fundraise.

New computing and communications developments which have redefined computers have also continued. The release of Apple's iPad in 2010 established a market for tablet computers in much the same way as did Apple's release of the technology of the personal computer in the 1970s (Griffey 2012). Although tablet computers had been produced earlier, Apple's iPad was the most commercially successful device, based on an operating system that was fast and flexible. Importantly, it enabled superior mobility to that of a laptop computer. Google soon followed with its Android operating system which a number of manufacturers used to produce new ranges of tablets and smart phones (Griffey 2012). While manufactured largely overseas, smart phones, too, were seen as the result of American technological superiority, due to their 'American-made operating systems and applications' (NTIA 2013, i). The impact of these devices has been significant on the market for both desktops and laptops. Rather than upgrade their computers, consumers instead purchased tablets and smart phones. For the first time in 2010, the combined sales of tablets and smart phones overtook those of personal computers (Manyika et al. 2013). In 2013, the pace of decline in the sales of desktops and laptop computers is accelerating (BMI 2013b).

Computer use and access to the Internet, particularly via broadband, have become widespread in the US. In 2011, 76 per cent of households possessed a personal computer and 69 per cent were able to access the Internet via broadband (NTIA 2013). Those with internet access at work were also more likely to use the Internet at home. Most likely to possess both a computer and broadband internet were families with children at school, of whom 84 per cent had a computer and 79 per cent a broadband connection, reflecting the widespread belief that a computer is a critical component of education (NTIA 2013). Children and young people are heavy users of the Internet, particularly teenagers, although use amongst younger age groups is growing rapidly. In 2006 and again in a 2013 survey, 95 per cent of American teenagers used the Internet. Of those, 93 per cent had computers in their home. However, access to the Internet took place across a range of devices and locations, with a trend to greater use of smart phones and to a lesser extent, tablets (Manyika et al. 2013).

As the Internet has been increasingly designated the technology for the future, government attention has shifted to the supporting infrastructure of broadband, both mobile and fixed. Regulatory decisions taken in the 1990s and the early 2000s meant that by 2010, the performance of the US in the provision of low-cost but high-speed broadband services was below that of a number of OECD countries, most notably Japan and South Korea (Berkman 2010). In 2009, 96 per cent of South Koreans had internet access, much of it high-speed (ABS 2011a). In 2009, 23 per cent of American households did not use the Internet at all (NTIA 2010).

However, there are also significant costs in the shift to web technology. For businesses, governments and the community sector, there is the cost of the technology itself such as building new platforms (Allard 2008). For governments, the infrastructure needs of web technology are growing, with pressures on broadband networks and on computing power. Issues of standards, property rights, including copyright and intellectual property as well as ownership of underlying structures, remain contested areas. The increase in complexity is significant as, ironically, the user interface is simplified. The very ease of use and expanding access, in itself promoted by government on equity grounds, means an increase in internet crime of all kinds and privacy concerns which remain unresolved. The explosion of social media use, particularly by children and young people, has attracted worldwide attention. In a pervasive atmosphere of moral panic, policies and strategies have been developed to protect young people from both real and perceived dangers.

The rapid development in internet technology and its diffusion through society is reminiscent of the speed with which personal computers were adopted. Internet technology also generated similar fears, as had personal computers, about the challenges it presented to young people in particular. The US Department of Commerce (NTIA 2013, 2) noted that 'between 2000 and 2011, household computer use increased by 49 percent, while home Internet use rose by 71 percent'. During that period, as in the early 1980s, calls were made for education to provide instruction and protection to children and young people in their use of computing technologies, especially the Internet. Unlike 1983, however, when personal computers were still rarities, these technologies are now embedded in a web of daily practices in almost every sphere of everyday life. Over time, governments as both promoters and customers, have contributed to the growth and adoption of computing and communications technologies in the belief that these 'are essential to economic growth' (NTIA 2013, i).

New internet environments have been developed to cater for mobile technology. Applications and the new services of cloud computing have been adopted increasingly by governments and corporations, further extending demands on broadband services, particularly wireless, which has been growing more rapidly than fixed line services (BMI 2013b). In the largest market for computing and communications technologies in the world, mobile internet-enabled devices and the web-based services such as cloud computing are projected to be the fastest growing segment in the immediate future (Manyika et al. 2013). The pace of change seems certain to accelerate.

Computers and education in the US

The growing numbers of computers in American workplaces during the 1960s and the rising number of people who had access to them led to pressure to employ computers in education, particularly from business, academic researchers, parents exposed to computers and governments. With the education system the responsibility of the states, and both decentralised and very diverse, the US federal government had limited involvement in education until the 1960s. The federal government, however, was crucial in providing funding support and thereby legitimacy for the use of computers in school education in the US.

The early years

The first commercially available mainframe computers were large and expensive, making it difficult to imagine them as teaching aids for school students. Yet in 1958, IBM leveraged off its involvement with government-supported programs and began to experiment with educational computing via a drill and practice program for school students (Aspray 1991; Baker 1978). IBM's initial experiments with computers and students formed the basis for the development of the computer-assisted learning program, PLATO, with funding support from the National Science Foundation (NSF 1971). Later bought by Control Data Corporation, the program was widely used for many years in schools, private corporations and also in the military for drill and practice training (Aspray 1991). From the early 1950s, more than half of IBM's research effort into computers had been funded by the federal government through the award of contracts to develop computers for specific purposes (CSTB 1999). Federal government funding partially assisted the production of a market for computer learning products.

More overt federal government support for educational computing began in 1966 when President Lyndon Johnson funded research into the potential uses of computers in education at the time of the Great Society program. The Office of Technology Assessment (OTA) noted that 'the "War on Poverty" looked to education as a means of creating social change, and computer-based education was seen as a potentially powerful tool for improving the educational opportunities for the disadvantaged' (US Congress. OTA 1988b, 175). The National Science Foundation was provided with a limited degree of funding to promote computing in education. In part this support for computing reflected a belief that a scientific and business technology could be used to improve education.

Government funding promoted the computer's potential educationally; but more importantly, the federal government's new activism shaped public perceptions of the computer as a modernising technology which could improve public schooling. Between 1965 and 1971, the US Office of Education provided over US$160 million to fund approximately 500 projects utilising computers in schools, the majority focused on the disadvantaged (Grayson 1971). Funding was channelled through the Office of Naval Research and the National Science Foundation (CSTB 1999). Additionally, the National Science Foundation awarded computers donated by commercial firms as prizes to schools, meaning that these firms could gain a foothold into a substantial new market in schools (Aspray 1991). Even obliquely, the role of federal funding was important in the earliest stages of computing research in education.

Some of the funding provided to the National Science Foundation was used to establish the Office of Computing Activities, led by Andrew Molnar, with the brief to promote computing in education. The National Science Foundation aimed to support academic computing because it contributed to the research base into computing and also educated professionals in associated disciplines (NSF 1971). The development of the programming language, LOGO, by Seymour Papert was assisted by funding for his research into artificial intelligence from the National Science Foundation and the Office of Naval Research (Papert 1972). Funding also supported educational researchers, particularly Patrick Suppes of Stanford University and Richard Atkinson, who conducted research into the teaching of mathematics and reading respectively (Aspray 1991).

Researchers such as Suppes and Atkinson were often educational psychologists, interested in the potential of the computer to improve reading and writing in elementary and secondary school students. Suppes, a researcher at Stanford University, had access to expensive and sophisticated computers. He advanced the metaphor of the computer as equivalent to a private tutor for wealthy children, emphasising the potential gains in education that could result from such individualised instruction (Suppes 1966). Its perceived capacities could provide rapid feedback and enable customisation for different ability levels across a range of subjects (Suppes 1966). The work of Suppes and Atkinson, amongst other researchers who examined the impact of computing in educational settings, was influential and widely cited. Their conclusions that learning with computers could be more effective in some tasks than traditional methods suggested for the first time that computers made better teachers than teachers themselves (eg, Fletcher and Atkinson 1972).

Yet the conclusions of researchers had not begun to influence the majority of schools and even less so, teachers. Computers were still an esoteric subject for many. A more persuasive tactic to ally the computer with school education came in 1972 when Andrew Molnar, of the National Science Foundation, employed the phrase 'computer literacy' (Aspray 1991, 10) to connect the computer first with literacy and through that, with the school: the place which has traditionally been associated with literacy learning. To connect 'computer' with 'literacy' was not just to link computers with schools, but also to assert that knowledge of computers was regarded by those in authority as essential to functioning in society. The multiple meanings attached to the concept of literacy (Snyder 2008), at the same time as computers were seen to be behind changes in work practices, ensured the power of the phrase. 'Computer literacy' became a very influential discursive construction to associate computers with schools, one with an enduring impact which echoes in the later permutations of 'information literacy' and 'digital literacy'.

However, despite the interest of researchers and some educators, few American schools were involved with computing. Interest in educational computing declined at the end of the 1960s, a feature of the difficulty of incorporating it into even a very few schools, its expensiveness and the perception that its benefits could not be confirmed (Baker 1971). In 1971, fewer than one per cent of secondary school students had access to a computer (Dieterich 1972). A plateau was reached where research continued, although at a much lower level than in the 1960s. In the economically difficult years of the 1970s, during recession and stagflation, funding for computer projects in education was significantly reduced (Aspray 1991). Some teachers retained their interest in computing, but cost constraints were substantial. If funding was withdrawn, as it was from so many projects, the project itself did not continue (Magidson 1978).

In these early years, the influence of federal funding was decisive, despite the fact that the approach of the federal government to computing in education was not straightforward, coherent or even planned with a goal in mind. In fact, it was often contradictory, piecemeal and at times counter-productive (Molnar 1971). However, that the loss of funding meant the loss of a program demonstrated the role of the government in enabling a program and legitimising it through that funding. When funding was withdrawn, the program was exposed as of uncertain value and thus marginalised. It was not until the dramatic appearance of the microcomputer that the interest of the US federal government in the potential of computers for school education was reignited.

The microstorm

Hobbyist teachers were the instigators of renewed interest in computer applications for schools following the development of the microcomputer and its first commercial edition in 1975. Mainframe computers, even minicomputers, were not just expensive but unwieldy and beyond the reach of most schools. Teacher-enthusiasts, typically mathematics and science teachers, had often built their own microcomputers from a kit at home and then introduced these into their classroom (Becker 1984). While these teachers were few in number, the microstorm changed views on educational computing in the wider American community. The stunning speed with which microcomputers were produced and purchased led to a resurgent belief that computers were changing society profoundly and therefore lives. The public was deluged with media articles and books that predicted revolutionary consequences for society from the widespread use of computers. The personal computer was portrayed as a magical device, akin to a wizard (Stahl 1995). Developing 'computer literacy' in the young became the new imperative and the microcomputer the instrument to produce it. Molnar (1978, 283), who had been influential in the promulgation and promotion of the term, proclaimed a 'crisis' if schools did not impart computer literacy. The National Science Foundation, where Molnar was a Program Director, funded projects that aimed to research and develop computer literacy.

As with computing more generally, the early 1980s marked a watershed for educational computing, in particular, the years from 1981 to 1983. Personal computers were extraordinarily successful, in both homes and businesses, leading to the rapid rise of a competitive consumer market with multiple players (US Congress. OTA 1982). The dramatic increase in sales of the computer and its proliferation across homes and businesses sparked concerns that young people should be prepared for a future in which computers would be pervasive. The extensive job losses during the recession of the early 1980s established a powerful connection between computers and the workplace, which flowed into a belief that schools must use computers if students were to gain jobs in the future (Birman and Ginsburg 1983). Computer manufacturers eyed the potential of the school education sector as a new market. Major manufacturers worked to promote school computing at the same time as they lobbied the federal government for tax concessions to apply to the computer technology they donated to schools (US Congress. OTA 1982). These were granted in the Computer Contribution Act of 1983 (Birman and Ginsburg 1983).

The storm of attention aroused the federal government's interest in the educational potential of the personal computer (US Congress. OTA 1982). In 1980, the Reagan administration had come to office promising smaller government. While federal funding for schools was limited, the administration decided to use its prestige of office as a way of achieving objectives, rather than to direct more funds towards areas which were the responsibility of the states (McDonnell 2005). Instead, the language of persuasion was used. The US Department of Education (1981) provided direction as to the means of achieving this aim:

> Through news conferences, speeches, and other information-disseminating devices, the Secretary of Education should help make the general public, professional educators, and lawmakers aware of the potential benefits of the new technologies and of the need for students to be educated about and with these technologies so that they may understand and control them, for their own purposes and for the good of our society. (US Department of Education 1981, ii)

Government legitimation of computers in education centred on the importance for students of learning to 'control' computers through their use, thus advancing the view that computers were a necessary part of education. Such an argument was not new. Earlier proponents of the use of computers in education had argued that the coming impact of computers on society demanded that school students acquire a working knowledge of them. Two primary reasons predominated: the predicted future demand for skilled labour and the necessity for each citizen to be capable of full participation in a computer-dependent society (eg, CBMS 1972; Molnar 1978).

Earlier approaches to educational uses of computing from the days of the mainframe, such as Papert's LOGO for programming, and the drill and practice of Computer-assisted Instruction continued, as they do in places to this day. Computer literacy, however, became the dominant concern of the period between 1980 and 1985, with considerable effort expended to define computer literacy and to establish practices that developed it (eg, Anderson, Klassen and Johnson 1981; Luehrmann 1981). The Reagan administration's release of the political document *A Nation at Risk* in 1983, in response to perceptions of American decline at a time of recession, heightened the sense of urgency in terms of educational computing. It recommended computer courses as part of a solution to the perceived failure of American education to prepare students vocationally (McDonnell 2005).

While some schools had used computers in the early 1980s, the spread of personal computers into schools was extraordinarily rapid, assisted by coordinated, planned government funding from the states in particular. From '31,000 microcomputers' in schools in 1980, the numbers rose to 'close to a quarter of a million microcomputers in elementary and secondary schools' in 1983 (Roberts 1983, 309). Nor did the momentum fade. In the following three years, so many computers were added to schools that 'between 1983 and 1986 the national average dropped from about 92 students per computer to about 37 students per computer' (US Congress. OTA 1987, 22).

New uses for computers had been enabled by the rapid development and commercial dissemination of personal computers. Continued technological advances meant that educational applications became possible. The comparative cheapness of personal computers compared to existing mainframes and minicomputers meant that they were affordable. The widespread belief that the new technology would revolutionise society – which had emerged with the first computers, then moderated when the technology was better known – was an important impetus to putting personal computers into schools, although previous uses of computers had prepared the way. There was also considerable public support for the teaching of computer literacy in schools (Becker 1984).

Within education, however, there was no unanimity over the role computers could play and there was on-going debate over the meanings and ways of achieving computer literacy. Teachers, administrators and teacher educators attempted the difficult task of repurposing the computer to fit into the school environment. Pressures on schools and teachers to provide computers and to use them in their classrooms increased, although the requisite funding for hardware and software did not necessarily follow (Becker 1984). Teachers who were computer-enthusiasts remained in the minority.

While these computer-using teachers were often the first to introduce computers to their individual schools, the role of governments, both state and federal, was crucial. In a survey of computer coordinators reported by the OTA (US Congress. OTA 1987), the two most common reasons given for prioritising the use of computers in individual schools were state government policies and money. While state government policies were undoubtedly significant, the legitimising function of federal funding on the way computers were perceived by the general public, by business and by school administrators should not be underestimated. In 1987, it was estimated that the federal government had provided US$89 million between

1980 and 1986 under the Chapter 1 program alone to purchase or lease computer hardware and software to students classified as disadvantaged (US Congress. OTA 1987). To do so also classified the computer as a worthwhile educational technology with real benefits, one which should not be denied to the disadvantaged.

Computing technologies as tools for learning

While new technology was a significant spur for government action to introduce and promote the use of computers in education, it was not the only one. Continuing technological innovation and the diffusion of computers into society were also important factors. However, political changes under President Ronald Reagan between 1980 and 1989 assisted the growth of computing through deregulation and the shift to smaller government. Larger firms increased their use of information technology to maximise their profits, including through outsourcing. At the same time, the use of technology by economic competitors internationally, particularly Japan, threatened American dominance, arousing anxiety over the place of the US in the world (US Congress. OTA 1988b).

Fear that the US was in danger of being overtaken technologically brought about a renewed emphasis on education to provide a trained and adaptable workforce (US Congress. OTA 1988b). That this threat was construed as technological in nature lent force to a push for an intensified use of those same technologies in schools. In *Power On! New Tools for Teaching and Learning* (US Congress. OTA 1988a), American society broadly is depicted as technologically rich in contrast to its schools which are portrayed as backward, unchanged in 50 years. By contrast, computing technologies are positioned as 'new learning tools', new tools for new times (US Congress. OTA 1988a, 18). Instead of computer literacy as the aim, the computer was envisioned as 'a tool for learning' which should be used across the curriculum for higher-order tasks such as writing and problem-solving, instead of the then dominant drill and practice (US Congress. OTA 1987, 1). In *Power On! New Tools for Teaching and Learning*, computing technologies were being reconceptualised as tools that were an integral part of teaching and learning, not just as a way of preparing students to live in a world of information technology.

Governmental authorities believed that advanced technology would predominate across workplaces in an information society in which traditional jobs were disappearing and new ones arising. Their focus was on the skills needed in the future workforce (Levin and Rumberger 1987). As computer technology afforded new possibilities within the workplace, through, for instance, networking and the incorporation of images and sound on video-disc, scholars of education were also rethinking the possibilities of the new technologies, suggesting that computing technologies should be recast as 'intellectual tools' or 'tools of the mind' for the 'Information Age' (White, 1986, 168). But thinking about computers as intellectual tools for the information society was also implicated with productivity, specifically, improving the productivity of individual workers at a time of perceived American decline.

To conceptualise the computer as a tool of the mind capable of enhancing learning was also to consider the student experience as one that could be re-engineered through the application of technology, as jobs had been, and to cast schools as lagging behind. The OTA noted that:

> Information technologies have transformed the worlds of business, science, entertainment, the military, government, law, banking, travel, medicine, and agriculture. The question is whether they will make as deep a mark on classroom learning. (US Congress. OTA 1988b, 200)

By 1993, however, when newer technologies were once more the impetus for renewed governmental interest and for new ways of representing computers in education, teachers found themselves blamed for failing to capitalise on the potential the technology represented.

Connecting teachers

Despite the proliferation of personal computers in schools, teachers' use of them had not increased substantially. In the 1990s, concerns began to be raised that teachers had failed to incorporate computers routinely into their teaching and learning. Newer networking applications and extended multimedia capacity for computers had become available at a time when existing regulations covering communications were challenged, as computing and telecommunications technologies overlapped (US Congress. OTA 1995). A Congressional committee commissioned a report by the OTA to investigate the reasons for this failure and the report, *Teachers and Technology: Making the Connection* (US Congress. OTA 1995, iii), begins with the premise that 'despite over a decade of investment in educational hardware and software, relatively few of the nation's 2.8 million teachers use technology in their teaching'. Attention was drawn to the disbursement of funds to equip schools with computers but also to the limited use of these in classrooms (US Congress 1995). Teachers were cast as lacking in technological skills, rather than exercising professional judgements on educational decisions with their students' best interests in mind.

Under President Bill Clinton, who was elected at the end of 1992, legislation promoting the use of educational technology in schools was passed and funds provided for the professional development of teachers. The numbers of computers in schools had continued to rise, reaching a ratio of one computer to approximately nine students (US Congress. OTA 1995). However, these were unevenly distributed and often incapable of running the latest software, meaning that their use in the classroom was often limited or impracticable. This meant that the expansion of telecommunications and the growing spread of the Internet presented significant challenges in terms of adoption and implementation for the very large and diverse school sector (US Congress. OTA 1995).

Importantly, the OTA envisaged educational technology as a necessity which would foster new ways of learning, make teachers more effective and better motivate students (US Congress. OTA 1995). Only the role of the federal government in the further promotion of educational technology was under question. The OTA argued strongly that through promotion of computing technologies, 'the federal government can move to fully legitimize the role of technology to enhance instruction, increase teacher productivity, create new teaching and learning communities, and support educational change' (US Congress. OTA 1995, 31). The changes occurring in technologies and the resulting re-regulation of the communications sector provided a powerful impetus to the report. Concern was expressed that education would be disadvantaged if it was excluded when new communications infrastructures and regulations were being put into place (US Congress. OTA 1995).

Embodied in these views was the belief that education existed in a world that had remained fixed in the past, when the rest of society was using the new technology of the Internet as a matter of course. For students, the ability to use technology was inextricably linked to their future place in the workforce. Without this ability, they would be relegated to lifelong unskilled labour (US Congress OTA. 1995). Teachers were characterised as reluctant to change, requiring pressure to impel them to use computing technologies in their teaching and learning, despite the obsolete equipment with which many of them were forced to work and the acknowledged lack of professional development in the area of technology.

A renewed push to integrate computing technologies into schools began as the Internet was commercialised. In his State of the Union address in

1996, Clinton promised that schools would be connected to the Internet (US Department of Education 1996). The first national plan for technology in education, *Getting America's Students Ready for the 21st Century: Meeting the Technology Literacy Challenge*, was released in 1996 (US Department of Education). A key goal was for teachers and students to have access in their classrooms to computers connected to the Internet. The plan foreshadowed a two billion dollar commitment over five years, much of it from private sources, to ensure a greater penetration of computing technologies into schools. In addition, the federal government deployed its authority to depict computing technologies as central to modern life and to learning, while at the same time asserting that 'for the most part, those technologies are not to be found in the nation's schools' (US Department of Education 1996, 7).

Computing technologies, according to the statement, were transforming every aspect of American society. Linking computer skills, including the Internet, with reading, writing and arithmetic, portrayed them as necessary and intrinsic to the purposes of education (Selfe 1999). The Internet was depicted as extending the capacity of the computer to allow access to 'the best libraries, museums, and other research and cultural resources at our students' and teachers' fingertips', a world of new information (US Department of Education 1996, 5). Instead of the computer as 'tools of the mind' (White 1986, 168), the 'finger-tip effect' had become the key to access more information, as if this in itself would deliver better learning (Perkins 1985, 11). A tap on the keyboard would open the screen to a cornucopia of cultural goods. Yet the amount estimated to be necessary to achieve this vision was around US$30 billion. Mustering community, business and private support was regarded as essential to achieve the aim of equipping the nation's schools with internet-connected computers and enhancing the ability of teachers and students to use them for learning purposes (Smith, Levin and Cianci 1997).

Over the next four years, the Clinton administration introduced several new programs which aimed at extending the use of computers in schools, particularly focused on use of the World Wide Web, and linked this access with future success in a competitive workplace (Roberts 1998). The federal government's provision of surplus computers for schools was one such program (Glennan 1997). A second National Education Technology Plan, *e-Learning – Putting a World-class Education at the Fingertips of All Children* (US Department of Education 2000), was instituted in 2000, although the funding attached to it was smaller than that of 1996. This plan built on the goals of its predecessor, although the focus shifted to digital technologies and networked applications. Digital content was identified as central to bringing about more effective teaching and learning (US Department of Education 2000). The internet technology boom that had followed the public listing on the stock exchange of the first internet companies, such as Netscape, appeared to be a powerful endorsement of the government's message.

Technology and accountability

Following the election of President George W Bush, the emphasis on federal support for computing technologies and their use in education shifted. The collapse of the internet stock bubble during the course of 2000 undermined a key argument which claimed that the Internet was transforming the economy. The Bush administration's educational endeavour took shape in the 'No Child Left Behind' (NCLB) legislation of 2001, as the renewal of the Elementary and Secondary Education Act was designated (Groen 2012). The focus of the legislation was standards-based: holding schools accountable to standards, testing students' levels of attainment in language and mathematics, and specifying levels of teacher qualifications (Shaul and Ganson 2005). The legislation was controversial as it represented an extension of the federal government's authority over the states in education, requiring adherence to prescribed standards and applying sanctions for failing to achieve these (Groen 2012). In the legislation, literacy with computing technologies was considered necessary for students, but the technologies were conceptualised as support for the curriculum rather than as a means of learning (Culp, Honey and Mandinach 2005). Grants of funds were provided by the federal government to the states for the purchase of computing technologies as educational aids (Metiri Group 2009).

The new National Education Technology Plan of the Bush administration, *Toward a New Golden Age in American Education*, focused on the failure of computing technologies to make inroads into schools or to transform learning. While recommending on-demand internet access for students, the plan considered computing technologies in the light of whether they would assist schools, teachers and students to achieve the standards required under the NCLB legislation (Wyzard 2011). The emphasis on accountability embodied in the legislation contributed to the greater adoption of computing technologies within schools for administrative purposes: to manage and analyse data in order to improve student and school performance on the prescribed testing (*Economist* 2013).

In 2009, as part of stimulus measures adopted in the US during the financial crisis, the Obama administration introduced the Race to the Top program of competitive grants for schools. Congress allocated an amount of over US$4 billion and schools could apply for grants for programs which supported four key areas. One of these was a continued focus on standards and assessment. The others addressed schools' data systems, teacher recruitment and underperforming schools (US Department of Education 2009). Funds from this program could be spent on technology if its projected use supported aims in these four areas. The vision of the Obama administration for educational technologies was presented in 2010 in a new National Education Technology Plan, *Transforming American Education. Learning Powered by Technology* (US Department of Education 2010).

Contrary to the plan produced under George Bush, which envisaged computing technologies as supporting and extending student learning, the 2010 plan conceptualised computing technologies as the tool to drive the transformation of schools. Education was identified as 'the key to America's economic growth and prosperity and our ability to compete in the global economy' (US Department of Education 2010, ix). The aim of education was to 'develop inquisitive, creative, resourceful thinkers' (US Department of Education 2010, 1). The plan noted that the use of educational technologies varied widely across the country but that children's and young people's lives beyond school were saturated with a variety of different technologies which enabled new informal learning opportunities. Yet the plan argued that by and large these new technologies had not been adopted within classrooms. Premised on the view of an education system which had failed to shift with changing times, the plan advocated greater use of digital technologies to enhance individualised learning through on-going feedback during learning tasks.

In 2013, President Obama initiated a new program, ConnectEd, to generate the momentum which would enable 99 per cent of students and teachers to access high-speed Internet within five years. The connectivity which could be delivered by high-speed broadband was explained as vital for school students but also for the nation. Faster broadband offered 'more rigorous and engaging classes' and furthered the individualisation of learning through tailored software (The White House 2013, 3). At a time of slow economic growth and high unemployment, it was claimed that connecting schools to high-speed broadband would stimulate 'a robust market in educational software' which would 'create American jobs and export opportunities in a global marketplace of over $1 trillion' (The White House 2013, 3). In addition, fast internet access held out the promise of the US once again resuming technological leadership over its competitors which were making 'aggressive investments' in digital technologies (The White House 2013, 4). Only with such investments could the American economy's competitiveness in the global economy be enhanced in the future.

Significant disparities in the outcomes of schooling amongst students are a feature of the diverse and decentralised American school system and have prompted successive federal governments to intervene in educational policymaking since Lyndon Johnson's administration marked a watershed in 1965. The authorisation of the NCLB legislation of 2001 has seen federal efforts to improve the quality of schooling intensify, despite resistance and political contestation. Control of schooling remains primarily with local districts and with the states, but the federal government has been able to advance some of its aims through its funding programs and advocacy (Vergari 2012). Initially peripheral, computing technologies have been asserted to be pivotal to the national project to improve schools and raise the quality of education. Ironically, those same technologies have been harnessed for other purposes: the collection and analysis of data from student testing by school and government education authorities (*Economist* 2013).

The possibilities opened by the ability to capture such data were explored in the National Education Technology Plan of 2010. One idea canvassed was that of enhanced student learning through greater self-direction in response to continuous feedback provided during assessments. Another was the projected benefit at the school level and beyond, at that of the educational authority, from the growth in information which could be analysed in terms of systemic performance: 'administrators and policymakers should be able to mine assessment data over time to examine the effectiveness of their program and interventions' (US Department of Education 2010, 35). In echoes of previous years, the potential of new technologies to deliver change in education is advanced as the key to achieving higher levels of educational outcomes for students.

Conclusion

The role of the US federal government in funding the development of computers and of the Internet was critical. Its role in supporting computers in education is less well known. While often haphazard, it was nonetheless significant in authorising the computer as not only a worthwhile educational technology, but also one that was indispensable. Two factors stand out as creating impetus for the federal government to promote computing technology in schools. The first was the widespread use of new computing technologies in the workplace. The federal government responded with interventions in education in the later 1960s when computers became widely used in business and in government, in the 1980s following the introduction of the microcomputer, and with the development of internet technology in the 1990s and in 2010. The second was a perception that the American economy was losing ground to foreign competitors, particularly in computing technologies, which led to federal government support for computing technologies in schools late in the 1980s and again in 2010 and 2013.

Governments responded in different ways. In the 1960s, large amounts of government funding were dispensed, with little accountability required, to portray the computer as a tool to improve the efficiency of learning. In the 1980s, governments deployed persuasion as a device to depict the computer as transforming society on the one hand and on the other, as offering new opportunities for learning. In the 1990s and between 2010 and 2013, the federal government actively positioned itself as a modernising government by adopting and advocating the Internet as a tool to transform both learning and schooling. All approaches were underpinned by the same key ideas across the decades, of schooling as inculcating the required skills in the future workforce and of new technologies as maintaining American supremacy in international competition. At each stage, the interplay of government, the academy, and business and industry, varied, but all were regarded as necessary, if unequal, partners in a joint endeavour.

Over many years, the US federal government lent legitimacy to the idea that the computer was an 'educational good' (Bigum 2002, 135). Its means included funding, the discursive framing of the computer in numerous reports, legislative acts, speeches and media appearances and its advocacy for particular roles that the technology should play in maintaining America's place in the world. That these efforts were haphazard over the years did not detract from the impact of government support. If schools do not now use computing technologies, they are undoubtedly regarded as backward. The US federal government was a significant actor that made this designation possible.

Chapter Two

The Computer in Australia

In June 1951, Australia's first computer performed a rudimentary version of the tune, *Colonel Bogey*, to an audience of local and international scientists at Sydney's inaugural computer conference (CSIRO 2011). Australia's first electronic computer was the world's fourth, built far away from those constructed in the US and the UK, and with limited knowledge of wartime developments in computers. Initially called the CSIR Mk. 1, then later the Commonwealth Scientific and Industrial Research Automatic Computer (CSIRAC), the computer was built between 1947 and 1949 by the Commonwealth Scientific and Industrial Research Organisation (CSIRO). The CSIRO employed an English scientist, Trevor Pearcey, who had worked on the development of radar in Britain during the war years. En route to Australia, Pearcey visited scientist Howard Aiken and the Harvard Mark I computer project in the US and, once in Australia, was behind the mission to build an Australian electronic computer (McCann and Thorne 2000).

Beginning operation in 1950, the CSIRAC carried out computations for the scientific community (McCann and Thorne 2000) but rapid technological developments in the computing field in the US meant that the CSIRAC, like other computers in both the UK and the US, was quickly superseded. With limited resources, the CSIRO discontinued its support for computing in 1954, focusing instead on radiophysics and particularly on agriculture (Pearcey 1988). Despite much pioneering work by a number of individuals in Australia, only small numbers of computers were built here (Pearcey 1988). The US soon dominated the computer industry, supported by its enormous defence expenditure. Most computing technology in Australia was, and remains to this day, imported.

The story of the CSIRAC illustrates the differences between the US and Australia with regard to computers. At the end of the Second World War, the US was the pre-eminent power, both economically and militarily. The American federal government had maintained its military spending after the war, creating a marketplace for computers. Importantly, following the end of the war, Australia's spending on defence rapidly declined, in five years falling 'from £536m in 1942–3 to £20m in 1947–48' (Karmel and Brunt 1963, 115). While it rose from this low base during the Cold War, as a percentage of GDP, Australia's defence spending was small in comparison with the US, whose defence expenditure effectively underwrote the computer industry. Nor did Australia have the large business and industrial domestic markets or the academic and skills infrastructure which existed in the US. The disparity in the academic base is demonstrated by the difference between the two countries in tertiary education. In the US in 1964, 12 per cent of the population undertook tertiary education, whereas in the same period in Australia, the corresponding figure was only 1.9 per cent (Shaw 1966).

While wealthy, Australia was at a disadvantage in the world trading economy. Small and distant from its trading partners, its emphasis was still overwhelmingly on agricultural products (Karmel and Brunt 1963). Accordingly, Australia's federal governments during the 1950s and 1960s judged the national priority to be economic growth rather than defence. The reweighting of the CSIRO's research focus to that of agriculture reflected the exigencies of the time. Scarce resources were being reallocated to face a different economic and social landscape, one in which agriculture comprised the bulk of Australia's exports (Karmel and Brunt 1963). Australia's small population, limited industry and commerce, and lack of scientific expertise meant that the establishment of an indigenous computer industry here was an unrealistic dream, but it is one that persisted for many years.

Beginnings

In 1955, the now outmoded CSIRAC was moved to the University of Melbourne Department of Physics and the university opened a Computation Laboratory (Pearcey 1988). Computers were also acquired by the University of Sydney and the New South Wales University of Technology (Thornton, Linton-Simpkins, Stanley and Locksley 1983). In 1957, the second Australian computer conference was held. A number of speakers were from scientific computing projects in Britain but the conference also hosted representatives from some of the large manufacturers of business machines which had begun to manufacture computers, including Ferranti, a British firm, and IBM. These overseas firms showed an interest in developing a market in Australia (Pearcey 1988). The conference was a means of disseminating more recent technical developments, but it also drew together those in Australia who were interested in computing. These individuals formed a nucleus that would go on to develop the first Australian computer societies which were influential in bringing together those interested in computing and in promoting computing to the wider public (McCann and Thorne 2000).

The conference of 1957 sparked the interest of large commercial users in data processing (McCann and Thorne 2000), although in some subsidiaries of British or American firms, typically the innovators in terms of technology in the Australian market, data processing was already underway (Karmel and Brunt 1963). The very different economic structure and small population size in Australia made the use of computers in the 1950s uneconomic for all but the largest and most information-intensive users. These were the government sector and large firms, both of which had growing volumes of data (Tatnall 1993). IBM opened a data processing centre equipped with 650 model computers in Sydney in 1958 (IBM, n.d.). The first computer to be used by the federal government is believed to have been in the Bureau of Census and Statistics in 1958 (Tatnall 1993). This was the same pattern of early civilian use as in the US. Census bureaus had a substantial need for information processing purposes (Campbell-Kelly and Aspray 1996).

From 1959, computers were installed progressively in most sizable federal government departments, including Treasury, Defence, Foreign Affairs and Taxation. State governments too began to install computers (Thornton et al. 1983). The federal government's actions in promoting the computer as a necessary tool for large-scale data processing were significant and had far-reaching implications (Tatnall 1993). One was the development in the 1960s of vocational computing courses in the Colleges of Advanced Education to meet the needs of the government for skilled personnel (Tatnall 1993). By the mid 1960s, the federal government was taking the lead in promoting the use of computers in the public service and, lacking skilled personnel, introduced training courses for its staff (Tatnall 1993). While the number of computers in use was still very few, approximately 200 in 1962, there was considerable interest in computers in the scientific community and it was expected that their numbers would rapidly increase (Hosie 1965). Amongst the general public, there was less awareness of computers, consistent with their limited penetration into Australian society more broadly.

Nevertheless, ideas about the changes computers were creating in American society were reflected by some commentators in Australia. The disappearance of work and the growth of leisure were predicted, but so too was the discomfiting prospect that in future workers would need to upgrade their skills constantly. In an early Australian example of the ambivalence computers could provoke, the 'obedient morons' were welcomed for their potential to eliminate mundane jobs thereby freeing people from monotonous tasks, at the same time as anxiety was expressed over the social dislocation which could result (Hosie 1965, 147). This oscillation between excitement and fear was a common feature in the US as computer technology became cheaper, more efficient and reliable and thus in more widespread use. In Australia, by contrast, in the same period the more limited use of computers meant that fear of their impact on society was more muted. Instead, at a time of rapid economic growth, Australian governments and businesses were much more concerned over a shortage of people with the requisite skills and training to work with computers (Tatnall 1993).

The demand for skilled labour

By 1967, the number of computers in use in Australia had grown to approximately 600. While still low, there was more demand for employees with computer skills than could be met, raising concerns from the head of the Commonwealth Public Service Board over student awareness of computing as a possible career choice (Thorneycroft 1967). Very fast economic growth in Australia of over five per cent per annum during the 1960s, large infrastructure projects and a resources boom had led to concerns over labour shortages, particularly in science and technology (McMahon 1968). Large commercial firms also used computers, including QANTAS, insurance companies, banks and international subsidiaries such as IBM (Goldsworthy 1980). The increased number of installations meant higher demand for staff trained in their use. At the same time, the lower number of tertiary graduates than in the US limited the number of skilled workers available (Smith and de Ferranti 1976).

Despite the rapid growth of computers in use in Australia in the 1960s, their numbers were far fewer than in the US. In 1970, 80,000 computers were in use in the US compared to an estimated 1,132 in Australia, the majority in private business (Wearing, Carss and Fitzgerald 1976). These figures meant that there were approximately 39 computers per 100,000 people in the US. In Australia, by contrast, in 1970, there were fewer than nine computers per 100,000 people (UN 1971). These statistics represent a much slower rate of penetration of computers into Australian society than in the US but also than in other OECD countries (Thornton et al. 1983). The more limited use of computers in Australian workplaces meant that fewer employees and members of the public were confronted with computers and the almost hysterical fear of change that had affected the US in the same period.

From government, where computers were used in information processing, key individuals moved into tertiary institutions in the 1960s and early 1970s and became influential advocates for the adoption of computing disciplines in universities and colleges and later, in schools. Attempts were made to encourage schools to raise awareness amongst their students of the career possibilities in various aspects of computing (Tatnall 1993). In the early 1970s, computers were becoming increasingly important for business and large organisations. Small and medium size enterprises were planning to adopt computers, amplifying an already acute shortage of skilled labour. Two purposes were envisaged for new courses in both higher education and in schools: to raise awareness of computers and to train the future workforce in an era of intensifying technological change (Smith and de Ferranti 1976).

While Australian workplace use of computers was more limited than in the US, the depiction of the computer in popular media and books disseminated American views widely. Works like Toffler's *Future Shock* (1970) meshed with claims that a '"Fourth Revolution" in education' would result (Smith and de Ferranti 1976, 30) and sparked some interest in educational computing in government circles. South Australia and Tasmania took early and concerted steps to introduce computing applications to schools, in 1968 and 1972 respectively, with Western Australia following (Zammit 1989). Victoria, Queensland and New South Wales, the most populous states, lacked central direction on the use of computers in schools, although programs within regions and individual schools were growing in size and reach (Zammit 1989).

The federal government's interest in the potential of computers in education was demonstrated in 1972, when Malcolm Fraser, then Minister of Education and Science in the Coalition Government, requested the Australian Advisory Committee on Research and Development in Education (AACRDE) to inquire into the possible use of computers in education. In the dying days of the Coalition Government, when the election campaign was underway, it possibly reflected a move to gain some electoral advantage. It also followed a number of reports from other federal government departments on the use of computers in the workforce. The first federal inquiry into the 'impact of computers on education' by the AACRDE resulted in the Wearing report, *Computers and Teaching in Australia*, released in 1976 (Wearing et al., iii). As well as investigating the potential for computers in education at secondary and tertiary levels, the inquiry also considered whether federal funding should be provided for educational computing.

In considering the issue of expensive mainframe computers and their possible applications, committee members also had to contend with existing views on the purposes of education and whether computers were consistent with these. Far from displaying unanimity on the role that computers could play in education, the committee members failed to agree on a position. One dissenter resigned from the committee altogether. The distance between them was noted in the report:

> Two extreme positions have been expressed with regard to computer applications in education. The one extreme is that the applications of computers is education's greatest hope. The other is that computers will destroy whatever is of value in education. (Wearing et al. 1976, 55)

Unable to adopt a firm view, the committee recommended a wait and see approach to funding any investment in computers in education, particularly in the school sector. In the US, the federal government had been funding projects to explore the use of computers in school education since the 1960s, but this funding was in decline when the Wearing report was released in Australia. While the Australian federal government provided funding for the acquisition of computers in the tertiary sector in the 1960s and 1970s, momentum to initiate a similar project for schools was lacking. The use of computers in Australian workplaces was much more limited than in the US. Importantly, however, the lack of a domestic computer manufacturing industry meant that computers and associated equipment were imported and therefore considerably more expensive in Australia.

The primary impetus for the development of computing courses in schools came instead from teacher-enthusiasts who had been exposed to computing as undergraduate students (Tatnall and Davey 2006). The first tertiary courses in computing had been established in the 1960s, with tertiary educated teachers beginning in schools in the early 1970s. These teachers were not simply focused on vocational preparation, but also on the perceived benefits of using computers for their students (Walker 1991). The introduction of the personal computer in the mid 1970s, however, brought about a sea change in attitudes, particularly within government circles.

The computer and unemployment

The boom of the 1960s came to an abrupt end in the early 1970s. Unemployment rose rapidly in an environment of stagflation. Until then, while there had been job losses as a result of the installation of computing technologies, these changes were almost invisible. People were absorbed into other positions within organisations while those who left through natural attrition were not replaced (Thornton et al. 1983). During the 1970s, it was estimated that 20,000 people per year in information processing jobs were displaced by computers (Thornton et al. 1983). Rapidly rising wages in the first half of the 1970s coincided with declining prices for computers as the newer microcomputing technologies were introduced. Many clerical workers in the early 1970s were women and the deployment of computers to automate clerical work coincided with the move to equal pay for women (Thornton et al. 1983). The intersection of these trends had a profound impact on the Australian workplace. Small businesses were able to afford a microcomputer and deploy it to replace labour.

For many Australians the arrival of the micro, or personal, computer crystallised perceptions that technology was the cause of the highest unemployment since the Great Depression. Fears, by no means overblown, of mass job loss as a result of automation led to governmental inquiries (eg, Myers 1980) and considerable media commentary. Routinely, social dislocation was sheeted home to 'technological change' (Myers 1980), a phrase which elided the individual decisions made in governments, businesses and industries to employ new technologies for the specific purposes of reducing labour costs and increasing the speed of operations (Thornton et al. 1983). This technological determinism was criticised by Barry Jones (1983, 216), then an ALP member of Parliament, who likened it to waking 'one morning to find a computer in the garden' as if it had appeared from nowhere but had come to stay.

For employees, the personal computer was no mere symbol. Its use by employers in government, business and industry brought about changes in working lives, or determined whether jobs were eliminated. In Australia, personal computers were acquired by small businesses which had not previously had access to computers, whereas in the US, initial uptake had been by consumers. The extension of computerised process control systems into manufacturing began only in the 1980s in Australia, unlike the US where it had been employed since the 1960s, and the job losses in manufacturing further highlighted the links between computing technologies and unemployment (Thornton et al. 1983).

For school leavers, the larger baby boom demographic, jobs were disappearing. Fears were expressed that some of these young people would never gain work (Thornton et al. 1983). The apparent link between unemployment and the deployment of computers in workplaces led to widespread public support for educational computing in schools. It was seen as a way of preparing students for a future working with computers and also of equipping them with the computer skills believed to enable certainty of employment. The states and territories too were sensitive to rising unemployment and the perceived association between the introduction of computers and labour shedding. Responsible constitutionally for the majority of education spending, they lacked further resources to deal with the problems they faced in schooling and struggled in particular to fund rising school retention rates.

The numbers of students staying on in school in the post-compulsory years had risen steadily. From 1969 to 1981, the number of students retained at Year 10 nationally increased by 14 per cent in government schools, in Year 11 by 11 per cent and in Year 12 by 5.5 per cent, with the majority of those retained being girls. In total, the increase was 30.9 per cent over 12 years (CSC 1983). Importantly, the states and territories assumed that this increased retention of young people in schools was the direct result of workplaces employing new computing technologies, thereby eliminating traditional jobs for school leavers. Their views were reinforced by the Commonwealth Schools Commission, a national statutory body, which argued that persistently high levels of youth unemployment were not just a cyclical phenomenon, but a structural one which was a 'worldwide political and economic reality' (CSC 1981, 12). Teenage unemployment had risen six-fold between 1966 and 1980 (Gregory and Stricker 1981). This new reality required higher levels of skills and education for young people, in effect mandating higher retention rates in schools.

In 1982 curriculum and computer education authorities from each state and territory met in Perth. They agreed that 'computing and information processing are now seen by every State and Territory Education Department as being of sufficient importance to require their inclusion in the education of every Australian child' (WCCIPAS 1982, 4). They pressed for federal assistance in funding computer education programs and supported a national approach towards computing in schools. In the federal election campaign of 1983, the introduction of computer education to schools was part of the policy platform of both major parties. When the ALP won the election, it moved quickly to devise such a policy. The policy text that resulted, *Teaching, Learning and Computers* (CSC. NACCS 1983), was significant. It developed a model for a National Computer Education Program, the first of its kind federally, and funding for the program was allocated by the minister.

The introduction of the personal computer was a powerful impetus to the policy, as were political considerations during an election campaign and pressure from the states and territories. The federal government, however, was a hesitant participant. The policy was small, almost experimental, and the devolution of implementation to the states and territories has tended to obscure the federal government's role. It was nevertheless important. It positioned computers as an essential part of the teaching and learning process and instituted changes that affected teachers, schools and students across the country. The first federal government initiatives with regard to computers in education in the US occurred in the 1960s. That the first federal government program to support computers in schools did not begin until 1983 in Australia is a reflection primarily of the different roles computers played in Australian society and the perception that Australia's comparative decline economically was linked to the use of advanced technology, including computers, overseas (Thornton et al. 1983). This is a theme that resonates through the following years.

Micro-economic reform

The ALP's election to government in 1983 followed a deep recession. In 1983 and 1986, economic crises during the ALP's first period of government led to its embrace of financial deregulation, signified by the landmark decision to float the dollar in 1983, which set in train a number of related policy decisions (Martin 1999). The economic situation provided both imperative and justification for a change in the government's ideology and the governmental practices it introduced to develop and implement new policies that aimed to restructure the Australian economy. Historically, the ALP had considered the role of government as central to the amelioration of disadvantage. Under the Hawke/Keating ALP Governments, the role of government was reconceptualised. The task for government was to ensure economic prosperity through transforming Australian society in a way that privileged the role of private businesses and individuals in economic activity, signified by 'the market'. Widely known as 'economic rationalism', although its progenitor was the neoliberalism of Thatcher and Reagan, this ideology extended to education which became viewed through the prism of its contribution to the national economy (Dudley and Vidovich 1995, 44).

Absorbed by the economic difficulties of 1986 and the election of 1987, the ALP Government withdrew funding for the computer education program which had been established following the NACCS Report of 1983. The federal government's discontinuation of the program was part of an exercise in cost-cutting, but one that did not detract from its initial acknowledgement of the computer as a necessary part of education. Instead, the focus of the federal government shifted to instituting reforms throughout Australian society, including education, that would make Australia more competitive, more market-focused and its people less dependent on government.

Within Australian society, computing technologies had become more prominent but also more diverse. Significant changes had taken place also in the now global computing industry (Industry Commission 1995). The development of the personal computer had enabled American multinationals to relocate their operations to different regions around the world in response to competitive pressures from other countries. The computer industry was an early mover but also an enabler of the globalisation of business and industry, which saw large firms and increasingly smaller ones move their operations to cheaper offshore destinations. The declining costs of computing technologies, including networking, and the stabilisation of hardware types led to a greater focus on services and software, increasing the usefulness and penetration of computing into all aspects of business and government and increasingly into the Australian home (Industry Commission 1995).

The federal government viewed computers as essential to making Australia competitive internationally. In 1977, under the Fraser Coalition Government, assistance to industries using computers had been provided through a bounty on computers (Parliament of Australia 1991). In 1984, this bounty was extended and included a wide variety of computer-related products and peripherals. Designed to expand the information technology sector in Australia and to reduce costs for users of information technology, much of the benefit however went to overseas subsidiaries of multinational computer companies (Industry Commission 1995). The information technology industry in Australia, while still producing and assembling computing technologies, was dominated by local subsidiaries of large international companies (Industry Commission 1995).

The high number of multinational firms in Australia, the dependence of local firms on these suppliers and their propensity to shift facilities to other countries left Australia vulnerable to decisions made elsewhere. Government assistance to industry was one tool to try to prevent businesses from relocating overseas with the inevitable job losses that would follow. The computer bounty was one such program. IBM Australia was one of the biggest beneficiaries, receiving nearly AU$10 million between 1991 and 1994 (Industry Commission 1995). A number of other forms of government assistance were also available for information technology companies, including from state governments. Taxation benefits were another means of assisting companies (Industry Commission 1995).

By 1987, computing technologies had become an intrinsic part of the local economy with sales of information technology products and services worth AU$7939 million (Parliament of Australia 1991). In 1989, the top

50 information technology companies in Australia reportedly had sales of AU$8.85 billion, out of an estimated industry total of AU$10.3 billion, and employed 36,855 people (Parliament of Australia 1991). Australian-owned information technology companies formed only a minor part of the industry. The top echelon of the 50 information technology companies were all multinational corporations, for which Australia was attractive as a substantial market in the Asia-Pacific region, exceeded only by Japan (Dedrick and Kraemer 1993). The purpose of tax incentives and other industry assistance measures was to promote investment in Australia but, above all, to provide employment through retaining such multinational subsidiaries in Australia.

While it is impossible to judge the degree to which such assistance added to the number of computers in business and industry, their use increased rapidly during the late 1980s and early 1990s. By 1993, the Industry Commission (1995, 61) estimated that Australia's 'per capita rate of PC ownership was 22 per cent, compared to 26 per cent in the United States of America'. In business, the numbers of computers were much higher, with 49 per cent of businesses possessing computers. Amongst businesses with more than 100 employees, fewer than one per cent did not have a computer (ABS 1994a, 1994b). Of those businesses with fewer than 19 employees, 46 per cent had computers (ABS 1994a). The federal government comprised more than 10 per cent of the information technology market, with state, territory and local governments also making up a significant proportion (Industry Commission 1995).

Government measures to assist business and industry to acquire and use computing technologies embodied a belief that they were crucial for Australian business. The federal government acted on different fronts to regulate and to shape the adoption and use of new technologies, in effect establishing and altering the 'rules of the game' over a long period (Galperin 2004a, 162). In 1947, the federal government included computer parts in items that were dutiable, acted as purchaser of computing technologies and introduced tax incentives for companies employing computers in their operations. Since then, successive federal governments deemed computing technologies to be both a threat and a promise. The use of computing technologies to improve the operations of business and governments overseas represented a threat to Australia's economic performance. More efficient foreign businesses could gain market share from Australian companies. However, the widespread adoption of computing technologies by Australian businesses and governments held out the promise of maintaining economic growth and status *vis-à-vis* other advanced economies. So the federal government regulated and contained computing technologies on the one hand, but encouraged and promoted them on the other.

The pursuit by the ALP when in government of policies to internationalise the Australian economy though micro-economic and structural reform created winners and losers in the economy, evident during the recession of 1991. For many employees, particularly in areas of lower skills, large numbers of job losses meant long-term unemployment as jobs for the less skilled disappeared. This was part of a trend that had begun in the early 1970s. Over a period of 25 years, from the 1970s to the late 1990s, full-time jobs declined by 20 per cent, while part-time jobs trebled (Lucarelli 2003). Rising use of computing technologies in skilled jobs and the elimination of unskilled jobs through computerised automation, attractive to Australian employers because of perceived high wages, led increasingly to the acceptance of a causal link between intensive use of computing technologies and a highly skilled, high-wage future (Dedrick and Kraemer 1993).

For government, computing technologies and their use in education came to be seen as key to enabling skill levels to be raised, thus leading to employment in the future knowledge-intensive industries. These industries were depicted as the employers of the future, already successful in the US and Europe and increasingly the suppliers of sophisticated technologies in Australia (Lucarelli 2003). At the same time, such industries appeared to offer a way to move the Australian economy from reliance on the export of commodities and the inevitable boom and bust cycles. The new technologies of the Internet and enhanced computing and communications technologies appeared to offer the tools to redesign education for a new era, thereby equipping students as future workers with new skills that would bring about enhanced competitiveness. That the US in 1993 was promoting the 'information superhighway' as the basis of a new knowledge society was also an important impetus to join the race.

Convergence

By 1993, dramatic changes were occurring in the technology and policy landscape at a time when media, entertainment and information technology companies, particularly multinationals, were exploiting new opportunities for profit-making. Previously separate communications, computing, broadcasting and entertainment industries were brought together in conglomerates through mergers and acquisitions to distribute services via the new communications technologies encompassed in the term 'broadband' (James 1994). International companies positioned themselves to deliver these services, employing the rhetoric of the 'convergence' of information and communication technologies as justification for their entry into industries which had been the domain of governments (Industry Commission 1995). New spheres for such companies had been opened up in Australia, but also in many countries overseas, through technological developments and widespread privatisations which allowed for market operations where they had previously been restricted.

Federal government interest in the new technologies of multimedia and communications, and the uses to which they could be put, was prompted in part by pressures on regulatory regimes from previously separate communications and computing businesses. The federal government regulated telecommunications and the broadcasting industry, but the computer industry was considered to be part of the commercial sector. The use of the new technology of broadband by companies to provide services across multiple platforms presented challenges to industries which had been previously separate (James 1994). In the period 1993 to 1996, the Keating Government initiated a number of enquiries in different departments to investigate the application of new technologies and the issues related to convergence. New infrastructures and regulatory regimes were required and the Keating Government also saw possibilities to position itself as forward-looking, with an eye to the next election (Joseph 1996).

The new regimes were underpinned by the justificatory rhetoric of the 'knowledge economy', which rendered the practices of the old economy, based on industrial manufacturing, obsolete. Computing technologies, seen through this prism, were again the drivers of a new world, but a world that superseded the old paradigm of industrial manufacture. The term 'knowledge economy' was used to signify necessary changes in societies, both internationally and nationally. The promise of the knowledge economy was the replacement of the jobs that had been lost from the old industrial economy with new, better paid and more satisfying jobs in the knowledge industries. These jobs depended crucially on computing technologies. Enhanced education was the key to employing the new technologies successfully in order to create knowledge industries.

At the federal government level between 1993 and 1996, a cluster of reports was produced that investigated different aspects of the new computing technologies. The cluster included whole-of-government approaches from broadband infrastructure, telecommunications, copyright, creative and industrial policy to employment and education policy. Technology was also connected to both employment and education in a substantial report,

Converging Technology, Work and Learning (NBEET 1995b), intended to consider the role of new technologies in these fields. Its preparation was supported by a separate report specifically into the use of technology at all levels of education in Australia, *Education and Technology Convergence* (Tinkler et al. 1996). Commissioned in 1994 by the National Board of Employment, Education and Training, the purpose of *Education and Technology Convergence* was to provide information on the use of computing technologies in educational institutions across the school, training and tertiary sectors. Both reports were to inform government on the application of new computing technologies and their potential to change work and patterns of employment, as well as the consequent changes that would be required in education to introduce the new skills needed by a future workforce (NBEET 1995a).

A central construct of *Education and Technology Convergence* was that the knowledge economy was vital to Australia's future in an age of globalisation and that the convergence of information and communication technologies was a crucial element of achieving this knowledge economy. For future workers, 'information literacy' was mandatory for success in the knowledge economy and therefore, at all levels of education, the new computing technologies should be employed to improve learning and develop the necessary skills (Tinkler et al. 1996, 73). The report was completed and released in the last weeks of the Keating Government's term in office and its impact was muted by the change of government. Nevertheless, its linking of informational skills with new technology and with education represented a current of thought that was popular at the time and has retained currency to this day in international policy circles (eg, UNESCO 2011). Globalisation and national educational performance were perceived as critically linked with the new technologies, as both driver and instrument of success (Galperin 2004b).

The information economy

In March 1996, the Coalition parties, led by John Howard, inflicted a landslide defeat on the Keating ALP Government, ending 13 years of ALP Government at the federal level. The new Howard Government moved quickly to distance itself from Keating and the ALP, slashing government spending in its first budget, reducing the size of the public service and moving rapidly to the privatisation of not just government businesses, but also of government services. These were an expression of the Coalition's and, in particular, John Howard's underlying beliefs in private enterprise, individual choice and small government (Aulich and O'Flynn 2007). The Coalition

Government's orientation to business was evident in these privatisations and its values were reflected in the government's policy statements and choices. Over time, these led to the privileging of the private over the public in all aspects of public policy (Aulich and O'Flynn 2007).

The Coalition Government regarded the state's role as supporting and 'enabling' business, the true engine of economic growth (Commonwealth of Australia 1997, 79). In this, it reflected a principle enunciated by former Liberal prime minister, Billy McMahon (McMahon 1968, 19), as far back as 1968, that 'government must be an ancillary to industry'. The Coalition Government systematically expanded the openings for private businesses while at the same time it reduced the federal government's role in a variety of operations. As Aulich and O'Flynn (2007, 372) write, the 'period immediately following Howard's election (i.e. 1996–8) represented the biggest disposal of public enterprises in Australian history'.

The partial privatisation of Telstra reflected the government's orientation to private business but was also a response to pressures from business within Australia and overseas. The new forms of computing technologies that had preoccupied the Keating Government during its second term, signified by the use of the term 'convergence', were now dominated by the Internet and the World Wide Web. Driven by large businesses, both overseas and in Australia, regulatory regimes in telecommunications were coming under attack (Brock 2003). The ability to combine communications and computing technologies in single devices in a competitive marketplace pressured existing models of telecommunications ownership and pricing. At the heart of this struggle were property rights in the area of communications (Brock 2003). At the same time, the new computing technologies offered enticing prospects for Australian society and for businesses. The Howard Government began a project to increase the use of these technologies throughout Australian society, but particularly within government itself and in education, and employed the term 'information economy' to signify its focus.

Education was one element of the proposed information economy. The first Coalition Government policy in relation to education and technology was *Learning for the Knowledge Society: An Education and Training Action Plan for the Information Economy* released in 2000 (DETYA 2000b). *Learning for the Knowledge Society* attempted to put in place policies to extend the reach of new computing and communications technologies and to position the educational sector as a consumer market for off-the-shelf digital products. This was reflected in the imperative to the educational sector that it 'must cooperate with the private sector to promote an active and productive content and services delivery market' (DETYA 2000b, 11). The needs of the business sector were an important influence on the Coalition Government and the Internet was seen as a powerful means of enabling more profitable businesses (Commonwealth of Australia 1998). Business adoption of the Internet was rapid when compared with that of households, as the table below demonstrates.

Year	Percentage of employing businesses with computers	Internet access
Jun 1994	49%	
Jun 1998	64%	30%
Jun 2000	76%	56%
Jun 2001	84%	69%
2006*	88.8%	81.3%
2009–10	Not stated	91%
Year	Percentage of households with a computer	Internet access
1994	24%	
1996	34%	7.5%
1998	44%	16%
2000	54%	33%
2002	61%	46%
2007	73%	64%
2010–2011	83%	79%

*Changes to sampling have an impact on comparability

Table 1. Business and household use of computing technologies.
(Source: Australian Bureau of Statistics 1994–2012)

The government's efforts were designed to improve business access to services, but also to markets. Australian households and schools were considered as potential consumers, thus internet access was a matter of enabling businesses to reach a larger market.

However, the transition from dial-up internet access to broadband was bumpy. In 2002, the majority of Australian schools did not have broadband access or alternatively sufficient bandwidth to enable them to use it effectively (NOIE 2002). The Coalition Government took the view that in the provision of broadband infrastructure and services, 'the market is the primary determinant' (NOIE 2004, 5). Government responsibility to provide infrastructure and services was limited to areas where it was uneconomic for commercial companies to do so, such as in rural and remote areas. In 2003 and 2004, education ministers from the federal government and the states and territories, working through the Ministerial Council on Education, Employment, Training and Youth Affairs (MCEETYA), developed plans to extend the bandwidth available to educational institutions. MCEETYA worked too with telecommunications providers to improve the bandwidth available to schools across the nation (MCEETYA 2004; MCEETYA 2006). While the federal government provided funding for broadband infrastructure, fixed, mobile and satellite, in rural and regional areas and in some limited metropolitan areas, its primary role was regulatory to ensure competition amongst providers. Such competition was vigorously resisted by companies, particularly the dominant provider, Telstra (Fahrer 2006), which was fully privatised by the government in 2006 (Gans and King 2010).

In 2005, broadband use in Australia was lower than in a number of other OECD countries and prices were generally higher for lower speeds (Fahrer 2006). While on the increase, broadband connections comprised only 30 per cent of internet connections. A majority of these connections were to households, although businesses and government were more likely to access higher-speed connections (ABS 2007c). As more services moved online, complaints about low speeds and high costs appeared frequently in the media. So too did tales of black spots where no internet access was available at all, even in metropolitan areas (*Sydney Morning Herald* 2007). These factors and the comparisons with high-speed broadband in countries such as Japan and South Korea made this dissatisfaction fertile ground for an ALP Opposition facing the Coalition Government in the election year of 2007.

The Digital Education Revolution

In 2006, the ALP had been in opposition for ten years. Following leadership turmoil within a dispirited party, Kevin Rudd was elected leader of the Parliamentary Labor Party in December of 2006. In the election year of 2007, Rudd set about remaking the ALP's image, releasing a number of papers under the rubric, 'New Directions', in which he outlined his planned policy positions. Education played a central role. In a paper released in January 2007, Rudd and his education spokesman, Stephen Smith, argued an economic case for increased federal government expenditure on education. In *The Australian Economy Needs an Education Revolution* (Rudd and Smith 2007), higher levels of education in the population were promoted as key to raising declining productivity. Also vital for engineering higher productivity was new technology, particularly broadband. In March 2007, the ALP's broadband policy, *A Broadband Future for Australia – Building a National Broadband Network* (Rudd, Conroy and Tanner 2007, n.p.), described broadband as 'a critical enabling technology that is currently driving substantial productivity gains around the world'. They pledged a 'revolution' if elected to government: the construction of a fibre to the node National Broadband Network (NBN) which would provide high-speed broadband services to 98 per cent of people in the country (Rudd, Conroy and Tanner 2007, 1). The new network would allow for speeds which were 'over 40 times faster' than those that were then achievable and would bring significant 'economic benefits' to the nation (Rudd, Conroy and Tanner 2007, 1).

Later, during the election campaign of 2007, Kevin Rudd announced that an ALP government, if elected, would bring about a 'Digital Education Revolution' through the provision of a computer for each upper secondary school student in the country as well as connections to the proposed NBN for every school (Rudd, Smith and Conroy 2007). Computers were depicted as a necessity to enable Australian school students to compete with others globally for the new high technology jobs of the future. The cost of the policy was estimated to be more than AU$1 billion. Following its election win, the ALP in government moved swiftly to implement its promises, including for the Digital Education Revolution. Consultations with state and territory Chief Ministers began almost immediately. Over the six years of the ALP's period in government, more than 950,000 computers were delivered to schools and students (DEEWR 2012). During this same period, changing computer and communications technologies saw different devices, tablets and smart phones, enter the Australian market. As in the US, use of both devices increased rapidly as consumers put a premium on mobility (BMI 2012; BMI 2013a, 2013b).

The proposed NBN, the ALP's signature policy, followed a different trajectory. Unable to deliver the promised network under the existing institutional, commercial and regulatory regimes, in 2009 the ALP instead announced a plan to build an entirely new network with fibre to the home connections for 90 per cent of Australian homes, at an estimated cost of more than AU$40 billion over eight years. In a country as large as Australia, this represented a massive undertaking and a level of government investment in broadband that was greater than any other underway in the world at that time (Berkman 2010). The project was controversial from its inception and its progress slow. At the time of the September election of 2013 a small number of households were connected in several trial sites but the bulk of the infrastructure construction still lay ahead. While committed to a NBN in opposition, the Coalition deemed fibre to the home too expensive, instead promising to deliver a fibre to the node network. Following the Abbott Coalition's victory in 2013, a review into the NBN project was announced. At the time of writing, the shape of the future NBN remains unclear.

In a number of countries, access to computing and communications technologies has been identified as critical to a nation's future and promoted for use in education as central to measures designed to lift national economic performance. Government policies and plans to enhance the use of computing technologies in schools are important tools which present a national vision for the future and aim 'to convene stakeholders and coordinate activities across levels of government' (Bakia et al. 2011, vii). To this end, considerable public and private investments have been made by governments, but also by organisations, businesses and individuals in many countries. In Australia, this investment has taken place over many years and the change in this period has been significant. From a country in 1976 in which computer penetration was much lower than in the US, by 2013, access to computers and to broadband was comparable. In 2013, 78 per cent of Australian households had access to the Internet and for 98 per cent of these households, that access was via broadband (ABS 2013). In the US in 2011, 76 per cent of households had computers, 69 per cent with a broadband connection (NTIA 2013).

More than 90 per cent of Australian families with school-age children owned a computer in 2012 (ACMA 2013), a figure which mirrors that in the US (Madden et al. 2013) and expresses a belief now common around the world that access to the Internet is essential for education. The number of children and young people using computers and accessing the Internet both at home and school continues to rise, particularly in the younger age groups, although use at home is still considerably more common than at school. Internet use is also more likely than in 2009 to be via a mobile device (ACMA 2013). There is growing dissatisfaction amongst policymakers, however, as such investments have not delivered higher levels of use of computing and communications technologies in schools. At the same time, the conviction remains that these technologies are the key to engendering higher levels of learning and sustained improvement in the quality of education (Bakia et al. 2011; UNESCO 2011).

Educational computing in Australia

The trajectory of educational computing in Australia differed from that in the US, where interest in educational computing began as a product of the computer's invention and dissemination through that society, assisted by substantial government funding support for experimentation with computers in education. Early experimentation with computers and school students in the US centred around drill and practice applications in reading and mathematics. By contrast, in Australia, the later penetration of computers into the country and the lack of a computer industry meant that initial interest in the role of computers in education focused on preparing students for living in a future world where computers would become more prevalent. The purely pragmatic necessity of imparting vocational skills at a time when there was a shortage of skilled labour to work with computers was another significant impetus. The example of Victoria illustrates a number of these aspects.

Expressions of interest

The push to use computers in schools in the 1960s came initially from academics working within computer faculties in universities and colleges of advanced education. A number of these academics had previously worked with computers in government departments or industry. Trevor Pearcey from the CSIRAC project, for example, joined the Caulfield Institute of Technology and Cliff Bellamy moved from computer firm Ferranti to Monash University (Pearcey 1988). Convinced that computer knowledge would be vital in the future, they also knew that there was a shortage of personnel trained to use computers. These academics wanted to encourage students to adopt future computing careers but were also keen to promote courses in their institutions at a time of expansion.

Teaching using computers was rare in Victoria in the 1960s. In a seminar for secondary school teachers in 1968 at Monash University, the Director of the Computer Centre, Dr Bellamy, described the potential use of the Monash MINITRAN system and the cost to schools of its use, which, while presented as affordable, was very expensive ('School Computer Seminar' 1969). Indicative, however, of the interest in computers in education was the attendance at the seminar of more than 200 teachers, as well as members of the Public Service Board who had an interest in measures to increase the number of people training as computer programmers and operators (Tatnall 1993). A handful of secondary schools in Victoria used computers through a program introduced by Monash University, but they were unusual (Tatnall and Davey 2004).

As in the US, the next push came from teacher-enthusiasts, typically mathematics teachers, who had had some experience with computers during their pre-service training (Walker 1991). In 1978 a group of these teachers formed the Computer Education Group of Victoria as a lobby group and as a means of providing collegiate support (Grover 1980). For most teachers, however, the computer was still mysterious and expensive. Few schools considered computers to be a viable or necessary technology. One report from Victoria suggests that in 1976 fewer than ten schools possessed computers (Grover 1980). That there was interest from students in computing, however, is demonstrated by the inclusion of a computing-oriented mathematics subject at Year 12 level in the 1970s. Between 1976 and 1978, the number of students completing the subject rose from 163 to 364 (Grover 1980). While the numbers of students were small in absolute terms, the growth in a short period was substantial.

The personal computer and computer literacy

Despite some interest in the use of computers in education, for the majority of schools the cost of computers was prohibitive. Following a period of increased funding for education between 1972 and 1974, funding for both new and existing educational programs in public schools tightened from 1975 (CSC 1982). A small minority of researchers, administrators, public servants and educators retained a remarkable continuity of interest in educational computing, believing that there was a strong future for it in schools. Their primary concern was to ensure that all students should be prepared to live in a world populated by computers (Tatnall and Davey 2006). For advocates of computing in schools, the arrival of the personal computer confirmed the necessity of such an approach but it also sparked a much wider debate over the role of the computer in society and in education.

The personal computer had many advantages over the existing mainframe and minicomputers: it was much cheaper but also smaller, and therefore could be installed in the school itself. The decision to use a personal computer was school-based, although it depended significantly on available staff and beliefs about the future of computers, as well as sufficient resources (Burt 1982). The first personal computers were purchased and employed in at least one Victorian school in 1976 (Walker 1991). The impact on the few secondary schools which used Monash University's Computer Centre was considerable. In 1978 there were 19 schools which used the Centre. In 1982, there was only one (Burt 1982).

The rapidity with which the personal computer spread throughout Australian society aroused fears about its impact on society. Advocates for computer education, such as academic Anne McDougall, argued that using computers at school would demystify them. When McDougall (1980, 3) made the case for educational computing in a report commissioned by the Victorian Department of Education, she cited community anxieties to buttress her argument, noting 'that most people outside the computing profession have attitudes of awe and fear towards computers, and feel helpless and powerless in a highly computerised society'. Indicative of the concern within the Department of Education at the spread of computers, the report was instrumental in allowing schools to introduce courses in computing (Grover 1980). Later, McDougall served on a panel reporting to the National Advisory Committee on Computers in Schools which recommended the National Computer Education Program. In 1981, Computer Science became a Higher School Certificate subject in Victoria, giving formal authority to a particular kind of computer education, of computing as a body of scientific knowledge (Burt 1982). The interest of enthusiasts was important in shaping approaches to computing in schools and providing expertise, but it was the actions of government that legitimised the use of computing technologies in schools.

The views of advocates for computers in schools differed on the proposed purposes of educational computing and how students could best be prepared for the future. Some argued that computers should be used so that students would become familiar with them and understand their potential, the 'computer awareness' approach. Others favoured their use to teach programming, particularly Papert's LOGO, for problem-solving purposes. Others pushed for the development of a discipline of computer science. As personal computers became more common in society, the approach of 'computer literacy', that computers should be used as a tool across subjects to train students to use computers, began to dominate (Moont 1984). The spread of the personal computer into schools in Australia mirrored that in the US, as did the frantic haste to equip schools with computers (Williams and Bigum 1994). The National Computer Education Program, begun in 1984, only added to the sense of a rush to put computers into schools, one that was intensified by the large number of vendors in a relatively small market (Burt 1982). There was also concern that expectations were too high for the educational improvements that could be delivered with computers, leading to the inevitable disillusionment when inflated expectations met reality (Penter and Sully 1984).

Despite the rhetoric, the numbers of computers in schools were still small and often confined to a computer laboratory for the use of students undertaking specific subjects, usually a form of information processing. While many teachers received some training in the use of computers, it remained substantially the preserve of enthusiasts. The National Computer Education Program, while it had imposed some restrictions, particularly on what equipment could be bought, was nevertheless devolved to the states and from there to local schools, which could make choices as to purpose, placement and use of computers. While the program legitimised the computer for educational use, its small-scale, almost experimental, nature made choices possible for schools. In the 1980s, teachers were still able to be active participants in the negotiation of meanings and the place of computers in schools (Bigum 1992). Even as *Teaching, Learning and Computers* authorised new meanings for computers in schools, the fact that few schools used computers allowed principals and teachers a degree of autonomy on where and when to deploy them. From the early 1990s, increasingly, meanings of computing technologies were being made for teachers, students and schools by others.

Education for a competitive workplace

During the late 1980s, a more assertive federal government attempted to exercise greater authority over the states and territories in the realm of education with the aim of instituting a national approach. At a time of high unemployment and continuing economic restructuring, the federal government believed that a national approach could reorient education to serve more fundamental economic aims (Sherington 1990). Through the deployment of the metaphor, 'the clever country', the ALP Government conjured up a vision of Australia securing its place in an uncertain world through its people's skills. These would be gained via an integrated education and training sector linked with a modern workplace (Dawkins 1990). This workplace was associated with the sophisticated use of computing technologies and required school leavers and university graduates with high level skills. In the Hobart Declaration of 1989, the federal government and the states and territories agreed for the first time on a set of national educational goals. One of these included the commitment to develop students' skills in 'information processing and computing' (MCEETYA 1989, n.p.).

Computing in schools, while more common than ten years earlier, was still limited in scope but the wider issue of the use of computing technologies in the workplace was responsible for increasing pressures on schools to use computing technologies. Business interests were enthusiastic advocates of computer use in schools and were strongly represented in the Australian Computing Society, an early proponent of the use of computers in schools (Tatnall 1992). For governments, the use of information technologies within workplaces was seen as enabling progress towards an 'information society' at a time of economic difficulty (Bigum 1992). Importantly, however, government and business views contributed to establishing the idea that the use of computing technologies was central to achieving a successful and rewarding career. During a deep recession, this was a seductive message. Teaching computer skills was viewed as insurance against unemployability (Arnold and Gilding 1994).

Also significant was the competition amongst schools for a declining number of students (Baldwin 1990), and in depressed economic times, of schools wishing to ensure their continuing viability. In 1991, these threads intersected with the release of portable computing technology, the laptop computer, which was made mandatory for new students entering Year 7 at a wealthy independent school, Methodist Ladies' College (MLC) in Melbourne (Shears 1995). MLC attempted to position itself at a time of declining enrolment as a leader and innovator through adopting a technology, the laptop, associated with the business professional to secure its place in an increasingly competitive environment (Arnold and Gilding 1994). It was also a way of introducing expensive technology for which parents, rather than the school, paid. Controversial at the time, it received considerable positive media coverage and spawned a number of similar programs in other independent schools.

While there was some belief in the educational merit of laptops and in the value of innovation, competitive pressures and the need to demonstrate progressiveness were also powerful incentives. In time, several state schools introduced similar programs, for instance, Frankston High School (Shears 1995). In Victoria, the introduction of laptop computers into these schools shifted the debate on computing. Rather than questioning whether computers should be used in schools, the debate centred around the type, either laptop or desktop. For several years, a number of studies focused not on the benefits of computer technology for education, but on the superiority or otherwise of laptops as opposed to desktops (eg, Newhouse 1998; Shears 1995; Stolarchuk and Fisher 2001).

The promotion of laptop computers was infused with the rhetoric of individual choice and the message that students would be motivated by having their own personal computers, resulting in more powerful learning

(Stager 2000). When allied to constructivism, as was common, an educational rationale was advanced to legitimise the use of the laptop computer and to position schools which instituted such programs as not just innovators, but also more sophisticated and knowledgeable, thus ensuring their continuing attractiveness to the elite parents they targeted (Arnold and Gilding 1994). Commercial interests were also clearly implicated and, on occasion, studies were supported at least in part financially by computer companies such as Toshiba, which were keen to promote their laptop computers (eg, Shears 1995). Laptop computers were more expensive and the potential market of individual schoolchildren both larger and more lucrative than that of cash-strapped public schools.

The conjunction of government and business pressures, competition within the independent school sector and the new technology of the laptop led to an entrenchment of the view that computers were essential for schools. At the same time, the computer's connection with privilege, status and success was reinforced, conferring on it a lustre that colours attitudes to it today.

Governments take the lead

In the 1990s, with rapid commercial and technological change, state governments acted powerfully to shift the direction of computing in schools and the culture of schooling itself (Lankshear et al. 2000). In Victoria, the Coalition Government, elected in 1992, instituted the 'Schools of the Future' program, designed to bring about a more market-based system in public schools. It aimed to reduce the cost of the central bureaucracy through the devolution of some functions to schools and to align school outcomes more closely with those demanded by business (Marginson 1997b). In 1994, the Victorian Government released *Technologies for Enhanced Learning*, known as the Smith report (Directorate of School Education) which rebranded computers as 'learning technologies', implying that they possessed the capacity to improve student learning (Lankshear et al. 2000). The policy expressed a strong technological determinism that celebrated computers' transformative capacities.

As with the introduction of earlier policies, the use of terms such as 'learning technologies' aimed to build support amongst members of the community by positioning computers as essential for children's future, particularly for their future employment. In that way, the expenditure of public and private resources was legitimised in the service of a particular view of the world, one that was presented as 'common sense' and which made it acceptable through connecting with people's everyday lives (Apple 1993, 53). Gaining community support was also in part an attempt to marginalise a particular constituency, in this case, teachers. Teachers, as professional educators, had lost their earlier influence over the direction of computer technologies. While only a small minority of teachers had been involved, the movement to introduce computers into schools in the 1970s and before 1983 had been a grass-roots movement (Tatnall and Davey 2006). By the mid 1990s, this was no longer the case. Technology was imposed top-down, in independent schools by principals, and by government direction in state schools in Victoria and in some other states and territories, on a much broader scale than had been the case following *Teaching, Learning and Computers* (Lankshear et al. 2000).

In 1998 further emphasis was placed on computing technologies with the release of the policy *Learning Technologies in Victorian Schools 1998–2001* (Department of Education 1998), which required all schools to incorporate computing technologies into their curriculum. Significant funding, a total of more than AU$100 million over five years, was allocated to achieve the policy goals. This funding included: the provision of laptop computers and training in their use for teachers in government schools at both primary and secondary levels; internet access to schools; the creation of websites; and the establishment of several 'Navigator' schools which were designed in part to promote the use of computing technologies in teaching and learning. There was increased focus on equipping primary schools with computing technologies, but the provision of funding was based on a subsidy basis. Schools were required to raise two-thirds of the funds for purchase of computing technologies, a process which built in inequities (Victorian Auditor-General 1999).

The Victorian Government's promise in 1998 to connect every school to the Internet echoed that of President Bill Clinton in the US in 1996. When the personal computer penetrated workplaces in Australia, the technology was depicted as transforming society. Similar rhetoric surrounded programs to extend the use of the Internet. Phil Gude, the Minister of Education in Victoria at that time, asserted on the release of *Learning Technologies in Victorian Schools 1998–2001* that Victoria was thereby positioned at the forefront of global innovation in education: 'It was great to hear one of the world's computer gurus, Bill Gates, specifically refer to what we're doing in Victoria and it's tremendous that school systems around the world are emulating what we've pioneered here,' announced Gude (1998, n.p.). That Microsoft benefited from the sale of licences for its products to all state governments, including Victoria, was obscured (Moyle 2002). Such statements served the interest of the government which attempted to portray itself as progressive and future-oriented at a time of restricted spending on public services and greater involvement of private for profit providers through outsourcing (Victorian Auditor-General 1999).

The internet boom and the rhetoric of the new economy contributed to the sense that the state government's provision for computing technologies in schools, including primary schools, was vital for a vibrant future. An expanded commitment to computing technologies and their role in schooling was made in the Adelaide Declaration of 1999 between the states, territories and the federal government (MCEETYA 1999). In this policy document, computing technologies were represented in ways that assumed their centrality in the future world and through the actions endorsed, contributed to making the world in that image (Fairclough 1992).

The Coalition Government's release of 'Learning in an Online World' in 2000, a policy negotiated with the states and territories, set the framework for the following seven years with regard to policy for computing technologies in schools. It moved further to tie the states into the promotion of computing technologies in schools by requiring them, as one of the conditions of their funding, to produce an 'ICT Statement of Learning' (Information and Communications Technologies) with an intended implementation date of 2008 (DEST 2007, 9). Sample assessments of students' learning in the ICT area were also required and were introduced in 2005 as part of the measurement of the states' and territories' achievement of the National Goals for Schooling (MCEETYA 2009). Following the election in 2007, the new ALP Government introduced measures outlined in the policy text released during the campaign, *A Digital Education Revolution* (Rudd, Smith and Conroy 2007), to equip every senior school student in the country with a computer. A slowing economy was no longer the impetus, as had been the case with several earlier policies. By contrast, in 2007 the economy was growing strongly. Instead, the policy worked to differentiate the ALP from the Coalition Government's policies, although it built on and extended similar policies from earlier years.

Conclusion

In the economic boom times of the 1950s and 1960s, Australia began slowly to employ computers, primarily in government and large firms for information processing. Computerised automation came later to the small manufacturing sector, coinciding with a severe worldwide economic downturn, one in which Australia felt a sense of precipitous decline. While educational computing emerged at the grassroots level, when countries overseas introduced computing into their schools on a large-scale basis, Australian governments were alarmed. Motivated by fears of further marginalisation in the world economy, they moved to institute computing policies for schools. Government intervention, both state and federal, generally followed the development of new computing technologies overseas but until the 1990s, was limited and often hesitant. Schools and teachers had a degree of autonomy to develop their approaches to computing technologies, ones that took account of their local circumstances. In the 1990s, state governments became more significant in setting the agenda for educational computing, following the commercialisation of the World Wide Web and its perceived advantages for schools.

From 2000 onwards, however, the federal government exerted considerable influence, attempting to define the role of computing technologies in schools as vital to Australia's continuing success. The task for teachers and schools, rather than determining the uses of computing technologies in their schools, was to implement government policy decisions. By tying the states and territories together into a national approach and through new funding and accountability measures, the federal government took control of the agenda on computing technologies.

Chapter Three

Teaching and Learning with Computers

> As Australia moves into an information-based post-service society, the greatest hope – perhaps the only hope – for a democratic and egalitarian community will be to effect a further revolution in education. (Jones 1983, 168)

So wrote Barry Jones in his 1982 book, *Sleepers, Wake!*. In *Sleepers, Wake!* Jones argued that technology, particularly computer technology, was being deployed in workplaces in Australia and in other wealthy countries to reduce the need for labour, resulting in rising unemployment. Jones pointed to the human calculation behind the decision to introduce computers into the workplace: 'computers are *intended* to displace labour' (Jones 1983, 114). The effect on work and the future demand for workers, he suggested, would be profound. Those most affected would be the unskilled and semi-skilled, particularly young people, for whom unemployment was already high. Jones noted the stratified nature of the Australian education system, where fewer than 15 per cent of young people from lower socio-economic backgrounds undertook education in the senior years. Higher levels of education were necessary, Jones concluded, to enable greater participation in society, particularly in work, for those from lower socio-economic groups at a time when jobs for those without skills were rapidly disappearing.

Barry Jones was well known to the public as a legendary quiz show winner from his eight years during the 1960s on the television quiz show, 'Pick a Box'. When *Sleepers, Wake!* was written, Jones had been an ALP member of the House of Representatives since 1977. A former teacher at Dandenong High School and academic from the University of Melbourne, he had had a long association with education. *Sleepers, Wake!* blended analysis, critique and proposals for future political action. While not populist, it proved popular. First published in 1982, it was reprinted twice that year and three times in the following year. The book tapped into fears in the Australian community that the world of work no longer offered the sense of certainty that it had once seemed to, nor would it for their children.

While Australia was initially slow to computerise, the gathering pace with which computers began to be used by businesses and government in Australia was accompanied by rapid job loss, accelerated during the recession of 1982. Where Jones saw in education the promise of the development of human potential in all its forms, including personal enrichment, others considered it instead the pathway to gaining secure jobs for themselves and their children. For them, technological change was represented by the computers appearing in every office and small business, meaning that preparation for work in the future necessitated education with computers. The mood of unease in the electorate across the nation was recognised by both major political parties, which incorporated policies to introduce computers into schools in their electoral platforms in preparation for the 1983 federal election. The ALP's promise was specific: the introduction of a National Computer Education Program with a funding commitment of AU$24 million over a three year period (Hawke 1983).

In 1983, the Fraser Coalition Government was defeated at a general election and the ALP, led by Bob Hawke, was elected. Jones was appointed as Minister for Science and Technology. The Hawke Government took office at a time of recession both locally and internationally. Interest rates nationally were high and the eastern states affected by a severe drought. In addition, the previous Coalition Government bequeathed a deficit substantially larger than anticipated (NAA 1983a). Mindful of the perceived economic errors of the Whitlam ALP Government between 1972 and 1975, the new Hawke ALP Government was determined to be seen as competent in the face of community uncertainty. Where necessary it would wind back expenditure. In the same month in which the Hawke Government was elected, the advice to Cabinet from the Treasurer, Paul Keating, and the Minister for Finance, John Dawkins, was 'that some of our lower priority election proposals will have to be deferred' (NAA 1983a, 7). Others would have less funding allocated to them than their new ministers may have hoped. One of these was the promised National Computer Education Program.

A federal and state/territory accord

The ALP's pledge in opposition to introduce a computer education program for schools responded to concerns in the electorate over the rapid growth of computers in the workplace and the link with job loss, but also to concerted pressure from state and territory governments. While state and territory governments in the Australian federal system are responsible for the delivery of school education, federal government recurrent funding provides the financial resources for the states and territories. Beginning in the 1960s, the federal government also increasingly provided specific purpose funding for particular programs and purposes which it deemed important. Demand for education had grown, as had the expectations of what it could deliver (Marginson 1997a). Education was also more politicised. The greater involvement of the federal government, and its ability to dispense special purpose funding, added a new level to this politicisation, in part through shifting the composition of flows of funds to schools and sectors under governments of different political persuasions. While the states and territories were responsible for schools, they were dependent on the federal government for revenue, which meant that they were more likely to request, but were also attracted to, funds which were attached to specific programs (Lingard 2000).

In the early 1980s, when the states and territories had difficulty re-sourcing schools adequately at a time of high inflation, the share of federal funding for government schools had been declining. Rising retention rates, particularly the more expensive senior secondary years, contributed to the demands on state government resources (CSC 1982). The paradoxical answer to the problem of rising school retention rates was an approach which raised the skills of all students, and increasingly encouraged stu-dents to stay at school beyond the compulsory years to improve their life chances. The states and territories believed that computer education would assist students to gain the skills that would be necessary for their future in the workforce but they lacked the ability to finance such a scheme. These concerns were channelled through the institutional framework of the Commonwealth Schools Commission, which comprised representatives from both the federal government and those of the states and territories.

The Commonwealth Schools Commission

Established by the Whitlam ALP Government following the Karmel report (1973), the Commonwealth Schools Commission was a statutory authority. Its role was to provide advice to federal governments on educational policy, administer federal programs and funding, and recommend future funding. It drew together a number of the interests involved in education: represen-tatives from state and territory governments, the Catholic and independent school sectors, universities, education unions, professional associations, parent groups and business. Ostensibly independent, the Commission responded to, and reported to, the federal government which could choose to accept or reject its recommendations (Lingard 2000). By placing the Commission at arm's length, the government of the day could distance itself from the political interests involved in the educational debate, which were significant and powerful. These included state and territory governments, schooling systems, universities, professional associations, teacher unions, parents, business and the wider community. Each had differing and often conflicting interests as well as particular points of view on the purposes and content of education which each believed should prevail. Fierce struggles, aimed at garnering political support for their programs, were commonplace amongst these groups (Johnston 1983).

The establishment of the Commission signified an enhanced role for the federal government in the state responsibility of education as well as the introduction of new ways of speaking about education in order to explain and justify changed policies for Australian schools (Johnston 1983). Educational policy, always contested, had become more so as the federal government took a more active role. One part played by the Commission was to bring together the differing views of education and the interests involved in ways that contributed to a 'settlement' around policy while at the same time allowing successive federal governments to distance themselves from the inevitable political battles (Johnston 1983).

The process of achieving such a settlement took time as the progress towards a computer education program for schools illustrates. In 1981, the Commission considered computer education in schools to be unnecessary, instead recommending that young people be taught new skills which would enable them to negotiate a changing workplace environment (CSC 1981). However, in 1982, school retention rates for boys rose sharply as apprenticeships were lost when Australia entered recession (Teese and Polesel 2003). In 1983, faced with rising retention rates and high teenage unemployment, the Commission focused on 'the nature, quality and direction of aspects of secondary education' which it blamed for not equipping young people with the skills they needed to gain employment (CSC 1983, 1). That those young people who left school after the compulsory years could not gain jobs supported the Commission's view that students required new skills to equip them for a changing future, and that these new skills should involve computers.

The link between the workplace and computing skills posited by the Commission depicted computers as essential. A primary purpose of education was to equip students with skills that would enable them to gain employment and computer skills were being proposed as the new necessity for the future. Rising retention rates as jobs for young people disappeared were seen as failures of the educational system, rather than of the economy itself at this time of recession. Instead of locating failure to provide jobs in the economic system, schools were blamed. The solution proposed by the Commission was a National Computer Education Program. Computers were already used in some schools and funds were allocated to support computing in schools by the states and territories and through ad hoc grants by the federal government, amounting to approximately AU$8 million a year (CSC 1983). The federal government had already provided funds through specific purpose programs at various times to selected schools and institutions for the purchase of computers (CSC 1983; Walker 1991). Many schools, however, had only one computer, usually for administrative purposes.

The unevenness of computer provision was a concern for the Commission, which led it to argue that a national policy to expand computer education and to ensure that all schools participated was vital:

> The development of a satisfactory program of computer education in Australian schools is regarded by the Commission as being of fundamental importance for Australia's future. This view was strongly supported by State and non-government school authorities with whom the Commission has consulted. (CSC 1983, 46)

Only the federal government could provide the 'initiative and leadership', as well as funding, for this essential national purpose (CSC 1983, 46). Should this not occur, the Commission predicted a dire outcome:

> The implications for Australia in terms of employment opportunities for the young, international competitiveness, and the relevance of schooling to future adult life and all its aspects will be very serious indeed. (47)

Accordingly, in 1983, in its funding recommendations for the school education sector, the Commonwealth Schools Commission proposed a very substantial allocation of funds for a National Computer Education Program, AU$125 million over five years, the largest single allocation of its existing joint programs (CSC 1983). A settlement had been reached amongst the majority of actors on the importance of introducing computers into school education. The responsibility to fund the program fell to the federal government.

Fulfilling an election campaign promise

In 1983 at the request of the Minister of Education, Susan Ryan, the Commonwealth Schools Commission established the National Advisory

Committee on Computers in Schools, or NACCS, to devise and recommend to the minister a national program for the use of computers in schools and allocations for funding. The committee's report, *Teaching, Learning and Computers*, was released later that year. It advanced a rationale for the proposed program, made recommendations as to the type and scope of the program, and advised funding allocations. The key recommendations proposed curriculum development to ensure that all secondary school students were given exposure to 'computer awareness and computer literacy experiences' (CSC. NACCS 1983, 52), professional development with computers for teaching staff, the establishment of support centres, the development of software, the standardisation of computing hardware and the establishment of coordinating committees at the state level. These recommendations were largely accepted by the Commonwealth Schools Commission and later formed the foundations for the National Computer Education Program which began in 1984 (Bigum 1987).

Representation on the NACCS comprised those in positions of power, predominantly from the upper levels of state education departments as well as the federal Department of Science and Technology. These representatives had already expressed a belief that computers in schools were necessary (WCCIPAS 1982). The voices of state and territory government bureaucrats dominated the NACCS at a time when these governments were under considerable pressure to resource greater numbers of students in secondary schools. The institutional framework of the Commonwealth Schools Commission and the NACCS ensured that the legitimacy of the states and territories in educational policymaking was reflected and consolidated (Ball 1997).

For the federal government, however, other issues were at play. The commissioning of the NACCS report by new ALP Education Minister, Susan Ryan, fulfilled the promise made during the election campaign. Even though the Commonwealth Schools Commission had recommended funding of AU$125 million over five years, the minister allocated AU$18 million over a three year period (CSC. NACCS 1983). Her decision to allocate substantially less funding reflected different priorities. The new ALP Government's central education initiative was the introduction of the Participation and Equity Program, to which it allocated over AU$40 million nationally in its first year, 1984 (Rizvi and Kemmis 1987).

The computer education program was in fact a small almost exploratory initiative, one that could be regarded as fulfilling a campaign promise. The funding for the program revealed it to be one of the smaller programs, comparable in size, although slightly larger, than the Multicultural Education Program with its annual allocation of just under AU$5 million nationally (CSC 1983). Governmental funding allocations signify their priorities. The ALP's priority was to encourage all students to complete secondary education as a way of providing 'more equitable outcomes of education for all young persons' (Commonwealth of Australia 1983, n.p.). Yet the aspirations of the Commonwealth Schools Commission for a much larger program could not be met with the funding allocated by the government. The NACCS was still deliberating when the funding budget for the program was released. The struggle to reconcile aspirations and reality is evident in the report. The Committee noted that 'both major political parties promised support for schools computing' (CSC. NACCS 1983, 1) and that:

> The cost estimates for all primary and secondary schools in Australia in the Commission's report Recommendations for 1984 were reasonable. It is therefore recognised that the amount allocated for 1984 will not enable all stated objectives to be met, and hence priorities have been considered in formulating a reduced program to make most effective use of the funds available. (2–3)

The committee began with an already established position that endorsed the use of computers in schools. It faced the challenge of making recommendations for a program that was funded at a much lesser level than the Commonwealth Schools Commission had proposed. Rather than beginning with a pre-determined budget and designing a program which could be achieved within that budget, the committee was forced to readjust its thinking during the process of policy development. Their struggle to do so remains embedded in the language of the policy text, *Teaching, Learning and Computers*.

A significant policy

Despite the funding constraints, *Teaching, Learning and Computers* was a significant policy. While it was one of a number of reports and studies on computers in education in a similar period (eg, McDougall 1980; Shears and Dale 1983), it was the first report on the subject of computers in education by a federal body since the Wearing report of 1976 (Wearing et al.) and unlike the Wearing report, it achieved a consensus on the necessity for a school computer education program and for federal government action. It allocated funding for the first time for a schools program which the federal government and the states and territories had determined to be of national importance. The purpose was to guide decision-makers on the design and implementation of a national computer program in schools. As a national approach, the policy attempted to standardise computer education programs across the country.

As the decision to introduce a school computing program had already been made, the task for the NACCS was to advance meanings for computers and preferred practices with them that would be acceptable to the majority of the committee members. While computers had been and were being used in Australian schools, the overt link between the computer and education had not been made so forcefully before in federal government policy. In this report, the computer as an object that is new in the sphere of education is explicated and its attributes and uses delineated, so that understandings can be formed both of the computer and of its place in education (Rose 1999). In *Teaching, Learning and Computers*, the authority of the state is deployed to invest meanings in what was a relatively new technology, to redefine existing uses and practices, and to initiate new ones (Rose 1999).

As an official report from a governmental authority, it carried weight. As well as advancing meanings for computers and preferred practices, the processes that should support the proposed program were outlined. The report strongly influenced the computing programs that were put in place at the state level, particularly in New South Wales and Victoria (Zammit 1989). The policy was also powerfully symbolic. It posited computers as central to schools, as evidenced in the title of the report, *Teaching, Learning and Computers*. Connecting computers with teaching and learning was an idea that had some currency, but was also controversial. The title attempted to naturalise the computer as an essential part of the teaching and learning process. At an early stage of educational computing, the assumptions, beliefs and values embedded in the language of the report shaped understandings of the new technology of the computer and its potential in education.

Teaching, Learning and Computers echoes the Commonwealth Schools Commission's view that schools should provide students with computer skills. The representation of the states and territories on the NACCS meant an alignment of views, despite the dissenting views of some members of the working parties which advised the NACCS. The assumptions about the role of computers that underpin the report are in part those of the Commonwealth Schools Commission, but also of the states and territories, as expressed in the Working Conference on Computing and Information Processing in Australian Schools (WCCIPAS 1982). The focus of *Teaching, Learning and*

Computers was on the technology of the computer. The insertion of that technology into schools was a modernisation project which was framed as urgent. The report thus began with the embedded assumption that putting computers into schools was both necessary and pressing. Constructed as requiring national impetus and support, the computer program was advanced as the solution to a problem which the Commission believed was located within schools rather than in the society more broadly.

For the wider educational community, the belief that computers were necessary in school education, despite its apparent popularity with the public at large, was not uniformly supported. *Teaching, Learning and Computers* reflected the political and institutional decisions to introduce a National Computer Education Program that had been made before the report was written. The committee which was tasked with developing the policy began from a stated position which supported the introduction of computers into schools and the text, *Teaching, Learning and Computers*, was the product of negotiations over several months.

However, the complexity of the interests represented within the structure of the Commonwealth Schools Commission and the NACCS created tensions between differing points of view over priorities. There were contending beliefs about the purposes of education and the as yet undemonstrated potential of computers in education as well as their place in society more broadly. Drawing these views together into a coherent policy involved projecting a vision of the future, mapping plans for implementation and prioritising some meanings and practices over others. The struggle to reconcile different positions is evident in the competing discourses within the document. Dissension as to what was important in education and where funding should be allocated meant that negotiation and tensions were central to the policy's formulation (Taylor et al. 1997). Traces of these tensions survive in the contending discourses in the text, revealing the different values and beliefs among participants in the process and which voices dominated. Rendered almost silent were the large number of practising teachers whose voices were scarcely represented.

The discourses of *Teaching, Learning and Computers*

Teaching, Learning and Computers proceeds from three premises which are advanced to support and to promote federal government involvement in computer education for schools. The first is that national competitiveness requires students to learn to use computers at school. The second is that only government involvement will bring about change in ways which are equitable. The third is that computers are changing society irrevocably. These three premises are drawn from particular world views which can be broadly ascribed to the economic, the social democratic and the technologically determinist respectively. These world views and the discourses in which they are expressed each had significant constituencies in Australia at that time and tying the computer into these existing discourses worked to give legitimacy to claims for a relatively new technology.

The economic

A critical element of the economic world view is the conceptualisation of education as serving the needs of the national economy through imparting knowledge and skills to a future workforce. In *Teaching, Learning and Computers*, an appeal to the national interest tied the computer into the effort to improve Australia's economy through teaching students to use computers in schools:

> It is essential to the well-being of Australian society that schools provide students with knowledge of the electronic information technologies and skills in their use. If this does not happen, Australia will be severely disadvantaged in relation to other countries. (CSC. NACCS 1983, 18)

To ally the computer with the national interest was to assert its necessity in an environment where other countries, such as the UK and France, were using computing technologies to improve their national competitiveness in the changing international environment, thereby damaging Australia's trading position. However, a program to place computers in schools offered another kind of economic promise to the nation, through giving impetus to the development of a local computer industry, rather than relying on imports of computing technologies:

> Many Australian inventions gain worldwide recognition, but often their development takes place overseas, with the benefits going to the country that develops them. A national program can be a means of encouraging the growth and development of the Australian computer industry, and could lead to sales of both hardware and software in the domestic market. (19)

This is the long-held dream of Australian policymakers, attracted by the lure of a captive and large market, that of schools and teachers, as a base from which to support and develop local industry. Such a view is evident in a 1983 cabinet submission from Minister Susan Ryan which supported the National Computer Education Program on the grounds of its 'potential together with domestic and business usage of stimulating over time the growth of a viable Australian computer hardware industry. It should also strengthen the local development of a software industry' (NAA 1983b, 5). The appeal to the national interest was based on economic self-interest, rather than educational benefit. The strategy of binding computer education to the national interest invested economic power in the computer so that it became the answer to the problem of Australia's decline.

The key assumption that underlies *Teaching, Learning and Computers* is that national economic malaise was the result of a failure to adequately prepare students for a more technologically-based workplace. At a time of recession and high job losses, it was a useful device. However, its use positioned schools as a necessary component of the economy, one that produces future workers who in turn can contribute to Australia's competitiveness through the use of the computer or handicap it through not providing the required skills. Placing the computer in schools thus became a way of improving the productivity of the nation. The general nature of the claim and its appeal to nationalism made the promise attractive. The nature of the threat and the possibility of Australia falling further behind its perceived peers in the wealthy world evoked fears of backwardness and enduring decline.

The social democratic

In *Teaching, Learning and Computers*, equality is tied to computers in schools. The Commonwealth Schools Commission was characterised from its inception by a social democratic world view which prioritised the aim of achieving equality (Johnston 1983). Education was regarded as a major means of improving the life-chances of those disadvantaged by socio-economic status, thus contributing to greater equality in society. As a potential partner in education, the computer is portrayed in ways that stress its benefits for learning, thus offering the promise of the computer as a means of ameliorating inequality.

Importantly, computers are constructed as an 'educational good' which confers educational benefit (Bigum 2002, 135), meaning that governments should be involved in their distribution to ensure equitable access for all:

> Governments will have to make deliberate efforts to enable students in all sections of society to participate fully in the developing information technology and its consequent cultural changes. (CSC. NACCS 1983, 18)

This construction of the computer as the means of improving learning ascribes power to it. The computer, once inserted into schools, will become the medium for remedying all kinds of disadvantage. At the same time, federal government intervention in schooling to bring about such change is regarded as legitimate. The computer is advanced as the means to achieve this goal. The report depicts the wealthy as monopolising computers, with the personal computer a consumer item that is acquired by professional families, thereby threatening progress towards greater equality in education.

> Computers tend to be acquired by the households of those students who already seem to gain most advantage from schooling. (18)

Computers in disadvantaged schools would also allow students to gain advantages which were then available only to those in wealthier schools. Paradoxically, the recognition that youth job markets were in long-term decline led governments to support expanded educational provision to equip young people with higher levels of skills so that they would be more likely to gain employment when they left school (Kennedy 1988). The appeal to equality, to special provision for the disadvantaged, was attractive to many, particularly those within the educational community, and the discourse here acted as a strategy to mobilise the support of these groups, which may not have welcomed the introduction of computers into schools. Resources that were put into computers were not then available for other expenditures, which may well have been viewed as more pressing.

A key term of the social democratic world view was 'equality of outcomes' (Johnston 1983), a phrase which occurs in *Teaching, Learning and Computers* (21, 22). In 1983, the goal of equality of outcomes was under challenge, at least partly because of a conservative resurgence which sought to reorient education (Johnston 1983), a challenge which appears in the report as a focus on '"access" to computers for the disadvantaged' (CSC. NACCS 1983, 29). This use of the term 'access' is important. The provision of resources, in this case, computer resources, was considered by policymakers as the key to overcoming disadvantage rather than the differential ability to make use of those resources:

> The use of computers in schools should be introduced in such a way as to foster the attainment of more equal outcomes of education... planning committees will need to make special provision to encourage access to the program by groups such as girls, Aboriginals, disadvantaged students and the disabled. (22)

In this moment of the report a shift can be observed. The task for government is recast as the provision of 'access' to different resources rather than to effect the improvement of the conditions which lead to disadvantage. As Luke (1997, 17) remarked, "'social justice' is being renamed "access"'. In this way, attention becomes focused on the resource itself, the computer, so that the provision of computers, in numbers, becomes a way of reducing inequality.

A discursive strategy that centred on ameliorating disadvantage through a government program to assist all schools, including the most disadvantaged, to acquire computers was likely to be persuasive for many. The premise of the computer as a resource monopolised by the wealthy worked to justify the government's introduction of computers into schools on social equity grounds.

The technologically determinist

The third world view is that of technological determinism in which the computer is considered to be an irresistible force, a neutral agent of change akin to a force of nature. As this force changes society, it changes the knowledge that is valued, as well as the skills people need to function effectively in the future. As a result, the people who invent, produce and wield such technology, and those who structure the 'rules of the game' as well as those who benefit from them, disappear (Galperin 2004a, 162). Instead, these attributes are conferred on the technology, obscuring the role of political and economic actions (Sussman 1997). So in *Teaching, Learning and Computers*, computers drive change, instead of change being brought about by the political and economic decisions of politicians and business people, who use computers to achieve particular ends. Assertions as to the nature of change and its consequences convey an air of inevitability:

> To stay in touch with the work and leisure activities that their students will undertake, schools must give them a chance to use computers and to learn about the way other people use them. Although teachers will use the computer to enhance their students' powers of thinking and communication, they must also teach about the changes computers are bringing to all aspects of society. (21)

Anxiety over the potential effects of computers on society was prevalent (Jones 1983; McDougall 1980). In the report, the task for education was depicted as teaching students about the computer and giving them experience with the technology, in order to train them for living in a future world in which computers would be pervasive. To gain control over their future, students' education had to include computers:

> Perhaps the main reason for teaching about computers is to give students greater understanding of the effects which computers and information technology may have on them in society and the means to gain greater power over their lives in a world increasingly dominated by sophisticated electronic technology. (22)

To dispute the view that computers should be used in education was to argue that students should face the future world unprepared to deal with its challenges, thus effectively silencing critics.

Negotiating meanings

The computer was in use in Australian society primarily for information processing purposes in businesses and government. The discourses that represented the computer in these contexts were the technologically determinist and the economic. To transform the computer into an educational technology necessitated the insertion of the computer into existing discourses of education in a way that could garner support in the educational community. Understandings of education, although contested, already existed. The meanings made for the computer's role in education needed to mesh with those understandings. The institution of education would have the task of implementing policy and eliciting the support of the wider community which had a stake in education. Thus discursive strategies which framed the computer as an educational benefit had to enter into different discourses, classifying the computer in ways that appealed to diverse constituencies. The strategic devices of identifying educational computing with the national interest and with the amelioration of inequality were deployed to link the computer into an economic and a social democratic discourse.

Linking the computer into the differing world views and their divergent beliefs about the purposes of education worked to garner the support of particular constituencies for a vision of the future. Another significant linguistic device, that of metaphor, is employed strategically in the text and works to construct a different kind of appeal. Through metaphor, particular characteristics are highlighted and identified with a known entity so that attributes from the known are transferred to the new in a way that can '"bring to life" or "vitalise" abstract entities, phenomena, ideas and imaginations' (Reisigl and Wodak 2001, 57). Metaphors also construct a particular view of the technology: who uses it, for what purposes and what kind of place it has in society. The power of metaphor is both its vividness and its ability to obscure. It invokes the old through a sleight of hand to intimate that the new is either an unquestionable benefit or a dangerous departure from the known.

Those with access to the public language of policy documents can deploy metaphor to shape the meanings of a new technology as people come into regular contact with it and before their views of potential use are fully formed (Reed 2000; Reisigl and Wodak 2001). Policy texts such as *Teaching, Learning and Computers* have mixed purposes: they provide advice to decision-makers but in doing so, they impose preferred meanings that attempt to define the field. The attributes applied to the computer, largely through implicit assumptions on the causal connections between computers and social change, and the qualities attributed to them through metaphor, are steps in the process of making claims as to what will eventuate in the future and what is required as an educational response.

Creating a vision

In *Teaching, Learning and Computers*, the computer is constituted as an instrument of power through the use of metaphor. The earliest publicity for the computer employed metaphor to enable the public to grasp the nature and attributes of the new technology. The name 'computer', initially used to designate the job undertaken by a person, was applied to the machine, linking it with a human being but also the task: that of undertaking computations. More potent still was the metaphor of the computer as itself human, the 'electronic brain' (Berkeley 1949). The personification of the computer as a powerful being with human attributes is the most striking metaphor of *Teaching, Learning and Computers*. Seldom overt, it is embedded in sentence constructions which position the computer as the active agent. In the report, this powerful being has two faces: one beneficent, the other malignant. The metaphors that the report employed proposed a seemingly natural link between computers and education, which was not then established.

The powerful being

In *Teaching, Learning and Computers*, the physical object of the computer is represented as a powerful being rather than an artefact which is to be inserted into schools. The computer acts alongside students, teachers, principals and administrators as if it were a human-like entity, suggesting an equivalent relationship. The computer is depicted as an intentional being interacting with the humans who are placed in relation to it (Bigum 1997).

The computer as active being is either positive or negative. It is never neutral. In roles where computers are known entities and can be used by individual students for social ends, such as improved learning or gaining new skills, computers are presented as positive beings which can improve on what teachers in schools offer:

> Because computers can store vast amounts of information, process data accurately, reliably, at great speed and at minimal cost in human time they are a powerful means for learning. (25)

> They have the potential to assist teachers to initiate teaching styles which are more effective and more appropriate to the needs of students. They can be highly motivational. (25)

The computer is envisioned as a constructive and independent force within the classroom. In relation to disabled students or those with special needs, not only is the computer powerful and positive, it is superior to the human teacher, because of:

> Its ability and power to provide software which will extend the special education curriculum to include skills not currently being taught, eg information handling. (29)

> Its capability to address the visual, auditory and tactile senses and its adaptability which allows it to overcome some physical handicaps. (29)

> Its motivating features and patience... (29)

The computer is depicted as a being with curiosity, intellect and capacity. Yet a being with intellect has the capacity to misuse it. Thus the computer is also portrayed as a potentially malign being which needs to be controlled. So students' learning in computer education courses should be of a particular type, one which should teach them to:

> Make informed and responsible judgements about those aspects of computer use that affect them and others in economic, social, political and physical contexts. (20)

> Recognise the sort of problems that are not amenable to computer solutions... (20)

The positioning of the computer as the agent in relationship to the student implies the potential for it to control the young person. To guard against this threat, education must employ the computer to enable the student to gain mastery over it. Students need both instruction and protection. In contrast to the agentic computer, the student is passive. The task for the student is to 'recognise', while the capacity to provide 'solutions' is the property of the computer. As the human characteristics of the computer are emphasised, students by comparison appear to lack the knowledge vital to their future. Propositions about education that may otherwise be contentious are represented as common sense. The space for questions and discussion as to whether computers are suitable for school use is not opened. Assertions that schools must use computers in certain ways valorise some over others. To argue against these is to deny students essential opportunities.

When the report proposes courses that should be developed and delivered to young people, the emphasis is on the student as passive recipient. The fear that the computer may control students, and in the future, society itself, is reflected in some of the suggested outcomes that students should gain under the program:

> An understanding of the social and personal implications of the widespread use of information technology. With this knowledge students should be able to understand and hence to exercise greater control over the effects of information technology on their lives. (26)

> An awareness of the fact that it is people who give computer instruction and enter the text or data... (26)

> Confidence that they can control the computer and communicate with it, to their advantage, in a variety of situations. (26)

> An awareness that those who design and implement computer applications have a moral and ethical responsibility to the community. (26)

Using computers in schools is justified to protect young people on the one hand, and future society on the other. The emphasis on gaining 'understanding' and 'control' of computers as well as 'advantage', echoes similar expressions from the Department of Education in the US in 1981 which claimed a 'need for students to be educated about and with these new technologies so that they may understand and control them, for their own purposes and for the good of society' (US Department of Education 1981, ii).

The effect of the metaphor of the computer as a positive being that can energise teachers depicts them as professionally deficient. Their knowledge of the world outside the school is portrayed as limited. Earlier in the report, the role of teacher-enthusiasts in introducing computers into the classrooms is acknowledged, if somewhat patronisingly. However, ignorance of computers is attributed to most teachers: 'a majority must be regarded as generally uninformed' (CSC. NACCS 1983, 37). The evidence of teacher interest in computers is denied and the pragmatism of teachers, in the face of an almost complete lack of computers in schools, is turned into a negative judgement on the profession as a whole. Compared to the powerful all-knowing computer, the teacher is depicted as wilfully backward. The attributes of power that have been applied to the computer through metaphor attempt to naturalise the computer and its two faces, both positive and negative, as human-like, therefore a part of the world, one to which people must adapt. Thus naturalised, the question as to whether the computer is as powerful or as pervasive as suggested is unlikely to be posed.

The force of metaphor

The metaphor of the powerful being with two faces is one of only several in the report although it is the most striking and aptly summons up the fear and anxiety surrounding the new technology of the personal computer as it was introduced into Australian workplaces and homes during the early 1980s (McDougall 1980). Other metaphors employed in the report portray the computer as an economic resource but also a tool, a long-standing metaphor for the computer which continues to this day (Bigum 1997). Presented as a resource, the computer is tied into the social democratic discourse, with computers depicted as a benefit which at that time only the wealthiest students were able to access. This association with wealth and future career prospects construed computers as a valuable social good with the ability to improve significantly the quality of education for those who might be disadvantaged financially. The metaphor of the computer as resource acts to further the view that more computers in schools will improve schooling for all. By using the metaphor of the computer as an economic resource that can be monopolised by the wealthy, *Teaching, Learning and Computers* positions the computer as an educational benefit which must be shared more equitably.

When the tool metaphor is invoked, the computer is rendered manageable in the hands of teachers and students, to allay concerns, to add legitimacy to the computer as one among other tools that teachers and students can incorporate into the classroom. This legitimacy reinforces other arguments for the introduction of computers into schools. It is not just necessary in the interests of the nation for students to use computers, but computers themselves are represented as a potent tool to enhance learning, particularly of higher-order skills. The effect is to designate the new technology of the computer as a necessary component of a good classroom and a good school.

Who uses it, for what purposes and what other resources may have been displaced by the provision of computers become questions which will not be asked. The debate is not over the worth of computers in education, but what type should be provided, the answer to which is provided in the text.

Overwhelmingly in the report, the metaphors used for computers suggest their power, which is often hidden and mysterious. The potential exists for computers to dominate people, whether as out-of-control machine/beings, or as the tool of unscrupulous and anonymous humans. The power of the computer, thus established, works as a rationale for promoting computers in schools through connecting these metaphors to two key beliefs about the purpose of education: education as the preparation of young people for the future and education as the imparting of knowledge and skills to students. In schools, teachers and students will gain knowledge of the computer and will use this knowledge to dominate the computer. Thus the computer will be rendered socially useful, at the same time as it prepares students for a future world in which the technology is pervasive.

However, the same metaphors that construct the computer as powerful also position teachers and students in relationship to it: teachers are represented as passive, ignorant of the world beyond schools, and reluctant to change. By contrast, students are depicted as passive, but sensitive to instruction and capable of learning. These metaphors conflict with each other at times, suggesting tensions or contradictions in the ways in which computers are envisioned. But the intertwining of some metaphors, that of tool and being, for instance, naturalises attributes of the computer that might otherwise be open to debate. The result is that they become accepted. The metaphors serve the function of creating a natural role for computers in schools: schools as teaching students to harness computers for socially beneficial purposes.

Found wanting: Schools and teachers

While *Teaching, Learning and Computers* is focused on computers, it necessarily also addresses education. It clearly presupposes the importance of education for the nation when it endorses a program for introducing computers into schools. If, as the report argues, 'computer education in Australian schools was of fundamental importance to Australia's future', so by inference is education (CSC. NACCS 1983, 1). However, negative evaluations are made of schools as a whole, particularly secondary schools. The computer offers the opportunity to improve 'the quality of schooling' (19). Yet a particular view of both schooling and computing is advanced, one in which education is a system which is controlled and directed from the top, the purpose of which is to transmit knowledge and skills to the next generation.

The report acknowledged that computers were being used in some schools. Decisions to introduce computers were made by individuals located within a particular school or school community, and this use of computers in schools, while small, was growing haphazardly. On balance, the report viewed this development as positive, with benefits for particular schools and school systems. However, the lack of control by governments over the ways computers were deployed and used in schools was conceptualised as problematic. The report disparaged teacher- or parent-enthusiasts, who were 'wanting to keep up with a nearby school, or just having a feeling that some computers are inexpensive and might be worth trying' (5). This approach provided justification for the committee to argue that only a coordinated approach by the federal government could 'help overcome the lag in the development of computing in schools' (19).

A particular practice was advised. Computers, the report proposed, should be used across the curriculum rather than constituting a discrete subject:

> If information technology is seen merely as another "academic" subject it will not address the experiences, needs and educational rights of young people. (25)

Such a prescriptive use further cast schools as lacking the ability to make decisions as to how computers should be used. Students are construed as young people with an entitlement to computers. However, the computer should not be a subject in the curriculum. The term 'academic' is used in a pejorative sense to suggest that the curriculum is remote from the world outside the school and the knowledge students would require in the future to navigate this world successfully.

Further, the competence of teachers is questioned. As a result, teachers should not be given responsibility for the development of curriculum materials to be used with and for computers in their classroom: these 'must be developed' by experts outside the classroom who will instruct teachers in their use. Expert construction and instruction will result in materials which will 'be of appropriate quality and interest to motivate the students' (25). This positions teachers as mere agents of delivery for materials developed by others, without the professional competence to determine these themselves. Teachers are targeted 'to be trained' and 'with limited funds' (32). The 'one or more teachers' who should be trained to 'become the resource persons for the school as a whole in the educational use of computers' are clearly seen to have significant responsibilities added to their existing professional duties, without consideration of the demands on them, compensation by way of extra pay, or the allocation of designated time within their workload (33).

Rhetoric and reality

Teaching, Learning and Computers emerged from within a particular set of institutional arrangements which no longer exists. In the importance that it ascribed to computers in education, *Teaching, Learning and Computers* and the Commonwealth Schools Commission more broadly were at odds with the politicians, traces of which remain in the report. The report asserted that 'a nationally funded program is needed… to provide students with the resources to learn about and to use computers and computing' (19). The ambition was for a large-scale program that was well funded, when the resources provided by the government were far below achieving this. It was not inevitable that computers should be used in schools. The NACCS report is valuable as an example of a moment in which a prior decision is justified.

Yet the representation of computers, education and its participants in *Teaching, Learning and Computers* is primarily instrumental. The decision to initiate the computer program by the new federal government responded to a new technology and rising community concern about the place of that new technology in society. The federal government, while demonstrating national leadership, was in part reacting to pressure from specific sectors, particularly state and territory governments. The allocation of funds was cautious, implying a desire by the government to be seen to be responding to this concern, and a lack of conviction that the new technology would bring about change in education. For a government unsure of whether the promised benefits would eventuate, a small funding commitment enabled it to be seen to be meeting an election commitment and to gain some kudos from supporting computers, but also to wait and see what resulted.

On the other hand, the funding allocated ensured that the program's aims, as outlined in *Teaching, Learning and Computers*, could not possibly be met. The rhetoric of the report was far removed from the reality. The message of the funding allocation and its complete withdrawal three years later was that computers in school education were marginal. This was not, however, the public view. In the minds of the public, computers had come to be viewed as a status good and as essential for young people's preparation for life and employment in the future. For teachers, constructed as deficient in the skills required to integrate computers into the curriculum, the policy recommendations in the text led directly to training requirements and to increased pressures on their time within and outside of schools.

Foundations laid

In October of 1983, the Victorian Education Department accepted the directions recommended in *Teaching, Learning and Computers*. The Victorian government matched the funding that was allocated by the federal government to the new National Computer Education Program (Zammit 1989). While the federal government devolved administration to the states, *Teaching, Learning and Computers* recommended the allocation of funds, the type of program and its administrative structure. The recommendations depended on the understandings of computers and their potential role in education which resulted from negotiation and compromise during the policy process. The claims that were made for computers in schools in the text were authoritative.

In 1984, the State Computer Education Centre was opened in Moorabbin, Victoria. Regional Computer Education Resource Centres were also established. As well, professional development courses to train teachers to use computers were instituted (Bigum 1987). In Victoria, more than 22,000 teachers were trained in this way over three years (Zammit 1989). The Department of Education in Victoria issued guidelines for the purchase of hardware and software, as had been recommended in the report. Two coordinating committees, for government and non-government schools, were established to administer program funds. The government schools committee chose a framework which selected schools for receipt of grants based on the premise that such schools would become a model for others. In 1984 approximately AU$700,000 was distributed among 87 schools, five of them to fund major projects (Bigum 1987).

The program itself lasted for three years and was no longer funded by the federal government after 1986, although schools' computing programs continued to be funded by state and territory governments. The program as it was delivered was modelled on the centralisation of expertise, which had been the perspective adopted in the report. Experts in educational computing were located in the computer education centres, which teachers attended for training. Committees chose schools to which grants should be awarded. While processes for administering funds and programs were necessary, these also reflected views and attitudes. As Bigum (1987, 26) points out, 'how the agenda is shaped will depend on who shapes it'.

The perspectives of the experts were often distant from those at the chalkface (Herszberg 1986). For teachers, one of the messages from this type of program was that they lacked important and valued knowledge. A national program, supported by both state and federal governments, authorised and legitimised knowledge and skills with computers as valuable and important for students (Grundy, Bigum, Evans and McKenzie 1987). The way in which this knowledge was transmitted to them was formed primarily by the understandings of computers that were embedded in the report. Meanings for the personal computer were made for teachers through the popular media, their own interactions with computers outside of schools, decisions made by educational authorities and in such authoritative documents as the NACCS report.

That these meanings were negotiated and renegotiated at the individual school and classroom level with individual teachers and students does not mean teachers had complete freedom to choose these. A set of meanings had already been applied: the computer was a technology that was important for children to master; it was in the national interest for children to learn to control the technology; and teachers in schools were responsible for imparting the knowledge that society considered important. Central to the report was an attempt to gain control over the essentially ad hoc nature of the spread of personal computers in schools to enhance the possibilities for Australian manufacturers and suppliers (NAA 1983b). That this occurred at a time of recession and of diminishing resources to schools generally but, more particularly, to government schools, was significant. Greater control over the ways computers were introduced into schools meant more opportunity to control costs. The fear of falling behind other nations in using new technologies was also a powerful driver. New computing technologies, it was widely believed, would improve national competitiveness in business and therefore living standards.

Conclusion

The policy for the National Computer Education Program can be seen as a political response in an election campaign to an area of community concern, rather than a sustained attempt to introduce a large-scale computing project into schools. The attention of the government, the discursive circumscription of the field, the allocation of funds, invested the computer with meanings that gave it power: the power to advance or retard the national interest and the power to improve education and thus society. The computer was constructed in positive terms as a means of ameliorating disadvantage, as a resource that would be spread evenly and in this way benefit Australia both at home, through greater social equality, and internationally, through improving Australia's performance. To the computer was attributed the power to improve education and through that, to contribute to national economic competitiveness and a more equal society.

The amount of funding allocated to the program, AU$18 million over three years, was small. At the end of three years, federal government funding was discontinued. The burden of adjustment and training fell on teachers. This burden was two-fold: it involved the use of teachers with some expertise in computers as resources both in their own schools and in others, much of it in their own time; and the in-service training over several intensive days of pairs of teachers from many schools, also in their own time. The expectation was that back in their schools, they would share the knowledge they had gained with others. At the same time as teachers were being treated as resources, they were also labelled as deficient.

Their understandings, though, were being framed through these processes. The decisions to introduce computers had been taken initially by small numbers of enthusiast-teachers and principals. Following the NACCS report, these decisions were influenced by others, with particular visions of computers and their place in society in mind. The ways in which teachers were introduced to these helped to frame their understandings not only of computers, but also of the ways they should be used in classrooms. In the 1980s, teachers still retained some say in how they should use computers, though views on the purposes of computers in schools had already been inscribed in the programs that trained them (Bigum 1987). These meanings continue to influence practice.

The divergence between the anticipated and the actual funding provided by the government for the computer education program illuminates an essential contradiction in the report between the claims made for the computer in education and the type of program proposed. The report asserted that computers in schools would serve the national interest by improving education and equipping young people for the future. On the other hand, the recommendations were for quite modest initiatives that did not match the future outlined for computers in schools. The interests of the NACCS, numbers of whom in the working parties were enthusiastic advocates for the use of computers in schools, were at variance with those of the government. As a policy which attempted to instantiate new practices, the report was hobbled by the divergence between the claims it made for the benefits of computers in schools and the minimal program for computer awareness which it advocated (Taylor et al. 1997).

Tensions over educational priorities were intensified at a time of economic downturn. They left imprints within *Teaching, Learning and Computers* which are evident in discursive strategies that attempt to balance different and at times competing points of view. These tensions can be traced in discourses that are recontextualised from disparate value systems and brought into sometimes uneasy conjunction. The report is characterised by the mingling of a number of different discourses which embody different values and beliefs about education, and the place of computers within society and school education. The embedding of these voices within the Commonwealth Schools Commission necessitated compromise to achieve a policy outcome and the use of particular strategies to achieve this compromise. Unlike the Wearing report of 1976, which saw a split decision, the NACCS report represented a settlement on the role of computers in education (Taylor et al. 1997). Within the report, different positions across the educational spectrum are brought together in an uneasy coalition through an unlikely medium: the computer itself. It is positioned as a bridge across these divides, through a set of discursive strategies that embody appeals to each of the different constituencies. Thus the political battle is preserved in the text itself.

Chapter Four

The Global Economic Arena

The information superhighway. Convergence. These were the buzz words of 1995. In 1983, the pages of the *Bulletin* magazine were filled with advertisements from numerous companies jostling to sell their variant of the personal computer: the Personal Business Computer from Toshiba, the Professional Computer from Wang, the Advanced Personal Computer from NEC, the Personal Technical Computer from Hewlett Packard (*Bulletin* 1983a–d). These were all targeted at business and immediately recognisable as computers. In 1995, the technology landscape was in a similar ferment but a new and wider range of technologies and services was available and aimed at the much larger home market. Computers with multimedia capacities. Pay television. Mobile phones. The Internet. The terms 'convergence' and 'information superhighway' were used to convey the interconnections between existing devices and the infrastructure which enabled previously discrete services to be delivered, however imperfectly, via the one device. Technological developments, regulatory changes and multinational media and advertising businesses were involved in a complex interplay which bewildered the consumer who faced purchasing decisions in big box stores.

While only the more affluent homes had computers, the capabilities of the new technologies and the hype surrounding their potential benefits were attracting more householders to consider their purchase. Articles explaining the mysteries of computers, their associated technologies and the multitude of possible applications abounded (eg, Rolley 1995). 'Parents who want their kids to have an edge at school' were amongst the keenest potential purchasers of computers (Rolley 1995). Nor was it only journalists who linked computing technologies with education. Prime Minister Paul Keating expressed his intention to place the issue of technology in education on the government agenda, telling journalists 'that exploiting the educational potential of the superhighway and the new electronic information networks would be an important element in government policy' (Korporaal 1995). Promises were made to the public about the benefits that the use of new technologies could bring. However, in the midst of changing regulatory landscapes, the services which might once have been delivered by a government-owned monopoly were to be provided instead by private companies for a small fee. The federal government set the example, happy to announce the provision of internet services for schools by Optus Vision, a private company, at a 'bargain price of $50 a month' (Potter 1995).

For the federal government, however, the new technologies and the corporate interests with which they were associated posed significant challenges and problems that were then unresolved across wide areas of its responsibilities: telecommunications, intellectual property, privacy and media regulation, amongst others. Concerns were raised too over the benefits which could be conferred on those who could afford ready access to information and services, further disadvantaging those already on the margins of society (Lowe 1995). The answer for many was to argue that inequities would be overcome through education: 'the educational system will help level out the playing field in the long term' (Lowe 1995). How this was to be achieved was seldom explained.

To canvass possible future directions for technology and education policy, in 1994 the government requested advice on the challenges presented to education, training and employment from 'the convergence of technologies' (NBEET 1995a, 170). Following the end of the National Computer Education Program in 1986, the ALP Government's interest in computers in schools had languished. Instead, the government's attention in the following years was directed to economic restructuring. The machinery of government too was reconstructed in pursuit of greater efficiency and control, meaning that the advice commissioned in 1994 emanated from a very different institutional framework than that which had produced *Teaching, Learning and Computers* in 1983, despite the continuance of the ALP in power during that period. The changes in the institutional framework within which this advice was produced provide an important backdrop to understanding the underlying values and the conceptualisation of computing technologies and education contained within the report that resulted.

Reconstructing policy frameworks

In 1985, the Commonwealth Schools Commission, which was created under the Whitlam ALP Government in 1974, was partially absorbed into the Department of Education as the Schools Commission. The Commonwealth Schools Commission had represented, however imperfectly, a wide range of interest groups involved in education but its influence was now diminished

(Marginson 1997a). Following the 1987 election, when the Hawke ALP Government was returned, the public service was reorganised, a response to the economic crises of the ALP Government's first term, and cuts to public spending ensued as a prelude to a restructure of the economy. New discourses that expressed the primacy of economics as the central focus of the government accompanied institutional changes and attempted to reframe the expectations the public had of government. This discourse, labelled economic rationalist, postulated the necessity of competition, of competitive markets, in a globalised economy and aimed to persuade the public to accept that the Australian economy should be restructured root and branch (Capling, Considine and Crozier 1998). Embedded within it was a strong view about the role of the state. Through altering 'the rules of the game', the government could enable a competitive marketplace in areas previously considered public (Galperin 2004a, 162).

The dominant economic ideology was given force in new institutional arrangements. Departments were merged and larger departments created, one of which was that of Employment, Education and Training (DEET), headed by John Dawkins. The aim of the merged department was to enhance employment outcomes through improving education and training and rearticulating the links between them (DEET 1988). The exercise of government power, enacted through legislation, established and prescribed ways of understanding employment, education and training, previously in separate departments, within the governmental field of policy and legislation. After the establishment of the new DEET in 1987, the Schools Commission, along with the other educational commissions, was abolished (Smart and Dudley 1990). The abolition of the educational commissions was an attempt by the government to assert greater control over policymaking, to reorient the purpose of education as primarily vocational, rather than liberal, and to control the expenditure of federal resources on education (Marginson 1997a).

The government viewed education through the prism of employment, which was its priority. At the government's behest, the prioritisation of employment over education and training was embedded in the title of the DEET, the Department of Employment, Education and Training (McMorrow 2003). Such a prioritisation aptly captures the way education was defined in economic rationalist discourse: education's purpose was cast as economic, excluding other purposes as well as voices from the profession (Dudley and Vidovich 1995). Officially, education was designated as an industry and incorporated into an economic discourse that presented

Australia as engaged in a mortal struggle to win international markets (Bryan 1991). In this struggle, education's role was to supply skills to the labour market, thereby growing national competitiveness. The primary purpose of schools, for instance, was the production of 'a more highly skilled, adaptive and productive workforce' for an economy which was 'part way through a process of substantial structural change' (Dawkins 1988, 1).

While the rebadging of education as an industry had occurred earlier in the arena of industrial relations, the designation of education as an 'industry' by John Dawkins had far-reaching implications (Knight 1992). New frameworks and language delegitimised earlier ways of conceptualising education as an institution, for instance, which provided a public good. Understood as an industry, education too could become the subject of industrial restructuring, a modernisation process which would transform the backward educational sector into one that could take the country forward into a more competitive future (Dawkins 1988; NBEET 1995a). Education was depicted as failing in the past to equip workers with the necessary skills, therefore requiring redefinition to ensure that it included teaching with new technologies. The new computing technologies would be employed as they had been in business and industry to improve productivity in the educational sector itself. Accordingly, work and education would become part of a continuum. Thus an economic discourse was blended with a technologically determinist one that ascribed power to the new technologies and saw them as a key factor in globalisation, a new and equally deterministic discourse.

Individual ministers were influential in setting directions and effecting change: Paul Keating as Treasurer, then Prime Minister, was committed to internationalising the Australian economy as was John Dawkins, the first Minister of the DEET. He assumed direct control over educational policymaking at the federal level, with the assistance of a small board, the National Board of Employment, Education and Training (NBEET). Established in July 1988 following the abolition of the educational commissions, the NBEET reported directly to the minister, providing advice on matters relating to employment, education across all sectors, and training and youth affairs (NBEET 1996). Responsibility for programs rested with the department (McMorrow 2003). Four councils of the Board were established to provide specialist advice – the Employment and Skills Formation Council, the Australian Research Council, the Higher Education Council and the Schools Council, with some of the personnel of the latter drawn from the Commonwealth Schools Commission (DEET 1988).

Advisory mechanisms were thus centralised within the public service, although separated from responsibility for programs (DEET 1988). Advice was also commissioned from outside the public service, but in practice the authors of this advice were often part of the existing policy environment (Taylor et al. 1997), members of interlocking networks among a number of government departments, often both state and federal, and also private consulting firms and academics. The result was a looser and more diffused policy environment. The formalised representation embodied within the Commonwealth Schools Commission and the different educational interests and voices that had played a part in shaping policy had vanished. Policy advice was shaped by the structure of the federal department, the DEET, and the subservient role of the NBEET within the department reflected not just a loss of autonomy of policy advice, compared with the Commonwealth Schools Commission, but also a narrowing of that advice (Marginson 1997a). The independence of the Commonwealth Schools Commission to advance policy positions, to recommend programs and to suggest funding allocations was not reflected in the NBEET.

The NBEET was relatively small, its resources were limited, and it was constrained by the legislative requirements which governed it (Lingard 1993). Its projects were determined first by its legislative requirements and second, through referrals from the minister, known as references. While board or council members could initiate projects, these were regarded as being of lesser priority (NBEET 1992). The NBEET issued a large number of reports in its eight years of existence, but it was up to the minister of the day to determine which reports would assist in framing policy. This meant that in many ways the NBEET was oriented towards ministerial priorities and distant from the education sector. This orientation is reflected in the policy advice which emanated from within this structure and bore the imprint of the government's economic orientation. Even if commissioned from sources outside the public service, these sources were often from within the policymaking orbit, reducing the need to balance the differing constituencies that had been encompassed by the Commonwealth Schools Commission.

Converging technologies, policy fluidity

Technological advances and the impact of new global businesses in the communications, broadcasting and entertainment industries stimulated the federal government's interest in computing technologies and education in 1994. The potential of new technologies for education was being lauded in countries such as the US. The further connection of computing technologies to globalisation in the economic discourses promoted by corporate interests and enthusiasts around the world worked to confirm and extend popular understandings of computers. New communications and computing technologies were eyed by governments internationally for their potential to enhance economic growth and to deliver services to a wider range of citizens (Galperin 2004b). In the states and territories, a surge of enthusiasm about the potential of newer computing technologies in school education was already underway, exemplified in Victoria by the Smith report, *Technologies for Enhanced Learning* (Directorate of School Education 1994). At the same time, significant technological changes were evident in both computer and communications technologies, enabling faster and more interactive communication and giving rise to the term 'convergence' to describe what had been previously separate and discrete technologies.

The federal government adopted the discourse of 'convergence' which linked computing technologies with economic growth. When in 1994, the Minister for the DEET, Simon Crean, requested advice from the NBEET on technology and education, his referral was cast as an investigation of the impact of 'the convergence of technologies' on the employment, education and training sector (NBEET 1995a, 170). The resultant report was published as *Education and Technology Convergence* (Tinkler et al. 1996) in January 1996 in the last months of the ALP's 13 years of government. *Education and Technology Convergence* was part of a response to the new computing and communications technologies of the early 1990s and the changing corporate landscape, but it was also shaped by the new ideologies and techniques of governing which had been established over the years of the ALP Government, particularly after 1987. The imprints of these changed values and ideology are preserved in the language of *Education and Technology Convergence*. Economic rationalist values lie at its heart and frame computing technologies as central to education and to future society, but in ways which were markedly different to those of 1983. At the same time, *Education and Technology Convergence* as a policy text constructed in this period and within this new institutional framework sheds light on how computing technologies in education were conceptualised (Lankshear et al. 2000), but also on the process of policy development and the factors that influenced this development.

As an educational policy which advanced new ways of conceptualising educational computing, the report argued that developments in computing technologies expanded the range of learning opportunities, but also provided both the means and the opportunity to remodel education to align it with market needs. As an example of the policy process, *Education and Technology Convergence* illuminates the complexity and fluidity of policy-making at the federal government level. It was part of a lengthy process through which policy was developed (Bell and Stevenson 2006). The report was intended to inform another more substantive report into the impact of new technologies on employment and education, *Converging Technology, Work and Learning* published in November 1995 (NBEET 1995b). *Education and Technology Convergence* was, however, also published separately. The authors of the report were already part of the policy environment, each of whom had a prior or concurrent involvement with other government reports or enquiries. The report itself is emblematic of policy as 'symbolic', designed not to allocate funds but to indicate a set of values which could provide the basis for a new direction for education (Taylor et al. 1997, 10).

The particular institutional framework within which *Education and Technology Convergence* was produced substantially shaped the nature of the problems to be considered and who should consider them (Galperin 2004a): the terms of reference outline the problem as it was envisaged by Minister Simon Crean and delineate its focus. The commissioning of a private consulting firm to investigate and present a report narrows the interests represented. It was notable, for instance, that the policy was constructed by academics and consultants, rather than the educational bureaucrats of the NACCS. Also, reflecting its uneasy location, the report was divorced from funding recommendations, unlike that of the NACCS. The process of policymaking federally had become more diffuse than in 1983 and it lacked the authoritative voice of the Commonwealth Schools Commission. As one of a number of reports which were to feed into another, *Education and Technology Convergence* was at risk of being ignored. However, its very location within the federal government policy sphere lent it a legitimacy which was recognised at the time (Lankshear et al. 2000).

In 1983, *Teaching, Learning and Computers* advanced a rationale for introducing computers into schools that was critically linked with the diffusion of computing technologies. Computers were co-located with teachers and students in schools, positioning them as integral to the teaching and learning process, as expressed in the title of the report. By 1996, the concept of using computing technologies in schools, if not always the reality, was established. The goal of policy was not to authorise and legitimise the use of computing technologies, but to intensify their use in order to institute change. The co-location that made the 'strange familiar' in

Teaching, Learning and Computers was no longer necessary in *Education and Technology Convergence*, where individual teachers and learners have almost disappeared (Noble 1999, 68). Instead, the report advances new views on the purposes of education and the way that computing technologies can be employed to achieve those purposes.

The discourses of *Education and Technology Convergence*

In *Education and Technology Convergence*, computing technologies link together the three dominant discourses: technological determinism, economic rationalism and globalisation. Education is portrayed as central to producing new knowledge workers for the economy, but also as in need of modernisation to achieve that aim. At the same time, education is represented as an item which is newly marketable because of the communicative possibilities enabled by the union of computing and communications technologies. The report constructs a new discursive framework that places computing technologies at the centre of education in two ways: as capable of enhancing learning and thereby workplace skills; and as enabling the export of education. Learning with computing technologies thus becomes central to the economy.

Two key premises underlie the report. The first is that the new computing technologies are a positive force that is changing all aspects of society for the better. The second is that the free market is a superior determinant of outcomes than governments. The first is evident in the technologically determinist discourse that pervades the report. The second is linked with two other world views and their discourses, those of economic rationalism and globalisation. The construct of the 'knowledge economy' is employed to connect each of these world views and to tie education into these discourses. Each of these is a determinist world view.

The technologically determinist

In the text, a technologically determinist discourse presents change as the product of technology rather than political and economic decisions (Sussman 1997). The technological focus of the report is explicit in its terms of reference which reflect beliefs at the political level. Technology rather than education is at the centre of the investigation and the impact of computing technologies on employment is the overwhelming concern. Thus the implicit assumption of the report is that rapidly evolving computing technologies are driving change in education. This is evident at the beginning of the report:

> Computer policy initiatives developed as recently as the early nineties
> have been overtaken by the rapidity of the technological changes. Hardly
> a week passes without some media release about a new development
> in communications technology that is likely to affect the delivery of
> education. Of singular importance is the increasing level of convergence
> between information and communications technology, and the computer
> remains central to these developments. (Tinkler et al. 1996, 6)

Computing technologies are foregrounded as the agents of change: this is
a world peopled by machines. The emphasis in the above paragraph is on
the speed of change. Metaphors of speed which equal progress and the
obverse, obsolescence, create a sense of time itself being sped up, driven by
the technology (Goatly 2007). 'Recently', 'the early nineties', 'overtaken',
'rapidity', 'hardly a week passes' build up a sense of urgency and inexorability.
By contrast, human policymakers have disappeared (Fairclough 2000b).
Instead, their products, 'computer policy initiatives' are rendered obsolete.
Computers spread as if they are independent. The machine is depicted as
acting, indeed performing, while the human behind the machine has
vanished.

The key metaphor of 'convergence' was employed to construct a sense
of the inevitability of technological change and its predicted outcomes.
Metaphorically 'convergence' conjures up a process by which apparently
abstract forces meet together in a union that is inevitable, irresistible and
irrevocable:

> The rapid convergence of computing, audio-visual media and com-
> munications technologies is starting to have a profound transformative
> effect on how people work, learn and play. (Tinkler et al. 1996, 149)

'Convergence' also functions to tie both education and computing technologies
into this process of change. The assumption that new computing technologies
are changing society means that they will therefore change education as well,
but these changes are represented positively as 'transformative'. Agency is
ascribed to the technologies themselves, consistent with their presentation as
an irresistible force. The use of 'convergence' to ally computing technologies
with education was a deeply political statement:

> In this environment it becomes vitally important that, to meet commer-
> cial and community aspirations, not only will there be convergence
> among the technologies, but between those convergent technologies and
> pedagogy. (70)

Implicit within the connection of the two is the opening of the domain of education to private profit-making enterprises, one that is obscured by the assumption of an irresistible process. 'Convergence' in the title of the report works as a naturalising device, asserting the inevitability of the process.

The economic rationalist

In *Education and Technology Convergence*, the discourse of economic rationalism is pervasive. The report is premised on the assumption that the new computing technologies which enabled the Internet would drive future economic growth as well as requiring new skills in the workforce. Focused at the level of the macro-economy, it employs the distinctive language of economics to construct a new model for education (Luke 1995). This is most evident in Chapter 4, 'The emerging new paradigm for the education industry':

> This chapter maps out a new paradigm for the education industry that is emerging from these forces of globalisation, the impact of the new technologies on design and delivery of education, and the international search for best practice in improving learning outcomes in students. However, this is not offered as a one-off major step change towards a new status quo, but as a process of continual learning in an increasingly complex and turbulent environment subject to continuing technological innovation and market, rather than supplier, criteria for learning services and products. (72–3)

In this paragraph, the authors postulate that underlying forces are initiating changes in education and they define and delineate that change premised on a belief that privileges the market. Education is no longer viewed as a public good, but as a business which sells 'services and products' and is therefore part of the global marketplace. The assertion that education will be transformed is abstracted from people or policy choices. The 'imperatives' for change in education are located in the powerful and irresistible forces of competition, shifting international markets, new technologies and globalisation as opposed to the substantial policy changes already introduced by the federal government.

The imperatives of the marketplace, particularly the global marketplace, dominate. Computing technologies act as symbols of this global marketplace, as instruments to enable access to it and as tools to restructure education to compete more effectively within it. In this model of education, teaching has been replaced by learning, a shift which is presented as the movement from a transmission to a constructivist mode of education focused on the learner. Eight specific learning principles are advanced as the underpinnings for this new mode of education. These have their origins in management theory (Peters 2001), recognisable by the terms, 'just-in-time' learning, 'customised learning' and 'collaborative teams' (Tinkler et al. 1996, 79). While there is an expanded view of knowledge proposed in the report, it is set within an economic framework.

In *Education and Technology Convergence*, as in 1983, the focus is on the computing technologies themselves. The purpose of using computing technologies in education is in part to develop new skills in the population, a human capital model, but more importantly, to position education as a part of the national project to enhance Australia's competitiveness in a ruthless globalised economy. Computing technologies are represented as more able to deliver on this than are people, because information is a property that is attributed to the computer, rather than the human who operates or programs the machine. The computer is represented as the engine of change and the tool which will transform the educational system.

The discourse of globalisation

An equally determinist discourse is that of globalisation. In the later 1980s, the term 'globalisation' began to be used by politicians, the media, business representatives and protesters, although from different perspectives and with different ends in mind. Used to describe the increasingly interlinked nature of nations, primarily western, through economic, political and cultural relations, 'globalisation' attributed the changes occurring within those nations to the action of global forces (Held, McGrew, Goldblatt and Perraton 1999). When deployed by politicians, the discourse of globalisation was used to justify political and economic change within and between nations with the aim of privileging market approaches in realms that were previously the preserve of governments. Deregulation and the privatisation of government agencies are prominent policy choices in this approach, one which has been particularly evident in the English-speaking nations (Fairclough 2000b). From the early 1990s, computing technologies became integrally linked in these visions of globalisation promulgated by politicians and espoused by business and corporate interests (Castells 2000).

In *Education and Technology Convergence*, the discourse of globalisation is woven into that of economic rationalism and technological determinism:

> The information society, flowing from the electronics revolution
> in the 1960s, as opposed to industrial society, is based on a global

> knowledge economy... World competitive advantage has shifted from
> ownership and exploitation of natural resources, such as minerals
> and primary agricultural products, to ownership and exploitation
> of created resources, such as knowledge, encoded in high value-
> added manufactured products and services and global marketing and
> distribution systems. (67–68)

Political and economic choices are presented as inevitable outcomes of both
technological change and the process of globalisation to which society must
adapt. The world of the past and the present is conceived of as having to cede
to the world of the future, one that will be characterised by the ubiquity
of computing technologies. This ascription of agency to an impersonal
force glosses the political decisions made and the struggle for ownership
and control in the areas of telecommunications and media which had
been continuing for some years. In all of these areas, large organisations,
particularly multinationals, and the government were participants and
decision-makers, with consequences for the public. Vital public services,
broadcasting and telecommunications, were being redefined as private and
for profit, with ownership being sold by cash-strapped governments for
private benefit (Galperin 2004b).

The construct of the 'knowledge economy' further ties *Education and
Technology Convergence* to the Keating Government's economic ideology.
Joining 'knowledge' to 'economy' connects education to the economy as its
servant. The construct of the 'knowledge economy' then becomes the link to
the discourse of globalisation through the causality ascribed to new computing
technologies. Competition and the extension of new technologies through
the workforce are thus justified. Despite the apparent emphasis on education,
globalisation discourse as employed in *Education and Technology Convergence*
is fundamentally an economic rather than an educational discourse.

The construct of the knowledge economy

The construct of the 'knowledge economy', drawing on economics and
management studies in particular, had currency amongst policymakers
internationally in the 1990s (Peters 2001). In *Education and Technology
Convergence*, the 'knowledge economy' is depicted as demanding uncom-
fortable change rather than the politicians who might arouse opposition:

> The knowledge economy demands a competency that links information
> management skills, system thinking and learning skills, and information
> technology competency at various levels of sophistication. (74)

The knowledge economy, the authors argue, has superseded the industrial economy. The 'raw material' that powered the industrial economy has become redundant (76). The new 'raw material' is information, which is thus designated the essential element of the new knowledge economy. Information is at once the property and product of sophisticated information technologies in a depiction that evokes the manufacturing process and a rupture of similar magnitude to the industrial revolution. To use information to create wealth, however, requires more advanced skills which will be produced by education. Education is allied with globalisation, because the information society is a globalised one. In *Education and Technology Convergence*, education is represented as operating on an old industrial economy model and therefore out of date. An intensified use of computing technologies is proposed as the solution to bring education into a more modern world.

Information literacy is presented as the new competence for the 'information society' (67). The term 'computer literacy', deployed to connect schooling with computers, had been widely influential in the 1980s. In *Teaching, Learning and Computers*, it was used to reinforce the notion that computers should be part of schooling so that students could learn computer skills to prepare them for work in a technologically sophisticated world. The term 'information literacy' draws from 'computer literacy' but it encompasses a wider range of meanings and draws on different assumptions to form the rationale for its adoption in the education sector at all levels. 'Information literacy' becomes the new 'competence' required in the workplace for which students should be prepared (Tinkler et al. 1996, 73). 'Competence' thus links education directly with the workplace but also to the federal government's policies in training which stemmed from the Mayer report, *Key Competencies* (Mayer 1992).

More importantly, the new information literacy explicitly ties computing technologies and school education into the discourses of the information economy and globalisation, in which the core notion of markets is naturalised. Knowledge has become a commodity that can be acquired through education in which information literacy is central:

> Students will require the development of information literacy to be effective citizens and workers in a knowledge economy, while teachers/ learning facilitators will require this literacy to be able to develop it in their students, and to carry out their professional responsibilities as knowledge workers. (Tinkler et al. 1996, 77)

The goal of education is to enhance productivity and to create 'comparative advantage' (76). The emphasis on national economic goals rather than social or personal ones becomes another way of linking computing technologies with the workplace and education and also the global marketplace (Galperin 2004b), recalling the depiction of the computer in schools as the architect of 'national well-being' in *Teaching, Learning and Computers* in 1983.

While an economic discourse was a substantial strand in 1983, in *Education and Technology Convergence*, the economy dominates. The 'national well-being' of 1983 was open to wider interpretations which could include social and democratic goals, but in *Education and Technology Convergence*, the term 'knowledge economy' signifies the primacy of economic views. What underlies these economic views are assumptions and values which reward some and penalise others (Blackmore 2000). The question as to who profits is elided. Yet the terms 'convergence' and 'knowledge economy' are linguistic choices which signify particular world views and their associated value systems. A more covert use is metaphor. In this report, the most striking metaphor is that of the global arena: one in which education is central to national survival.

The global arena

In *Education and Technology Convergence*, the key metaphor of the global marketplace as an arena of Darwinian struggle connects the report to the central theme of the Keating Government between 1993 and 1996, that of the global competitive struggle. The international marketplace is depicted as the neutral stadium where participants fight to survive with only the strongest winning the prize of market share. This central metaphor obscures the role of human agency in constructing the rules that govern commercial activity, the institutions which regulate it and the political and commercial choices that are made (Galperin 2004a). Instead, the hardships which individuals may experience are justified through the representation of this struggle as both a national imperative and one which is externally imposed.

At the heart of the global economy is the arena, where competitors struggle for supremacy. Achieving victory in the global struggle is the only base from which all economic growth, and therefore prosperity, can emerge. But the global arena is a fierce place. Organisations, and through their success or failure, nations, must fight continually for survival:

> The knowledge economy, with its global impetus for relentless organisational and product innovation to both gain international share and defend domestic share, has placed a premium on the development

of human capital, not only through a preparatory education and training system, but through processes of continuous lifelong learning across multiple career paths. (Tinkler et al. 1996, 69)

'Gain' and 'defend' evoke battle, victors and losers, the powerful and the defeated, a strongly emotive threat to the nation which struggles to 'defend domestic share' in a 'relentless' battle that takes place outside national borders. Yet this arena is presented as a depersonalised and deterritorialised place, where the struggle is between forces outside of human control. Tertiary education is identified as an area of comparative advantage for Australia as a provider of export services. Universities are portrayed as participants who are already positioning themselves in the global arena, ready to begin the race, with the prize being foreign students. To gain students, they will use the new technologies to enable them to communicate across distance. These 'convergent technologies' are themselves powerful, 'with the ability... to overcome the barriers of distance and physical access' (71). Again, technologies are positioned as the agent. The power of these technologies has a global reach from which individual educational institutions, 'the educational multinationals', will be able to profit (70).

The metaphor of the global arena builds the concept of a global struggle and positions tertiary education as central to Australia's success. Other forms of education, particularly school education, are envisioned as forming the basis for the development of this industry. The authors evoke a more sophisticated argument than in 1983 to explain the relationship of computing technologies to the national interest, but it is also a more narrowly-based economic argument that excludes other considerations as to what that relationship might comprise. Instead, their argument draws on strategies appropriated from the corporate world which are then adapted for different educational sectors in order to garner support for propositions related to the future of education.

A corporate model for education

The corporate model expressed in the term 'multinational' is presented as the prototype for education. Education is compared unfavourably to corporations and the way they have adapted to the challenges of the global arena. Corporate techniques such as downsizing and outsourcing are posed as potentially useful techniques to be applied 'when considering the prospective transformation of the education industry' (72). The comparison works to devalue existing educational practices, while an overtly economic rationalist discourse delegitimises the institution of education as it was then configured:

> At present the industry operates largely as a State or quasi-State monopoly industry, subject to bureaucratic centralised control and planning, supplier-driven, with weak market signals for the expression of consumer preference and a low capacity for change management to achieve high levels of consumer preference. (72)

The portrayal of education as an industry, as opposed to an institution, for instance, means that it can be defined in economic terms as a 'monopoly', with its state ownership a barrier to change. If depicted as an institution under threat, by contrast, the mounting of a defence might be a likely outcome. Rather than a conception of education which encompasses multiple purposes, in this construction education is construed as illegitimate because it does not meet consumer needs. Absent the discipline of the market, institutions are not forced to adapt their curricula to meet student preference. Homogenised, placed in binary opposition to the commercial world and its supposed benefits, education is seen to be inadequate, outdated and unresponsive to demands from a changing world outside a closed system. Self-interest is attributed to any voice from within education as 'supplier-driven'. Earlier in the report, teachers had been framed as an obstacle to change. Together with the views of education outlined above, the framing of teachers as an obstacle seems more ominous.

Views on education necessarily entail beliefs about teachers and their practices, their authority and their professionalism. The authors have already identified information as central to the society of the future and as an object of value which will require new skills to use. The skills to manipulate information are therefore important for students to gain for their future lives. Teachers, however, are depicted as lacking in these skills:

> Today's students will need these skills... Teachers will be required to teach these skills – teachers who, in many cases, may first have to acquire many of the skills themselves. (54)

Teachers are evaluated as deficient, unable to teach what they do not know, therefore handicapping children for the future. An economic discourse is employed to construct teachers as the obstacle and therefore dispensable:

> An aging teaching force offers the opportunity to consider using staff turnover as a means of restructuring the composition of the human

resource applied to education and the mix of human and capital resources. (51)

People and resources are deemed to be equivalent. Teachers are generalised, then abstracted, into a 'teaching force', a rewording of the more familiar labour or workforce. The 'aging' workforce and its implied enfeeblement is in fact an opportunity to employers of teachers, primarily government, to hire fewer teachers. As teachers 'turnover', 'the composition of the human resource' can be subjected to 'restructuring', a euphemism for reducing the number of employees in an enterprise. Teachers are depicted as backward, aging and unwilling to change in contrast to the widely held view, which still pertains, that young people find it naturally easier to use computing technologies. A more powerful assumption which underlies such claims is that technology will improve learning and that teachers are to blame for not making the effort to understand and use new technologies.

Such assumptions serve as justifications for measures to achieve a particular view of change which will lead into the new information society. So the authors suggest ways of impelling a greater take-up of computer technologies: the establishment of targets and benchmarks for teacher competencies and the incorporation of information technology as an essential subject into curricula for trainee teachers. Coercive measures are dressed up as 'a strategic approach' (57) and buttressed through the use of terms drawn from the Mayer report (Mayer 1992). The potential cost is justified by the familiar appeal to the national interest: 'the national and personal cost of not doing so, while less quantifiable, is certain to be greater' (67). Again, the new technologies are strategically equated with the national interest, while the difficulty of measuring their benefits is mitigated.

However, while teachers have been positioned as deficient and backward-looking, the authors raise a number of questions that indirectly reveal the situation that still prevailed within education institutions more than a decade after the National Computer Education Program of 1984 to 1986. Educational facilities were generally inadequate for the numbers of staff and students using them. Teachers were overworked. Schools did not have sufficient access to computers, nor appropriate software. Schools, in particular, had less technology available than existed outside the school. There were wide variations between institutions and considerable inequities within sectors and also between sectors.

While in the report education is generally considered as a whole, rather than by sector, the authors' judgement of sectors is apparent in one linguistic choice, that of the word 'computer'. The many more terms used in *Education and Technology Convergence* for computing technologies reflect in part changes in the technologies, but also changing conceptions of them. In *Education and Technology Convergence*, the term 'computer' is much less common than in *Teaching, Learning and Computers* in 1983. When used, its meaning is more specific. It refers to the object, the computer, often in reference to the number of computers or the use of computers. The domain of the 'computer' is in schools, both secondary and primary. When used of schools, the term 'computer' focuses on the hardware rather than its uses in learning in ways which cast schools as backward and old-fashioned. By contrast, in TAFE and higher education institutions, 'computer-based instructional courses' and a 'computer-assisted language learning laboratory' are advanced as sophisticated uses which are 'exemplars of change' (49). A positive evaluation of the use of technologies in such institutions is made, but it is one which schools have yet to embrace.

The impact of the report

The report was published in January 1996, although it had been completed some months earlier. Its publication came just weeks before the Keating Government lost the federal election of March 1996. Before it was released, however, events had already overtaken it. In April 1995, Prime Minister Keating announced a National Strategy for Information and Communications Services and Technologies. The prime ministerial statement pointed to government consideration of the 'ways in which we can stimulate the use of information and communications services and technologies in various sectors of the economy including industry, education, employment, social services and other areas' (Keating 1995, n.p.). As part of this strategy, the federal government established the Education Network Australia (EdNA), with the agreement in May 1995 of MCEETYA (NBEET 1995b). The EdNA process was designed to establish a framework for networking the education sector and for the provision of online content, and thereby to foster the growth of networked communications in the education sector (NBEET 1995b). Later that year, the Employment and Skills Council, following receipt of *Education and Technology Convergence*, recommended that 'a national strategic framework to achieve adequate technology, workforce capability and high quality education and training materials' be developed (NBEET 1996, 15). This followed policy steps already taken.

The major report which *Education and Technology Convergence* was commissioned to support, *Converging Technology, Work and Learning* (NBEET 1995b), accepted some of its findings, particularly its definition of information literacy. It was less in accord with the notion that learning with computers was central to education, arguing that:

> This is a contested area. There is no current learning theory which adequately incorporates current computer technologies and which would allow one to argue that learning is made unambiguously more efficient or that teaching is more productive as a consequence of such technologies. (NBEET 1995b, 80)

By contrast, it noted that 'good learning outcomes are reliant on the relationship (i.e. quality of interaction of teacher and student' (80). The question of personal interactions, relationships and their association with learning is one that receives little attention in *Education and Technology Convergence*. The dominant discourse of the report is an economic one. The conclusion that was drawn from the report by the NBEET was evident in its judgement that 'the Employment and Skills Council, in its commissioned report, *Education and Technology Convergence* observed that the intensity of labour inputs to education and training will change as converging technologies are applied to the learning process' (NBEET 1996, 15). While the report itself never states this baldly, its adoption and use of the dominant economic rationalist discourse enables the conclusion to be inferred that more widespread use of computing technologies in the education sector could save money through reducing the number of educators.

The voices that were represented in the report were fewer than in *Teaching, Learning and Computers* because of the new policymaking structures. This is reflected in the nature of the discourses represented within the report which are overwhelmingly economic in nature. The same policymaking formations also reduced the capacity for influencing policy from those outside the policymaking sphere. Factors which contributed to the narrowing of policy advice include: the reduction in scope, size and independence of the policymaking bodies in education; the control over policymaking vested in the minister; the subservience of education to employment in the DEET; and the commissioning of advice from private consultants. The academic nature of the arguments within the report demonstrated another change compared to 1983. Those considered experts in education were more likely to be drawn from academia and existing policy circles than in earlier years, a trend that was also evident during these years in the US (Culp et al. 2005).

While the report had little impact on the structure of education in Australia, its construction of educational computing was influential. The vision of change propounded for education which would usher in the 'knowledge economy' reflected views expressed by policymakers in other parts of the world. These views survive to this day and embody the belief that computing technologies will transform education in the same way that businesses and industry have been transformed (eg, Kozma 2011). That such ideas can survive and retain influence suggests that the promised transformation still lies ahead.

Chapter Five

We're All Online Now

At the beginning of 2000, wild euphoria over the potential of the Internet gripped investment markets around the world. Breathless talk of the 'new economy' that was initiated by the Internet pervaded the popular media. The technology boom was most extreme in the US where the Internet and the World Wide Web had been developed, then commercialised in 1995. New companies, often with only a passing association with internet technology, added '.com' to their name, floated on the stock exchange and watched their stock prices soar following their listing. Central to investor interest in these companies was the belief that the technology of the Internet would enable the growth of vast new markets which were hitherto untapped. The Australian investment market was also infected by the enthusiasm for internet stocks, despite the limited number of technology companies. As journalist Barbara Drury commented at the end of 1999, 'It seems only fitting that The Lucky Country should finish the 20th century with a wild punt on Internet stocks' (Drury 1999).

Education was one of these new markets. Rising numbers of educational institutions and households with access to the Internet gave rise to a belief that educational materials, indeed, whole courses, could be delivered online and prove commercially successful. Some Australians saw the potential for commercial gain from online education and their efforts were remarked on in the media. 'Online education companies are planning to teach the market a thing or two,' wrote Russell Baker in the *Sydney Morning Herald* in March 2000 (Baker 2000). Several small Australian companies were formed to offer online services or content for school students as well as for tertiary students. One of these, Isis Communications, was listed on the Australian stock exchange at an estimated value of AU$55 million in 1999. The company planned to deliver online courses on a subscription basis to senior school students in New South Wales and Victoria, with students to be recruited through promotions and advertising in their schools and online (Lowe 1999).

By March 2000, the company was capitalised at over AU$300 million (Baker 2000). Another company, Worldschool.com, which intended to offer online tutoring services to school students, planned to list on the market in 2000. The educational services to be offered by each company were only one part of the commercial appeal. Companies recognised the value they would gain from harvesting the information of their young subscriber base and the potential to target this market directly with advertising, as well as the opportunity to increase their revenue through selling subscriber details to third parties. Those behind such companies included former educators, but were predominantly business people, particularly from media, finance and advertising companies. Promoters spoke glibly of how internet technology would transform teaching and learning and the value that could be created for shareholders of companies entering this new market (Baker 2000). The reality, however, was markedly different.

In March 2000, the internet technology bubble began to collapse. In the US, dozens of companies failed and millions of dollars were lost. Australian companies were also affected, although to a lesser degree as the technology boom had been a smaller phenomenon in Australia than in the US. Online education companies which failed to produce the promised revenue were forced to downsize their staff and turn to other forms of business to survive. The dream of the vast market of students which could be tapped into online for wealth creation purposes turned out to be a chimera. However, two of the features evident in this period resonate with themes evident in the technology policies of the federal government of the day, the Howard Coalition Government: the belief that the Internet would have a transformative effect on schools and school systems; and that private businesses should play a role in the provision of digital educational services and content to schools.

New government, new ideology

In 1996, the Liberal–National Party Coalition, led by John Howard, was elected, defeating the ALP Government which had held power since 1983. A key aim of the new government was to recast the role of the federal government to expand the opportunities for business, built on an ideological belief that business could more effectively provide goods and services than government (Lingard 2000). The implications of such views were not spelled out in detail to the electorate, particularly the reduction in public spending that would result. From its first days in government, using the justification of the 'so-called budget black-hole of $10 billion' (Lingard 2000, 48), the

Coalition Government instituted a program to shrink the role of the federal government and to prioritise that of the private sector. What could be done by private business, metaphorised as the 'market', should be done by business.

An important tool to determine the redefinition of governmental boundaries was the National Commission of Audit, which was established in 1996 by the Treasurer, Peter Costello, and the Finance Minister, John Fahey. Promoted as an independent review of the state of the federal government's budgetary position, the Commission's task was to outline and justify new principles and purposes for government, including in the contested areas of federal and state government responsibilities (Lingard 2000). Embedded within the 'principles' which the Commission advanced to guide the newly elected government was the belief that the role of government should be minimised and that many of the functions then performed by government would be better undertaken by the private sector. The Commission's report (NCA 1996) provided an apparently neutral means to justify to the public both substantial spending cuts and the further sale of public assets. However, it also had considerable implications for the provision of policy advice.

The Howard Coalition Government distrusted the public service and dismissed a number of permanent department heads after it took office, prior to reorganising the public service. Previously core functions of the public service were contracted out and privatised (Prasser 1997). In education, the government disbanded the NBEET (Prasser 1997), established under the ALP for the purpose of providing policy advice, and both the funding and staffing of the new Department of Employment, Education, Training and Youth Affairs (DEETYA) were very substantially reduced (DETYA 2000a). Instead, the Howard Government extended the EdNA process established under the previous ALP Government. Educational policy was developed through MCEETYA, where the federal government and the states and territories worked at the ministerial level to achieve a more integrated national approach. Education policy thus came more directly under the control of ministers, both federal and state, than had been the case under previous federal governments (Lingard 2000). The role of the public service in providing policy advice as well as that of other organisations within the education sector such as the teacher unions was diminished.

Action agendas and action plans

In its first term, the new government focused on reducing public debt, shrinking the size and scope of the federal government and expanding the role for private business, particularly small business. Privatisation was a key tool to achieve these aims. The Howard Government extended the privatisation program begun by the ALP to large numbers of previously government-owned businesses or authorities, including the partial privatisation of Telstra (Aulich and O'Flynn 2007). However, the scale of privatisation and the potential for rapid price rises and the loss of services, coupled with the decline in the number of jobs in the previously secure public sector, meant negative reactions in some sectors of the community. This was reflected in the government. The structure of the Coalition, formed by the alliance between the Liberal Party and the smaller National Party, meant that there was a political necessity to balance different constituencies both inside and outside the government. While the National Party also professed a business orientation, it came from a rural base which feared marginalisation and which saw the potential for services in rural Australia to suffer from the privatisation of government services. It was not, however, the only constituency which exerted influence within and over the Howard Government.

Significant cuts to business in the government's first budget in 1996, the year it came to office, provoked reaction from the business community and prompted the government to commission the Mortimer report, *Going for Growth: Business Programs for Investment, Innovation and Export*. The report recommended greater assistance for business and industry and the formation of 'action agendas' to be developed by government working in concert with business, with the aim of enhancing business and trade opportunities (Richardson 1997). In 1997, in reply, the government committed AU$1.26 billion over four years in measures for targeted assistance to business in the policy statement, *Investing for Growth* (Commonwealth of Australia 1997), which was intended as a whole-of-government approach. *Investing for Growth* adopted the Mortimer report's 'action agendas' which then provided a discursive framework for other policies across diverse areas of government activity (Richardson 1997). The identification of areas to be targeted for 'action agendas' was the prelude to the development of 'action plans' within these sectors.

These terms shaped future policy documents across a range of government domains by focusing attention on particular areas at the same time as excluding others from consideration. The government's purpose in the adoption of the 'action agendas' was 'aimed at clarifying the balance of responsibilities between government and business and at enabling both parties to pursue the removal of impediments to growth' (Commonwealth of Australia 1997, 79). One of these 'impediments to growth' was identified as 'education and training' (Commonwealth of Australia 1997, 79). It is no accident that education was one of the areas targeted for the development of 'action plans'. Education was depicted in the Mortimer report as failing to provide suitably skilled workers for business and industry (Emmery 1999).

The potential of 'the information age' and the incorporation of computing technologies into education were seen as key to enhancing Australia's prosperity. Committed in opposition to a policy which focused on commercial applications of computing technologies, in particular, of online technologies, the Howard Government's focus was on infrastructure and regulation to enable business to use computing technologies for e-commerce (O'Regan and Ryan 2004). In contrast to the ALP's use of 'knowledge economy', the Howard Government adopted the rubric of the 'information economy' in 1997 to denote new directions in terms of policy for computing and communications technologies. As part of measures to advance its objectives in this area, the government established the National Office for the Information Economy (NOIE) in 1997 (Stewart 1998). In December 1998, the government released a statement, *A Strategic Framework for the Information Economy*, which aimed to persuade Australian sectors to adopt the Internet for everyday use (Stewart 1998). It was based on the view that 'Australia will be at a serious disadvantage in the global knowledge economy if it fails to produce workers, professionals and managers with the skills to work in the online environment' (Commonwealth of Australia 1998, 11).

The information economy and the role of education

The construct of the 'information economy' was deployed to both shape and justify policies which would introduce change across a range of areas the federal government judged to be strategic, one of which was education (Commonwealth of Australia 1997). The information economy was portrayed as global and requiring high levels of skills in computing technologies in order to be internationally competitive. While this was similar to beliefs which had shaped *Education and Technology Convergence*, there was a fundamental difference in attitude towards computing technologies and their place in society between the ALP and Coalition Governments. Substantial change in technologies and shifts in governmental focus had occurred in developed countries around the world. The multimedia capacities of networked computers were no longer celebrated as they had been in the shifting technological landscape of 1994 to 1996. Instead, the Internet was identified as the key technology of the future. The 'information economy' was linked by the Howard Government with 'the global communications and online technology age that is dramatically and rapidly changing our economy and society', change that was altering the structural basis of life in Australia, making computing and communications technologies critical to future prosperity (Commonwealth of Australia 1997, 65).

The Internet was depicted as the primary driver of the information economy, disrupting existing ways of conducting businesses, communicating and providing services, for governments as well as businesses (Commonwealth of Australia 1997). The Howard Government envisioned the information economy as a private business enterprise. The role of government was to provide light-touch regulation aimed at stimulating the private sector to build the information economy of the future because 'the driving force for the information economy is the private sector responding to market forces' (Commonwealth of Australia 1997, 68). Information was the property of the industrial and business sector, which was to be assisted by other sectors of the economy, such as education and training, portrayed as a 'producer, consumer and export earner' (DETYA 2000b, 17). Behind the rhetoric of the coming information economy lurked a palpable fear of Australia as a laggard compared to other countries regarding the gains that would be achieved through the enhancement of competitive advantage from effective use of computing technologies. At the same time, the rubric of the information economy was also underpinned by the perennial belief that Australia could benefit economically through developing local technologically sophisticated industries (Alston 1999).

In 1998 the federal government expressed its intention of moving towards web-based delivery of government services by the year 2001. This was a part of the strategy to intensify the use of information technologies but also to provide openings for business, thereby becoming a major customer (Commonwealth of Australia 1998). 'Enabling' became a key term, expressing an ideological view: that the task of government was to put in place structures and regulations that allowed businesses to deliver services to consumers as opposed to governments delivering services to citizens (Aulich and O'Flynn 2007). One element of this was to stimulate industry and business through funding them to achieve government ends. Another was through the application of public funds to create a market where one had not existed, or was in its infancy. Education and training were considered as offering an opportunity for the market to provide 'high quality, locally produced online content' (Commonwealth of Australia 1998, 11).

It was inarguable that many technological changes were driven by businesses, rather than by governments. The growing hyperbole in the US over the potential of the Internet to change education, business and government, as well as leisure and entertainment seemed to be a harbinger of a new world, a 'new economy'. In this new economy centred around services, the Internet would be the central technology to facilitate business interactions with consumers and with other businesses. Governments around the world rushed to respond (Willingham 1998). The OECD worked to bring together the wealthy countries to assist governments to prepare the ground for electronic commerce, releasing its policy statement *OECD Action Plan for Electronic Commerce* (OECD 1998b), as *A Borderless World: Realising the Potential of Global Electronic Commerce* (OECD 1998a) at a Ministerial Conference in Ottawa in 1998. The term 'action plan' in its policy statement recalls that adopted by the Howard Government and demonstrates the widespread currency of the term and its accompanying genre. The OECD too stressed the importance of education 'as a fundamental key to wealth creation and competitiveness in the current global information economy' (OECD. CERI 1998, 3). Embedding internet technologies in educational institutions and bringing them within the orbit of the expanding services offered via the Internet was one of the planks in the development of an electronic architecture.

The expensive nature of a commitment to expanding access to the Internet for educational institutions was recognised by all levels of government and by education authorities in Australia. Collaboration to enable the most efficient use of scarce government funds was acknowledged as the way to achieve the best outcomes (Mason 2000). In 1999, following consultations with the educational sectors on the federal government statement, *A Strategic Framework for the Information Economy*, priorities for action were determined (White 2000) and incorporated into the Howard Government's first policy document on computing technologies in education, *Learning for the Knowledge Society: An Education and Training Action Plan for the Information Economy* (DETYA 2000b). The statement was conceptualised as a whole-of-government approach to intensifying the use of computing technologies within education in order to further the development of the information economy. Its format as an action plan, however, was the outcome of a process that began with the Mortimer report and its recommendation to adopt action agendas to target change to particular sectors. A report into measures the government could introduce to assist business thus formed the basis for the policy text, *Learning for the Knowledge Society: An Education and Training Action Plan for the Information Economy*. The government's prioritisation of business values is evident within the text in the sector's designation as 'the business of education and training' (DETYA 2000b, 3).

A new approach to educational policymaking

Learning for the Knowledge Society was neither produced within a statutory authority, as was *Teaching, Learning and Computers* in 1983, nor commissioned from private consultants, as was *Education and Technology Convergence* in 1996, although it drew from previous reports commissioned by the DEET, such as *Real time. Computers, Change and Schooling* (Meredyth et al. 1999). *Learning for the Knowledge Society* was produced by the Schools Advisory Group through the EdNA process and agreed to by all education ministers at MCEETYA. It was an instance of the 'ministerialisation' of policymaking, bringing policy under direct political control (Lingard 2000, 49) but the process of the policy's production also illustrates the greater assertiveness of the federal government in the way in which it negotiated and outlined new boundaries with the states and territories. Far from representing a withdrawal from its role in the state and territory responsibility of education, instead, it was a reorientation that saw the federal government position itself as the national policy leader (Lingard 2000). Its continuing provision of substantial funding offered the federal government opportunities to influence education in the service of its own ends, be they national or political imperatives. It was prepared to use the power of the purse, with the Department of Education, Training and Youth Affairs (DETYA) noting that 'the Commonwealth's contribution gives it the leverage to influence national policies on schooling' (DETYA 2000a, n.p.).

This 'leverage' was given force in greater accountability measures imposed on the states. In 1996, the Howard Government had legislated the requirement for the states and territories to participate in 'a national report on the outcomes of schooling' as a condition of funding (Commonwealth of Australia 1996, n.p.). In 2000, states and territories were required by the federal government to meet 'a commitment... to the National Goals for Schooling prepared by the Ministerial Council on Education, Employment, Training and Youth Affairs'. Another stipulation was a 'commitment by the States to achieve the performance measures (including the performance targets)', as well as other measures that the Commonwealth Education Minister might consider 'appropriate' (Commonwealth of Australia 2000, n.p.). One important goal for the federal government was to increase the use of computing technologies in schools in order to progress the information economy. The government asserted that 'the most effective way of raising students' ICT awareness and skills will be to ensure that ICT pervades schools' curriculum practice in the same way that it is permeating other areas of community life' (DETYA 2000b, 21).

The states and territories were not powerless in their negotiations with the federal government. They retained control over the administration of responsibilities within their respective territories (Parkin and Anderson 2007) but they strongly supported the use of computing technologies in schools and were enthusiastic about the possibilities for the use of the World Wide Web. Their interests and that of the federal government, as they had been in 1983, were aligned as is demonstrated by the new set of National Goals for Schooling agreed to in Adelaide in 1999 (MCEETYA 1999). Revised and extended from the first National Goals for Schooling of 1989, they set out 'broad directions to guide schools and education authorities in securing these outcomes for students' (MCEETYA 1999, n.p.). The goals represent a compromise between ministers from different political parties and different levels of government to present a statement that embodies 'common and agreed goals for schooling' (MCEETYA 1989, 1999). Given their views on education often differed, endorsement of the policy by ministers from the states and territories and the federal government represented a settlement amongst them (Taylor et al. 1997). In the 1999 goals, Goal 1.6 designated computing technologies as one of the priority areas for MCEETYA for development in the following ten years. The aim of Goal 1.6 was for all students to:

> Be confident, creative and productive users of new technologies, particularly information and communication technologies, and understand the impact of those technologies on society. (MCEETYA 1999, n.p.)

In this one sentence in Goal 1.6, three themes common to previous policies on computing technologies are evoked: the determinist view that computing technologies are an irresistible force reshaping society; the vocational one, that of equipping students for the future workforce; and the social rationale that sees schools as the place to prepare students to live in a world in which computer technologies are pervasive. The future world thus created is one which naturalises the use of computer technologies (Selfe 1999). Presented as a given, the implications of such a goal for schools and school systems, both government and non-government, do not need to be specified. An image of student use of computing technologies as both necessary and straightforward is constructed. Nor was it a goal empty of meaning. The states and territories were required to report their progress towards meeting

Goal 1.6, along with others, with performance indicators that were to be prepared by the National Education Performance Monitoring Taskforce (DETYA 2000a).

The National Goals were endorsed in the same year that consultations for *Learning for the Knowledge Society* took place. The first report on Goal 1.6 took place at the end of 2005, where measurement was focused on 'ICT literacy', an evolution of the term 'computer literacy' that had emerged during the 1970s and the later 'information literacy' from the 1990s (MCEETYA 2005c). The functional view embodied in Goal 1.6 is represented in the *ICT Literacy Report Years 6 and 10* (MCEETYA 2005c), consistent with the goal of *Learning for the Knowledge Society*, that the primary purpose of education is the vocational preparation of the future workforce.

Designation, demarcation, distance

The policy text, *Learning for the Knowledge Society*, was described as 'the education and training industry's response' (DETYA 2000b, 6) to the earlier Howard Government statement, *A Strategic Framework for the Information Economy* (Commonwealth of Australia 1998). It presented an overarching vision and rationale for the use of computing technologies in the education sector and policies and plans for each tier within the sectors to foster greater use of computing technologies. The purpose of *Learning for the Knowledge Society* is stated as the provision of 'a common agenda' to 'work jointly to achieve common national goals' (DETYA 2000b, 18). The 'common agenda' was developed through consultations amongst educational authorities and levels of government through the EdNA network and in particular, with the Education Network Australia Reference Committee (ERC) (DETYA 2000b, 6). Set up in 1995, the ERC had both an oversight and advisory role with representation from all educational sectors. Its purpose was to advise MCEETYA on matters to do with the use of computing technologies in education (White 2000). 'Learning in an online world', the policy for the school sector contained within *Learning for the Knowledge Society*, represented the outcome of negotiations within the different parts of the educational sector, through the EdNA process, with the representation of the states and territories.

Learning for the Knowledge Society as an education policy statement at the federal government level encodes the new process of policy development. The use of the terms 'action plan' and 'information economy' in the title of the text symbolised a different approach and construct respectively and draw from previous government policy statements.

The task of the education action plans was to outline changes required, to demarcate the responsibilities of the different levels of government and to designate priorities. The use of the term, 'action plan', however, enables a reorganisation of the genre that had been the norm for policy statements. As the previous example from 1983, *Teaching, Learning and Computers*, best illustrates, conventionally policy texts included an outline of the problem, the reason for its importance, the terms of reference of the inquiry, and a proposal, followed by the rationale for the proposal. In the policy for schooling, 'Learning in an online world', which is contained within *Learning for the Knowledge Society*, the text is constructed differently.

'Learning in an online world' begins with reference to the key governmental statements which underpin the text, the *National Goals for Schooling* (MCEETYA 1989, 1999) and *A Strategic Framework for the Information Economy* (Commonwealth of Australia 1998). These endorse the centrality of schooling, particularly in terms of 'Australia's prosperity in the global economy' (DETYA 2000b, 48). The text is the embodiment of the 'shared national vision' to increase the use of computing technologies in schools, one which is agreed to by the different levels of government. Through its structure, the text expresses the agreements which have been reached, the targets set and the measures to achieve these (DETYA 2000b, 49). The responsibilities of each level of government are outlined. The federal government is responsible for 'the legal and regulatory framework'. The states' and territories' responsibilities are identified as 'school infrastructure, teacher professional development and the development of curriculum' (DETYA 2000b, 49). In this way the boundaries between the levels of government are delineated.

Headings structure the text, identifying and categorising particular areas as 'Action areas' which are targeted for change. Within these, 'Priorities' evaluated as pressing are set:

Key action areas

People

Infrastructure

Content and services

Supporting policies

Enabling regulation

Priorities

Bandwidth

Professional development

Content (DETYA 2000b, 50)

Thus identified, these areas are elaborated further and strategies advanced to achieve the goals. The responsibility for action is then assigned to a particular level of government. The 'key action areas' fall largely within the orbit of the states and territories. Two of these five action areas, that of 'Infrastructure' and 'Content and services', illustrate important differences in terms of the type of action proposed and the jurisdiction responsible for action.

Key action areas: Infrastructure

In 'Learning in an online world', effective teaching and learning are linked with internet access, a connection which equates use of the Internet with educational benefit:

> Every school must be able to access and afford connections to online services that enable them to teach young people effectively. (53)

The policy text advances three goals to steer government actions for the provision of infrastructure to extend the use of the Internet in schools. The first focuses on bandwidth, the second on the costs of telecommunications to schools and the third on the equipment and support required to embed computing technologies into school curricula. The provision of internet access to schools was acknowledged by all levels of government to be a significantly expensive undertaking (Mason 2000), yet there is no recommendation in the text as to how this provision will be attained. The language of 'goals' suggests aspiration rather than intention. The individual school is positioned as the actor which will deliver the 'online services', but the services themselves are presented as the key to effective learning rather than the professional expertise already existing in schools.

Importantly, these services must be provided in an environment which was markedly different from that of 1983 and of 1996 and following the partial privatisation of Telstra by the Howard Government. In rural areas access to the Internet was more expensive, if it was available at all. This was a key issue for the National Party, the junior party in the Coalition. For educators as a whole, however, the issue of infrastructure was much broader than simply access to online services. Yet their concerns over the maintenance of equipment, technical support and pedagogy were instead dismissed as the unavoidable result of greater social complexity. Instead, the task proposed for governments is the larger field of telecommunications infrastructure, rather than the provision of hardware, software, maintenance and the host of other issues that concern educators on a day to day basis when using computing technologies in schools. The crucial question as to who will provide the levels of infrastructure required is directed away from government:

> Infrastructure decisions need to be informed by research into the classroom organisation and computer and network configurations that best support the learning process. More also needs to be done to capitalise on opportunities for collaboration between schools, local businesses and community groups in providing schools and the community with improved access to ICT resources and network facilities. (54)

The strategies proposed to bring about change in this area suggest that action may be slow. Governments at each level should 'consider', 'review', 'investigate', 'undertake studies', 'commission a national study' and 'consider increasing investment' (DETYA 2000b, 54). These involve the postponement of action until studies are completed and are in any case dependent on the outcome of government considerations. Yet the substantive nature of the task is revealed:

> The Commonwealth consider a short-term injection of funds by the Commonwealth to modernise school buildings and facilities across Australia to accommodate new technologies. (54)

This circumlocution expresses and defers the significant and expensive undertaking required. While governments are demanding that schools intensify their use of computing technologies, they are not prepared, or do not recognise the need, to supply the resources which schools require to achieve that aim.

Key action areas: Content and services

Central to the policy, 'Learning in an online world', is the aim to establish a market for 'content and services' to be delivered to schools (54). Education is conceptualised as a potential market for online content, a commodity-type view of learning:

> Government and non-government school education authorities, together with the Commonwealth, need to support the development of a viable education marketplace that will supply the online resources and tools needed to support teaching and learning across all curriculum

areas. This requires a comprehensive strategy to stimulate an Australian market for the generation of quality online curriculum content. (55)

Within this paragraph is embodied the belief that the Internet enables schools to serve as customers for new types of business opportunities which then becomes the justification for action to create this marketplace.

Online curriculum content had been identified as necessary in *A Strategic Framework for the Information Economy* in 1998. In a paper by the Curriculum Corporation (1999), referring to the draft of 'Learning in an online world', a proposal for a strategy to develop online resources for schools is advanced. It expresses the view that 'online content has a transformational role, which... can be compared to the change in pedagogical possibilities after the invention of the printing press' (Curriculum Corporation 1999, 6). Online resources, commercially produced, mean that 'the marketplace enters both the school and the home' (Curriculum Corporation 1999, 6). In October 1999, after 'Learning in an online world' was finalised, but before it was published by DETYA, the proposal to develop an online content market was forwarded to MCEETYA for 'approval out of session' (Curriculum Corporation 1999, 1). Included in it was a proposal for business plan development and costing for an initial budget of AU$500,000. It, too, focused on the need for 'initial government intervention... to stimulate market activity' (Curriculum Corporation 1999, 5). A more detailed report which further developed the case for online resources was *Delivering the Promise* (Trinitas 2000), prepared by a firm of consultants and published in January 2000 (Moyle 2002).

When 'Learning in an online world' was released in 2000, moves were already underway to bring about the development of the marketplace for online materials. An important background influence on this push to develop online resources was the 1998 OECD Ministerial Conference, *A Borderless World: Realising the Potential of Global Electronic Commerce*, in Canada. While dealing with the emerging issues related to the development of electronic commerce, the OECD highlighted the significant role of governments in establishing regulatory frameworks and building trust. Governments as users of computing technologies could then model such use to citizens. At the same time they would assist business through developing the regulatory framework that would allow business to build and profit from the architecture for electronic commerce. The influence of the conference is embedded in 'Learning in an online world' which begins with a quotation from a paper prepared for the conference by the OECD's Centre for Educational Research and Innovation (CERI), *New Developments in Educational Software and Multimedia* (OECD. CERI 1998).

The tension between private and public funding sources that is evident in 'Learning in an online world' is referred to in *New Developments in Educational Software and Multimedia*, which points out that 'nations will come up with different models for allowing commerce into the educational system' (OECD. CERI 1998, 15). The same document concludes by noting 'the importance of creating a successful educational market' for which it is necessary to involve the private sector as well as governments (OECD. CERI 1998, 18). *New Developments in Educational Software and Multimedia* was premised on the belief that the amount of public funds available for education in member countries was limited at the same time as demand for education was growing significantly. The same belief underpins *Learning for the Knowledge Society* and its policy for the schooling sector, 'Learning in an online world'.

'Learning in an online world' needs to be viewed in this context. It is part of a whole-of-government strategy, initiated with *A Strategic Framework for the Information Economy* (1998), that is aimed at putting in place the architecture for electronic commerce. 'Learning in an online world' built on the OECD's view that electronic commerce via the Internet was a potentially transformative tool with the power to drive growth within and between nations across the world in future years, a view that accorded with the Howard Government's own ideas. The focus in 'Learning in an online world' is therefore on telecommunications infrastructure, the regulatory framework, intellectual property such as copyright and the development of a market in online educational material. Copyright and an online market are identified as 'key issues for the school sector' (DETYA 2000b, 51). It was a policy by governments for governments in order that these objectives, which crossed state boundaries and linked Australia into global frameworks, could be achieved.

While other outcomes flowed from the strategy initiated in 'Learning in an online world', for instance, standards for teachers, performance measurement and a program to distribute surplus government computers to schools, the most significant outcome in terms of funding allocated was the *Schools Online Curriculum Content Initiative*, or SOCCI, which became The Le@rning Federation (Kearns and Grant 2002). In a government statement of 2001, *Backing Australia's Ability*, the federal government allocated AU$34 million over five years to the development of online educational content (Commonwealth of Australia 2001). In the same year, MCEETYA agreed that state and territory governments would match the federal government's contributions for this project. 'Learning in an online world' was centrally concerned with teachers and students using off-the-shelf digital educational materials, thereby creating a private market for digital content. 'Content provision' had been identified as one of the 'huge opportunities' for Australia to profit from internet applications (Alston 1999, 2). The school sector was envisioned as a platform for the development of such an industry.

While there was no commitment to government intervention to achieve major changes in infrastructure provision, by contrast, there was a clear indication that governments would intervene to create the marketplace that they had identified as necessary. The strategy to achieve these goals reflected decisions that had already been made. Governments were prepared to allocate substantial funding for an initiative that would open the school sector as a market for private business.

The discourses of 'Learning in an online world'

The primary discourse of 'Learning in an online world' is a straightforward technologically determinist one which posits the Internet as a force which is changing the world. Managerial and vocational discourses are intertwined in an 'information economy' discourse which bears some resemblance to that of *Education and Technology Convergence*. It lacks, however, the Darwinian struggle for competitive advantage that characterised the latter, reflecting both different values and better times economically.

Online: A call to action

Technological determinism dominates 'Learning in an online world'. Embodied within the central metaphor of the online world is the belief that the Internet and the World Wide Web are reshaping the world and therefore education must be reshaped to adapt to this change. In the foreword to *Learning for the Knowledge Society*, DETYA Minister David Kemp asserts that 'the business of education and training is itself being transformed' as a result of technological changes occurring throughout society (DETYA 2000b, 3). 'Learning in an online world' argues that:

> Educators acknowledge that information and communication technol-
> ogies have the potential to transform all aspects of school education and
> to contribute to the achievement of all learning goals. The capacity to
> manage, share and create knowledge is a fundamental requirement for
> Australia's prosperity in a global economy. School education provides

the foundation for the knowledge society and for the development of citizens who are creative, confident and enterprising. (48)

The paragraph presents assumptions on change which are couched as the almost reluctant acceptance by educators of the transformative role of computing technologies, but excitement over these technologies is evident in the text, as in the policy of 1983. However, the new technologies are depicted as offering only promise in contrast to the ambivalence expressed in *Teaching, Learning and Computers* in 1983. So the technologies are linked with 'achievement' and a shared commitment amongst the states, territories and federal government which encompasses 'improving student outcomes' and 'supporting the progressive transformation of schools' (49). The result of employing 'learning technologies' will be 'equity of access' and 'educational benefits' (49). The term 'learning technologies' was employed in Victoria in the 1994 Smith report, and its juxtaposition with the positive attributes expressed in the phrases above works to position computing technologies as both powerful and constructive.

That there was community concern and a sense of threat over the further penetration of the Internet into schools is only acknowledged late in the text, with a brief and oblique mention of the 'other areas that concern school sector interests' (58). These include 'protection against illegal and inappropriate materials', 'privacy and data protection' and 'security of electronic transactions' (58). Although significant areas of concern for both schools and the wider community, the determinist discourse of 'Learning in an online world' portrays computing technologies in a much more benign light.

The role of human agency, however, is clearly posed as the domain of policymakers. It is 'the States and Territories, the Commonwealth and non-government school education authorities' who articulate a vision and 'share responsibility' for decisions (49). The emphasis on collaboration at all levels of government to achieve shared goals in the implementation of the new technologies works to reinforce the significance of these for school education. These were a reflection of decisions taken at the top, at the governmental level.

The government as manager

Consistent with the technological determinism of the text is the representation of government as manager, evident in a strong managerialist discourse. If forces such as the economy and technology drive schools as autonomous agents, then the government's role as manager is to enable this interaction (Taylor et al. 1997). The genre of the 'action plan' is modelled on business management practices and applied to the development of the education plans. The text itself is organised under headings such as 'goals', 'key action areas', 'overarching strategies' and 'monitoring progress' (DETYA 2000b, 50–51). While the move to greater regulation and measurement was evident in the previous ALP Government, managerialism was a much stronger discursive strand under the Howard Government. The use of terms such as 'effectiveness and efficiency', 'maximise the benefits', 'outcomes', 'efficiencies in business practices', and 'continuous improvement' signify this managerialist approach (DETYA 2000b, 48–50). They imply a greater focus on controlling costs and measuring results (Taylor et al. 1997).

Technology is positioned as central to this purpose, particularly the Internet, which will make schools more efficient, although the way this will be achieved is not explained. The new technology is equated with efficiency as before it had been with learning. The cost of this technology, however, is a central concern. The deregulation of telecommunications with the partial sale of Telstra meant that the costs of internet access were more expensive for schools. At the same time, the text argues that 'the cost per student should be competitive in the global marketplace' (53). This construction places the student in the marketplace as a product with technology as an input cost. The future world imagined is one in which schools are separate units, acting as individuals rather than on a systemic basis. Working together with businesses, managed by governments from a distance, they take their place as both customer of business and market for business, reflecting the value placed on the individual under the Howard Government.

The metaphor of the online world: The computer becomes invisible

The metaphor of the 'online world' is the key construct of the school education action plan. It is employed to denote that 'online' has not just its dictionary meaning of being connected to a computer, but also the popularly understood meaning in 2000 of being connected to the Internet (Moore 2004). As educational policy texts necessarily include a conception of the future for which school students must be prepared, the policy conveys a sense that the future of learning is to be found on the Internet. The Internet is altering the world in a profound way. Learning, as part of that world, is altered too. The title of the text, 'Learning in an online world', implies that the whole world is now on the Internet. While this was patently untrue in 2000 as in 2013, the sense of a future world that is radically different frames the policy.

The title works also to distinguish the policy from that of the earlier Keating Government and its emphasis on the multimedia capacities of computers. It signifies the Howard Government's awareness that technology is changing, with the growth and rapid adoption of the Internet by businesses, governments and the public at large. But it also assumes a particular vision of the world, one in which computing technology is dominant and ubiquitous at the same time as its technological underpinnings have become invisible. It is as if the computers, the hardware and software, and the other components necessary to form this 'online world' already exist and are only waiting to be put into service.

In 'Learning in an online world', the computer itself has been obscured, removing attention from the inadequacies of existing hardware and software. The word occurs only four times in the text and then in relation to networks and access to the Internet. The computer has become the invisible support for the 'online world'. Indeed, the text expresses the view that schools 'increasingly operate online to improve their effectiveness and efficiency' (DETYA 2000b, 48), a managerial perspective that embodies a belief in the capacity of the technology to force efficiencies on a schooling sector that is a recipient of substantial government funds. However, and importantly, it expresses an unspoken belief that the levels of previous investment in hardware and software have created the conditions for the Internet to play a greater role in school education.

The workforce of the future

In education, the Coalition Government prioritised vocational skills, particularly those with computers (Alston 1999). Education was identified as the supplier of skilled workers who would enable Australia 'to compete in the information economy' (Commonwealth of Australia 1997, 71). Information technology skills were central to this future workforce. In 1996, President Bill Clinton's release of *The Technology Literacy Challenge* (US Department of Education 1996) to extend use of the Internet into schools had been influential in associating it with education (Lankshear et al. 2000). That the Internet was regarded as increasingly important by the Howard Government was signified in the title of the policy text, 'Learning in an online world'. One factor that influenced the government in the context of the technology boom in the US and 'Y2K compliance' was a shortage of IT professionals (Alston 1999, 2). The role of the federal government was represented as 'enabling' a pro-business environment, whilst in terms of schooling it 'plays a fundamental enabling role in the growing information economy' (DETYA 2000b, 49). Thus the primary purpose of education was positioned as vocational.

Underpinning this belief was the assumption that the primary purpose of education is to produce students with skills for employment and for 'lifelong learning' (51). It is taken for granted that education has not been delivering the required outcomes, consistent with the earlier identification of education and training as 'impediments to growth' (Commonwealth of Australia 1997, 79). The first element of the vision shared between the different levels of government is 'improving student outcomes' and the second is 'supporting the progressive transformation of schools' (DETYA 2000b, 49). The tool to achieve both goals is the use of computing technologies. To embed such a use requires overcoming barriers to change within the educational system. 'People' become a key 'action area'.

Students, teachers, school leaders and school communities are all targeted for change, expressing, by implication, a sense of deficit. The goals that are advanced for these groups suggest that shortfalls exist. So students 'will have access to educational programs that provide a technology-rich experience and environment' (51) in order that 'all students will leave school with the employment-related skills needed in the information economy' (51). Teachers 'will be competent users of information and communication technologies and able to apply these technologies to improve student learning' (51). By contrast, school leaders 'will understand how information and communication technologies impact on learning and will have the confidence and capabilities to lead and manage the changes required to maximise the benefits of these technologies in school education' (51). Information and communication technologies are prioritised as it is these that will improve student learning, rather than teachers. Nor can it be assumed that these technologies are simple to use, as even from leaders, they require 'confidence and capabilities to lead'. Teachers are rendered functionaries, who must be 'competent', but only 'able to apply' the technology, rather than 'understand' its 'impact on learning'.

For students, 'educational disadvantage', construed in the document as lacking 'a technology-rich environment at home', prevents the achievement of these goals (51). Students in this situation are the Indigenous as well as 'those with learning difficulties and students who live in remote areas' (51). Those previously considered amongst the disadvantaged, the poor, girls, and the disabled in 1983, are no longer categorised as such. Instead, disadvantage has been redefined to exclude inequities associated with socio-economic conditions or gender, but to include those in rural areas, evidence of the influence of the National Party. Nor is the connection between lacking a 'technology-rich environment' and poverty made, despite the almost ironic use of 'rich' (51). Instead, 'schools must actively promote equity of access to such skills'. This contrasts strongly with the suggestion of 1983 that schools had a responsibility to contribute to 'equality of outcomes' (CSC. NACCS 1983, 21).

The responsibility to address disadvantage, even narrowly construed as it is above, becomes the duty of schools, reified as unitary actors. The task of redressing disadvantage has been shifted to the individual school rather than being the province of governments. The conditions of disadvantage are not to be considered as the target of government action and the role of schools is one of 'ameliorating' the effects (51). Schools instead have only the duty to provide 'equity of access' to technology skills (51). The conditions of disadvantage that may make these skills difficult to acquire for groups of students are elided as inequality is accepted. The solution for disadvantage is the acquisition of technological skills, as 'information and technological literacy are now essential pre-requisites to work in almost any career' (51). The assertion is presented as common knowledge.

The place of computing technology in schools and the purpose of education promoted are narrowly vocational. Schools become merely mechanisms for the transmission of 'skills and attitudes', crucially amongst them, the ability of students 'to adapt and learn throughout their lives', creating the autonomous individual who will not burden governments (51). For students to gain these skills, the prerequisite is that 'school leaders and teachers' must be 'committed to a vision for the integration of new technologies into practice' and 'have the skills to use the technologies appropriately and effectively' (51). Teachers are positioned as lacking, with their failure ensuring the failure of their students. The text notes that 'progress is taking place, but not at the pace or depth required to effect major change' (52). This 'major change', while not spelt out, is the improvement of school outcomes in computing technologies and by implication of teachers, who 'are developing basic ICT skills' (52). That these skills are categorised as 'basic' assumes a lack of competence on the part of many teachers for which no evidence is provided.

The 'strategies' put forward to achieve the desired ends are limited. For students, more career advice and more skills training in senior years are recommended. For teachers, the focus is on 'pre-service education to improve the ICT competence of commencing teachers', to 'develop teacher competency standards in using ICT' which will be linked to 'recruitment and promotion practices' and to 'strengthen teacher professional development' (52). The development of standards and the consequent linking of the attainment of these standards to recruitment and promotion entails an element of coercion. Principals themselves are targeted to have their awareness raised of 'the key role ICT plays in changing learning environments and improving learning outcomes' (53), a depiction which represents the technology as the agent of effective learning rather than teachers or students as active learners. Leaders will have to 'incorporate ICT planning and change management skills into person and job descriptions for personnel at all levels' (53). For schools, 'increased computer and Internet access to parents and the wider community' will assist, as will 'school-business partnerships' (53). Schools must seek and accept business support.

While pressure will be applied to teachers, in particular, underlying the text is the assumption of enough technology, enough software and hardware, enough resources, and suitable facilities for these goals to be achieved. The problems that exist do so because teachers, primarily, and school leaders to a lesser extent, do not apply themselves to the task of passing on the required skills. The application of standards, monitoring, professional development and research into good practice, will shift teachers into wholesale use of computing technologies. Thus the desired outcomes in students, new skills which they will take into the workforce, will be realised. The vision that is presented of the impact of computing technologies on learning is simply this: as narrow a view as that of education itself.

A template for change

The commitment to *Learning for the Knowledge Society* as a whole from ministers working in collaboration led to the growth and formalisation of processes to achieve the aims of the action plan for education. In July 2001, MCEETYA established the ICT in Schools Taskforce to advise it on matters to do with computing technologies and schools. The EdNA Reference Committee became the Australian Information and Communications Technology in Education Committee (AICTEC), a cross-sectoral national body with representation from governments and all education sectors, including the non-government. It was responsible for policy development and advice on computing technologies in education with a focus on online technologies (AICTEC 2006).

Learning for the Knowledge Society formed the template for future plans. Thus the 'key action areas' shaped not just the initial 'action plan', but also later plans and other approaches (eg, Kearns and Grant 2002; MCEETYA 2005a). The designation of key action areas, for instance, infrastructure and content and services, problematises some areas and ignores others. Curriculum is a notable exclusion. So too is funding, a perennially contested issue between levels of government. What was omitted from the original action plan is also omitted from later plans which were based on the template established in 'Learning in an online world'. Over the next six years of the Howard Government's term, MCEETYA released a number of follow-up plans and strategies to achieve the aims of the action plan. One concern in particular was internet connectivity, with the recognition that in Australian schools, access to the Internet was limited because of inadequate bandwidth when compared to other developed countries (MCEETYA 2003). To respond, a *National Bandwidth Action Plan* was developed and endorsed by MCEETYA in 2005 (MCEETYA 2006).

In February 2005, MCEETYA issued a *Joint Statement on Education and Training in the Information Economy* (2005b), which replaced that of 2000. Later that year it also issued *Building a Knowledge Culture. An Education and Training Action Plan for the Information Economy 2005–2007* (2005a), a new action plan which built on the foundations established in *Learning for the Knowledge Society* (AICTEC 2006). It was noteworthy that this was released by MCEETYA, rather than by the Commonwealth Department of Education, Science and Training (DEST), as it had become, unlike the first action plan. Following the release of *Learning for the Knowledge Society*, responsibility for driving change shifted to MCEETYA rather than federal authorities, consistent with the delineation of responsibilities outlined in the action plan. The focus of both the *Joint Statement* and *Building a Knowledge Culture* remains on the power of computing technologies to achieve lasting change in education, and to 'lay a foundation for our future economic and social prosperity' (MCEETYA 2005b, n.p.). This use of computing technologies is explicitly linked to online technologies: 'information and communications technology empowers teachers and trainers by increasing options for improving learning outcomes through access to new types of quality digital content, training, networking and advice' (MCEETYA 2005b, n.p.).

Measures of ICT literacy and tests for students' proficiency were devised with testing undertaken at the end of 2005 to monitor the achievement of Goal 1.6. It was notable that literacy was again linked with computing technologies, as it had been since the 1970s. In 2007, the results of the first tests of students' skills with computing technologies, *The ICT Literacy Report Years 6 and 10* (MCEETYA 2007), which was based on a sample undertaken as part of the National Assessment Program (NAPLAN), was released. The report found that proficiency in 'ICT literacy' was demonstrated by 49 per cent of Year 6 students and 61 per cent of Year 10 students sampled.

However, levels of proficiency were greater amongst students from higher socio-economic backgrounds and from metropolitan areas. Indigenous students, particularly from remote areas, demonstrated significantly lower proficiency (MCEETYA 2007). On the one hand, these results confirmed the relationship between those students identified in 'Learning in an online world' and locational disadvantage. On the other, students in both year levels reported using computers more often at home than at school. Such home use was significantly associated with students from higher socio-economic backgrounds.

Conclusion

The commitment to introducing web-based services into schools was not taken in isolation. Other countries around the world were also committed to introducing these into education for a range of purposes and through a variety of means (Bakia et al. 2011). It was, and remains, an expensive and complex process that necessarily involves other issues, such as telecommunications infrastructure and regulation. In 2005, the MCEETYA ICT in Schools Taskforce noted the cost, remarking that 'many billions of dollars have been invested since 2000 to upgrade the ICT infrastructure in Australia's school systems' (MCEETYA ICT in Schools Taskforce 2005, 9). Acquiring computing technologies for schools can require difficult trade-offs. The nature of some of these was pointed out by the NOIE (2002, 19): 'for small schools to pay more for bandwidth, they would need to cut teaching staff and increase class sizes'. The key reason for the investment in internet access was the belief amongst federal and state and territory governments in Australia that 'just as transport opened up new economic horizons in the last century, advanced communication networks will pave the way for productivity gains across global economies in the new century' (Commonwealth of Australia 2003, 5). This was, and remains, a commonly held belief in the wider community, as well as in governments.

Yet it is important to note that this is primarily an economic world view that regards knowledge as a commodity and education as a provider of human capital. In 'Learning in an online world', computing technologies are envisioned as a means to: engineer change in education through offering greater individualisation; improve skills which will enable people to take on the responsibility for their own future and on-going training; achieve greater national consistency and reduce costs; extend opportunities to the disadvantaged; and expand exports, particularly of education.

These are the visions of computing technologies in the service of governments to achieve particular ends. The belief that the use of computing technologies can bring about these ends embodies a utopian view of the capacities of technologies that sits squarely in the realm of technological determinism (Moyle 2005). Yet the overriding theme is economic. Even the emphasis on skills for lifelong learning is aimed in part at relieving government pressure to retrain workers whose jobs are lost through the process of technological change. What is embodied in this economic world view is a belief in the role of governments as 'enablers', rather than as 'providers', and of education as preparation for individuals to be responsible for themselves in their future lives.

Chapter Six

The Digital Education Revolution

In 2007 in a speech to the lobby group, the Business Council of Australia (BCA), its president, Michael Chaney, contrasted the Australian economic environment to that of 20 years earlier:

> A couple of decades ago the language of prosperity was almost like a foreign language – hard to understand, let alone discuss with any fluency. Now, phrases like full employment, stock market highs and the commodities boom roll off the tongue. The language of prosperity is now the second language of many Australians. (Chaney 2007, 1)

Chaney expressed sentiments that had become almost commonplace, particularly in the media, amongst conservative politicians and business-people. In 2007, economic growth was strong, unemployment was low and jobs were well paid. Despite this prosperity, however, there were those who had failed to share in it. Disadvantage had persisted, particularly amongst young people with low educational attainments. At a time of national emphasis on skills shortages, Chaney argued that education was failing in its task to equip these young people with the necessary skills.

Education was on the agenda in an Australia that had changed markedly even since 2000. While jobs were more plentiful, competition within Australia and from abroad meant that young people could not be assured they would attain their chosen careers. The *Sydney Morning Herald* drew attention to these fears: 'With hungry tradesmen of the Third World flooding into skilled work under the 457 visa scheme and white-collar jobs being moved to other countries, anxiety about prospects is high among the young and their parents' (*Sydney Morning Herald* 2007). The Internet and the high-speed broadband which would enable access to it were portrayed by a range of commentators as vital to enable Australia to gain the competitive edge which countries such as South Korea were already on track to achieve.

High-speed broadband would mean that school students would have access to a wealth of educational resources via the Internet. Such access was deemed essential for children and young people who were depicted as natural users of computing technologies, especially the Internet. Education researcher and writer Dale Spender argued that children were growing up in a technologically more sophisticated world with access to a range of devices in their homes. They were arriving in schools not so much as blank slates but as 'digi-kids' with new skills already in place to form the foundation for higher-level learning. Yet old computers and slow internet speeds within schools did not enable them to engage readily in ways that were natural for them to learn (Spender 2007). Nor was lack of up to date technology the only barrier which inhibited internet use in schools. Parents and the wider community shared fears over the new social media applications such as Facebook which enabled communication with strangers over the Internet, leading to sometimes fatal consequences. A more pervasive issue was cyberbullying of young people by their peers over the Internet or by mobile phone. This was addressed by state and federal governments through education campaigns and restrictions on internet sites within schools (Tarica 2007).

Education in which the Internet was central was the common thread that tied these disparate issues together. For people from groups across the spectrum, education with computing and communications technologies, particularly the Internet, offered promise in a range of areas. A future workforce with skills which businesses wanted was one potential outcome. For parents and the wider community, the prospect of new technologies located in schools was seen as important to teach students to manage the negative aspects of communication via the Internet and social media. Educators envisaged the potential for computing technologies to enhance higher-order learning. Schools, however, with their outdated equipment and old-fashioned learning styles, represented a formidable impediment. Despite the supposed national prosperity, it seemed they had been unable to grasp the way of the future.

The ALP and education in an election year

In a nation in which education was already under scrutiny, ALP Opposition Leader Kevin Rudd promoted education as central to the ALP agenda from the start of the election year of 2007, beginning with the paper, *The Australian Economy Needs an Education Revolution* (Rudd and Smith 2007). The paper served different purposes. On the one hand, it painted the ALP as economically responsible. The presentation of an economic case for greater expenditure on education was based upon evidence selected from authorities accepted as credible: Treasury, the Productivity Commission, the OECD, economic consultancies and think tanks, and individual economists. In this way the ALP could counter the electorate's commonly held perception that it was less capable of managing the economy than were the Coalition parties. On the other, an argument for more investment in education played to the ALP's perceived strength in that portfolio area. The economic justification for greater government expenditure on education was a coherent argument to counterpose to the Howard Government's apparent neglect of it.

In *The Australian Economy Needs an Education Revolution*, Rudd and Smith stressed their support for the macroeconomic policy settings in place under the Howard Government but argued for their refinement. They accepted that 'Australia is a prosperous economy' (Rudd and Smith 2007, 6) but noted that productivity had declined under the Howard Government. Productivity, they argued, was central to the maintenance of prosperity into the future. Under the Howard Government, they asserted that government funding for education had been reduced, leading to lower productivity. As a result, Australia's global competitiveness had weakened, portending lower living standards in the years ahead. Evidence of this decline was supported by recent international rankings which showed that Australia's educational achievements were surpassed by countries such as Singapore, Malaysia and Taiwan. Higher levels of investment in education by the federal government were portrayed as the solution to Australia's declining productivity:

> Australia needs nothing less than a revolution in education – a substantial and sustained increase in the quantity of our investment, and the quality of our education… We need to set for ourselves a new national vision – for Australia to become the most educated country, the most skilled economy and the best trained workforce in the world. (Rudd and Smith 2007, 5)

This view of education was based on a human capital perspective which held that raising workers' knowledge and skills would improve their productivity and hence that of the nation (Marginson 1997b). While Rudd and Smith accepted that there were social benefits from education for individuals and the wider society, they asserted that 'education should be understood as an economic investment and not simply a social expenditure' (Rudd and Smith 2007, 24). Education in this conception was central to the economy.

New computing and communications technologies, particularly broadband, were proposed as key to furthering productivity. The ALP's broadband policy, *A Broadband Future for Australia – Building a National Broadband Network* (Rudd, Conroy and Tanner 2007), announced in March 2007, identified high-speed broadband as the source of productivity in other countries which were using the technology to improve their economic competitiveness. Businesses, education, health and also consumers needed access to better quality broadband which could only be delivered through 'government leadership' and 'investment' (Rudd, Conroy and Tanner 2007, n.p.). The policy highlighted the slow speed and high cost of broadband in Australia compared to other OECD countries and the lack of any broadband access for many Australians, even those in major cities. The ALP argued that underinvestment by the Coalition Government meant that Australia was lagging behind its competitor countries. The Coalition's preferred private solutions to the provision of broadband infrastructure had led to slower investment in broadband than in comparable countries (*Sydney Morning Herald* 2007).

If elected, the ALP pledged to 'revolutionise Australia's internet infra-structure' through delivering a National Broadband Network (NBN), a fibre to the node broadband infrastructure, financed by both government and the private sector, at a cost to a future ALP government of AU$4.7 billion (Rudd, Conroy and Tanner 2007, n.p.). The many potential benefits to dif-ferent sectors in the economy were outlined in the policy text, including the possibility of 'e-education', especially important in a large country with a dispersed population. The ALP's planned NBN, a fibre to the node broadband infrastructure, was one of its signature policies which it took to the election of November 2007. Oppositions, lacking the benefits of incumbency, work hard to present themselves as new, with fresh ideas. Policies advance plans for change but they are also strategic political documents, designed to represent parties – and leaders – to the electorate. Through promoting broadband investment, the ALP positioned itself as a party which understood new technology and the necessity for government investment in infrastructure for public benefit. Both technology and education were tied into a narrative which posited them as fundamental to economic growth. The narrative also enabled the ALP to call on a range of symbols to reinforce its broader platform to the electorate. These symbols included computers.

Early in the election campaign in October 2007, Kevin Rudd captured media attention when he announced a tax rebate for families with school children to purchase computers, school books and internet connections for the home. At a press conference, Rudd held up a laptop computer and declared it to be 'the toolbox of the 21st century', one which the rebate would make available to families on modest or low incomes (Davis 2007). The Howard Government's response was to expand its existing focus on delivering trades training at a time of skills shortages during the commodities boom. Shortly after Rudd's announcement, the Howard Government countered with a plan to construct and fund another 30 technical colleges on top of the 28 already planned. These would target students in Years 11 and 12 for trades training in areas of skills shortage. Up to another 70 schools were also offered AU$10 million to become technical colleges in a move reporter Farrah Tomazin described as a 'metaphoric spanner' to 'Rudd's hi-tech hijinks' (Tomazin 2007). Trades education, a focus of the Howard Government since the election campaign of 2004, was counterposed to the hip-pocket appeal of tax rebates for computers.

The contrasting messages delivered by the ALP and the Coalition illustrate the powerfully symbolic aspect of policy in addition to the plans of action entailed within them (Taylor et al. 1997). Rudd's use of the metaphor of the 'toolbox' signalled different understandings of the purposes of education from that of the Coalition, as did the Coalition's emphasis on trades training. On the broad area of the economy, the views of the opposing parties were in alignment (Rudd and Smith 2007). Their positions on education were one area where the contending parties could deliver contrasting presentations to the electorate. At the ALP's campaign launch on November 14, 2007, in his home town of Brisbane, Rudd reaffirmed a number of existing policies, including that for the NBN, which he called 'one of our first nation-building investments' (Rudd 2007, n.p.). Declaring education to be the centrepiece of his 'vision for Australia's future', Rudd also announced that the ALP would ensure that all schools in Australia would be connected to the NBN, thereby gaining access to faster broadband than was available at the time.

Further, he promised a 'ground-breaking reform' if the ALP were to be elected: the provision of a computer for each school student in Years 9 to 12, at a cost of AU$1 billion over four years. His aim, Rudd said, was to 'provide every secondary school student with the foundations to move into the digital economy of the future'. He contrasted himself with Prime Minister John Howard, positioning Howard as a traditionalist with an outdated view of education: 'Mr Howard seems to believe that providing young people with computers is exotic. Mr Howard just doesn't get it. Around the rest of the world, providing young people with computers isn't exotic – it's mainstream' (Rudd 2007, n.p.). With education 'the engine room of the economy', computers were essential to enable a future workforce to compete against other countries which were 'making huge new investments in education' designed to make them 'the wealthiest economies of the future' (Rudd 2007, n.p.). Rather than an expense, Rudd argued, education was a 'national investment' which required a 'revolution' in funding to bring about improved performance, in order to raise Australia's living standards into the future (Rudd 2007, n.p.).

The reporting which followed the campaign launch was positive. The ALP's pledge of AU$1 billion for its digital education package was considered moderate compared to the cost of the Coalition Government's promises (Grattan 2007). A key message from Rudd's campaign launch had been that the Howard Government was engaging in 'reckless spending' to retain power. The ALP, Rudd promised, would be 'economically responsible', offering targeted and smaller spending measures which were intended only to improve Australia's economic competitiveness rather than to reward specific sectors of the electorate. The Howard Government, which was trailing the ALP in the polls, responded to the ALP's schools education policies by announcing a tax rebate for the parents of school children, one which could also cover private school fees. The proposed rebate was not means-tested and at an estimated cost of AU$9 billion, it was much more expensive than that promised by the ALP (Grattan and Murphy 2007). Kevin Rudd responded by describing John Howard as 'a political leader increasingly stuck in the past' (Grattan and Murphy 2007).

The ALP's policy on computers for schools which had been announced at the campaign launch was detailed in *A Digital Education Revolution* (Rudd, Smith and Conroy 2007). It built on the earlier policy statements on education and broadband, *The Australian Economy Needs an Education Revolution* (Rudd and Smith 2007) and *A Broadband Future for Australia – Building a National Broadband Network* (Rudd, Conroy and Tanner 2007). Its centrepiece was the pledge to provide funding of up to AU$1 million per school to purchase new computing technologies. The policy also announced the National Secondary Schools Computer Fund (NSSCF), the primary funding vehicle for the Digital Education Revolution. In *A Digital Education Revolution*, computers and broadband were linked together, drawing attention to the ALP's signature broadband policy, the NBN. AU$1 billion was to be provided via grants to secondary schools in all sectors. From the NSSCF, AU$100 million would be employed to connect schools to the ALP's proposed NBN. The policy text explained that the NBN would be required to provide connections to schools and to deliver them the fastest possible internet speeds, up to 100 megabits per second, far in excess of what was then achievable. Provisions for teacher training and online content were also announced and the policy concluded with a statement projecting costs for the Fund over the following four years, noting that it was 'fully costed and funded' (Rudd, Smith and Conroy 2007, 13). Recognising the reality of the federation and the political promise to work cooperatively with the states and territories, thus ending 'the blame game', the policy pledged a 'partnership with State and Territory Governments' (9).

Above all, the policy boldly proposed that:

> A Rudd Labor Government will revolutionise classroom education by putting a computer on the desk of every upper secondary student and by providing Australian schools with fibre to the premises connections, which will deliver broadband speeds of up to 100 megabits per second. (2)

This was a tangible promise: the provision of both a computer and broadband for every student would result in a revolution in school education. What this revolution would achieve was less clear.

The ALP's pledge to 'revolutionise classroom education by putting a computer on the desk of every upper secondary student' can be interpreted as not just another way of depicting the party as forward-looking (Rudd, Smith and Conroy 2007, n.p.), but also as a reaction to the Howard Government's increases in spending on education, particularly as the education tax rebate for computers had already been announced by Rudd the previous month. However, the lack of focus by the media or the government on the individual elements of the ALP's computer package ignored the substantial expenditure that was promised for the nation's schools. The proposed funding to equip schools with computing technologies was more than had ever been offered before by a federal government for such an initiative. The promise of federal funding for computers and for the NBN symbolised to the electorate a changed view of government from that which had prevailed under the Coalition: while the market was important, there were some things only government could deliver. The high-tech goods of the future would be provided by an ALP Government which stood for intervention, presented as investment.

A Digital Education Revolution

In *A Digital Education Revolution*, the ALP spelled out its plan to fund every school to purchase computing technologies and broadband connections to its proposed NBN. The plan was not presented as an expenditure, nor as an intrusion into the domain of the states and territories, but rather as an investment which would deliver dividends, the productivity growth promised in *The Australian Economy Needs an Education Revolution* (Rudd and Smith

2007). The framing of technology in *A Digital Education Revolution* draws also on *A Broadband Future for Australia – Building a National Broadband Network*, in which broadband is asserted to be 'a critical enabling technology that is currently driving substantial productivity gains around the world' (Rudd, Conroy and Tanner 2007, n.p.). In *A Digital Education Revolution*, 'computers and broadband are critical enabling technologies that are driving substantial productivity gains around the world' (Rudd, Smith and Conroy 2007, 3).

The importance of using the word 'computer' and allying it to broadband in *A Digital Education Revolution* cannot be overstated. The word 'computer' had almost disappeared in the Howard Government's 'Learning in an online world' in 2000, reflecting a greater focus on the Internet. The same disappearance of 'computer' is also evident in the Australian Bureau of Statistics (ABS) surveys, *Business Use of Information Technology* (ABS 1997a, 2007c). Focused on the term 'computer' in the year of its first survey in 1993 to 1994, by 2005 to 2006, the ABS surveyed instead access to and use of the Internet (ABS 1997a, 2007c). In October 2007, Rudd had revived the term 'computer' when he used the material object of a laptop computer as a prop at a press conference to attract attention to the ALP's policy for tax rebates. In *A Digital Education Revolution*, the text points out that 'a critical component of a world class education system in Australia will be use of a computer and access to reliable, high-speed broadband' (Rudd, Smith and Conroy 2007, 3). The word 'computer' conjures up the physical object and denotes the ALP's largesse towards school students and, by implication, their parents. Importantly, however, the word 'computer', linked as it is to 'broadband', also reminds the electorate of the ALP's broadband policy and provides a symbol of the access that will be provided to high-speed broadband. The computer symbolises a portal, one that is easily imagined when the broadband network might be more difficult to grasp.

A Digital Education Revolution is built on the assumption that intense global competition to gain market share, driven by the use of computing technologies, is beginning to threaten Australian jobs, particularly high-wage jobs. Improving Australia's competitiveness depends on higher levels of education in the future workforce. Existing educational attainments are presented as falling behind those of other countries, most notably, the Asian economies. Education is constructed as in need of improvement which necessitates federal government intervention. The provision of access to both computers and broadband is depicted as the means of effecting the desired improvement. Nor was the largesse of individual computers and broadband connections confined to the government schooling sector. In the Australian system in which nearly one-third of all secondary school students are educated in private schools, funds were promised to all schools, making a broad appeal to all parents across sectors. By contrast, ALP policies in the election campaign of 2004 had focused primarily on public schools. The intervention proposed by a future ALP Government was justified on the basis that 'a world class education system' necessitated 'significant government and private investment' (Rudd, Smith and Conroy 2007, 3). However, the ALP presented this investment as one which was responsible through requiring schools to block purchase computers, with the aim 'to maximise value for money' (Rudd, Smith and Conroy 2007, 9).

At the time of the election in November 2007, Australia had experienced 16 years of economic expansion. Politicians and the media considered prosperity to be widespread and unemployment was officially low. A ready indicator of Australian prosperity was the All Ordinaries index on the Australian stock market which peaked in October 2007 at 6779.1 points, having risen every month for more than a year (ASX 2013). The language of finance was as commonly used by politicians as that of economics as the references to 'investment' in *A Digital Education Revolution* make clear. *A Digital Education Revolution* is embedded in its time. In a period when the federal government received greater revenue from company taxes than it had for many years, a more expansive role for government was outlined than in the policies on educational technology from 1983, 1996 or 2000. However, the shift in the role of government and government expenditure planned by the ALP was camouflaged by the use of terms drawn from economics and finance. Often tagged as the party of higher government spending, the ALP in opposition presented itself as an investor in the national economy. It was this investment which would engender a 'revolution'. The promised outcome of the revolution was change which would benefit the country as a whole and which only the ALP, after 11 years of a Coalition Government, could deliver. The computer as depicted in *A Digital Education Revolution* was a mechanism both to symbolise and to drive change.

The discourses of *A Digital Education Revolution*

Of the policies examined in this book, *A Digital Education Revolution* is the shortest. Its function is different from the earlier three which were produced within government circles and bore the authority of that positioning. *A Digital Education Revolution* was a policy text constructed in opposition by a political party in order to present the ALP's plan for action in education to the electorate. Released during an election campaign, it was a document that was at once political and symbolic (Taylor et al. 1997). Politically, the policy attempted to persuade the electorate to support the ALP at the polls by announcing a program which promised benefits for some in the community but in a way which also presented the ALP as responsible and fit to govern. In a symbolic sense, the policy expressed a set of values and projected a rosy vision of the future under the ALP and its leadership.

Produced for the media and the electorate as one of a collection of texts, each with the same branding of 'New Directions' and the photograph of Kevin Rudd on the front cover, the document itself is 'mediatized' (Rizvi and Lingard 2010, 19). It is part of an attempt to assert control over the narrative presented to the public and is linked to its companion policies to recall these to the electorate and to the press. The title of the policy, *A Digital Education Revolution*, recasts the key theme of the 'education revolution' announced at the start of 2007. The term 'revolution' implies the governmental change the party anticipates, but it is emptied of the original meaning of overthrow. Instead, its use is a piece of hyperbole to suggest that changing the government will bring enduring benefits. However, the text also works as a 'material' policy, should the party come to power (Taylor et al. 1997, 33). It mapped directions, outlined plans for action and allocated funding to achieve its ends.

Technological determinism

One constant in federal government policies on computers and education since 1983 is technological determinism. In *A Digital Education Revolution*, a technologically determinist discourse is as pervasive as in earlier policy documents. Not only is it pervasive, it is expressed in similar terms although in 2007 the term 'broadband' has been added, reflecting the newer fibre optic technology. So:

> Computers and broadband are shaping the 21st century… Computers and broadband will not only increase efficiency, help reduce costs and create new markets for Australian business. They also have the potential to transform the way our schools operate in the future for the better. (3)

As in earlier policies, the computer is represented as the agent which acts independently of people and with the capacity to bring about change, 'as a driver of productivity and growth across all sectors of the economy, from farming and mining to manufacturing and services' (1). Its effects on education will be profound: 'few doubt the potential of computers and broadband to revolutionise the classroom' (3).

The claims in the 2007 policy for the educational benefits of computers echo those of 1983, 1996 and 2000. In *A Digital Education Revolution*:

> Computers will enhance the learning experience of every high school student in the country, giving them the tools they need to engage more effectively in the classroom and with the world. (4)

So important are computers and broadband that they must be available to every student from Year 9 to Year 12:

> Australian schools must have a computer on every desk and high-speed, reliable broadband access to drive a digital education revolution. (3)

Designated 'digital infrastructure', these technologies in schools will compel change in a sector which has so far seemed unresponsive, unlike those of government and business. The personalised access signified in 'a computer on every desk' places the emphasis on the equipment rather than the students. With control delegated to the technologies, the students are not just rendered passive but invisible.

Human capital

Allied to the technologically determinist discourse is that of human capital. It is linked to the ALP's earlier paper, *The Australian Economy Needs an Education Revolution* (Rudd and Smith 2007), which was subtitled the 'New Directions Paper on the Critical Link between Long Term Prosperity, Productivity Growth and Human Capital Investment'. This document posited a causal relationship between investment in human capital and higher productivity leading to economic growth.

Human capital theory has an extensive history dating back to the 1960s. Based in economics, its influence on education lapsed to some degree in the 1970s but resurfaced in the 1980s and 1990s when it was reworked in line with the new growth theories (Stedward 2003). Human capital discourse as it is used by politicians and policymakers draws on the concepts of investment and profitability. These concepts are then applied to education, the outcomes of which are construed as raising individuals' skills, in turn rendering them more productive for the economic benefit of both the individual and the nation (Marginson 1997b). Deploying a human capital discourse enables politicians to restrict or to expand their expenditure on education for particular purposes, depending on their perceptions of national or political need. Governments keen to reprioritise education spending can, for instance, claim that education as currently practised is insufficiently vocational and therefore wasteful as it does not contribute to enhancing human capital, with consequential results for educational priorities (Luke 1997). Alternatively, education can be targeted for greater intervention and expenditure for specific priorities which are politically determined, as in the UK under New Labour. This may well include the incorporation of computing technologies into education in order to raise national competitiveness in a globalising world (Stedward 2003).

In human capital discourse, education is considered valuable only for its contribution to the individual and the national economy rather than a means of personal and/or social betterment or the formation of a democratic citizenry. Terms which suggest value and efficiency, adopted from economics and finance, are commonly used (Bell and Stevenson 2006; Marginson 1997b), as they are in the opening statement of *A Digital Education Revolution*:

> To have the best job and life opportunities in the future, Australian students must receive a world class education today. (1)

> A world class education system requires significant government and private investment, quality subjects to study, well-trained and dedicated teachers, and the best classroom facilities such as computers, laboratories and workshops. (1)

'Best', 'world class', 'investment', 'quality', 'well-trained and dedicated' suggest value, with computers depicted as an integral component of a quality education system. It is notable that the funding to be provided for this purpose derives from government which will 'invest' in the future of the nation's children. While reference is made to the private sector, the text's focus is the ALP's intended funding of the computer initiative. The computers and broadband will form the 'digital infrastructure', a term which situates the required expenditure in the realm of government. The positive outcomes of educational use of computers and broadband for individual students are further justification for this expenditure:

> Students with better access to technology can receive a stronger education and achieve better academic performance. (5)

The nation will also benefit:

> Information and communications technology is no longer just another subject taught by schools, it is a means of learning across all subjects...

It is also a driver of productivity and growth across all sectors of the economy, from farming and mining to manufacturing and services. (1)

By implication, the Howard Government's educational effort and its impact on the nation are represented as deficient:

It is critical that Australia increases the accessibility of computers in schools and improves how they are used to maximise their benefit in the classroom. (5)

While human capital discourse is influential in policy texts from other countries, in this text the emphasis on value is striking. The terms 'world class', 'quality', 'sophisticated', 'enrich', 'well-paid', and 'best' recur and are allied with 'high-speed', 'fast', 'latest' and 'reliable' to position computers and broadband as key ingredients of a future education. Such an education, however, is also an individual financial benefit. The dividend will be 'well-paid jobs across all industries' for the workers of the future. Underneath this lies the assumption that finding a highly skilled job in an intensely competitive global economy is dependent on using computing technologies.

The 'toolbox of the 21st century' and the 'tool of the trade'

Two complementary metaphors depict computers and broadband as essential to education and also to the contemporary world of work but there is an important distinction between them. The computer, as in Rudd's earlier press conference, is portrayed as the 'toolbox' while high-speed broadband, by contrast, is the 'tool of the trade'.

The 'toolbox of the 21st century'

The metaphor of the computer as a tool has a long and controversial history dating back to the 1980s. However, in *A Digital Education Revolution*, the metaphor of the toolbox conveys a shift in meaning from earlier policies. On the one hand, it is a political jab at the widespread use of toolbox by the Howard Government to indicate its focus on vocational and training education. The policy of the ALP, by contrast, is presented as sophisticated, technological and inclusive, encompassing all upper secondary school students. On the other hand, the concept of the tradesman's toolbox is superseded by the computer which becomes the new necessity for the 'jobs of the future' (10). Under the heading, 'Computers: the toolbox of the 21st century', computers are represented as embedded within every workplace:

Whichever industry, trade, skill or profession they work in, Australia's children will need to be equipped for computer applications such as word processing, spreadsheets, and making presentations. These are the basic skills of the 21st century. (4)

The tradesman's toolbox is effectively relegated to the previous century, with 'the basic skills' for the new century those enabled by the computer.

Notably, the types of applications suggest a professional workplace. For students, these applications are 'the tools they need to engage more effectively in the classroom and with the world' (4). The toolbox, the computer, contains these applications which offer not just one 'tool' for students, but numerous different types with a range of uses. In the text, a table which enumerates examples of computer applications and their accompanying classroom applications evokes a visual representation of an open toolbox and its tray of tools. The computer that was depicted as threatening in earlier times has changed: now commonplace, it has been mastered. Its mastery has occurred in the workplace where its use is integral, particularly in highly paid and skilled work, and therefore vital. Computers are used by managers 'to boost productivity', by architects, engineers and doctors (5). Students' higher achievement in mathematics is said to be correlated with more sophisticated computer use. A high technology future, based around the sciences and technical professions, is conjured up. The skills students gain with the technology at school are the pathways to these careers:

> The computer skills that our children will gain from their school education will be invaluable to help them secure their future jobs. (5)

Yet computers are not available to all students. The policy notes that '34 per cent of students are in schools where principals report that instruction is hindered by a shortage of computers' (5), a sentence which references a similar one in the OECD's 2005 analysis of PISA data. The OECD report notes that in Australia, the schools most likely to report a lack of computers were those in rural areas (OECD 2005). While the same report suggests that there are associations between socio-economic advantage and access to computers, there is no mention in *A Digital Education Revolution* of the characteristics of these schools which have insufficient computers. Instead, the ALP's promise is to give 'access' to these skills through provision of the computers, with access to resources once more designated as the solution to the problems of social inequities.

The 'tool of the trade'

In *A Digital Education Revolution*, computers, now mastered, are no longer depicted as the transformative technology of earlier years. Instead, it is broadband for which the term 'revolution' is invoked. Broadband is about 'plugging into the digital revolution' (5). In the overview of the policy, broadband is explained as the 'internet network infrastructure' which will 'plug our schools into the information superhighway' (1). The 'information superhighway' is a phrase that was used widely in the 1990s, particularly in the US, to denote the invisible structures of the Internet. It was dated by 2007 but served as shorthand to evoke an image of rich technological infrastructure. More significantly, the heading implies that broadband, rather than the computer, is the truly revolutionary technology. Broadband connection enables participation in the 'digital revolution'. Nor is it simply broadband, which already existed to varying degrees across the country, but high-speed 'world class' broadband:

> Access to world class broadband will revolutionise classroom education and enable students to engage more effectively with the resources from around the world. (5)

Rather than the toolbox or the computer applications which will provide students with the means to carry out school tasks in the present and work tasks in the future, broadband will be the component without which these tasks cannot be undertaken:

> High speed broadband will also mean that Australian students have access to world class infrastructure that is the 'tool of the trade' for jobs of the future in computing, information studies, engineering, and across the sciences. (6)

'Tools of trade' refers to those items that are required by an individual to carry out their job (Butler 2013). The 'tool of the trade', as used here, suggests that high-speed broadband is the primary technology of the future in high-status jobs in the STEM disciplines, science, technology, engineering and mathematics. Ensuring sufficient graduates from these subjects is often regarded as crucial to enable a country to achieve an edge in the competitive global economy. Rather than positioning this as primarily in the nation's benefit, the threat of losing in the global race is portrayed as facing the individual student:

> If Australian students cannot access broadband of the same speed or quality as students in other countries, they may struggle to compete in the labour market against better trained students from overseas for the most highly paid, satisfying and secure jobs. (6)

In earlier policies, the provision of computer skills for school students was seen as enabling the nation to compete against others internationally. In this policy, high-skilled jobs are projected to be at risk and other students in competitor countries with higher educational achievements are portrayed as winners. While the improvement of national economic performance may be an underlying aim, the language of the policy suggests the real risk of individual failure to achieve success in the race for jobs, with the clear implication of a second-rate outcome should high-speed broadband not be provided. The national threat identified in earlier policies has become a threat to the future prospects of individuals, and only by implication, to the nation. Yet it is only access to broadband that is promised, with 'access' equated to good learning.

The majority of the potential uses of broadband in the classroom, as outlined in the policy, however, involve the student as passive user, much as in 1983: classroom uses such as listening, viewing and reading are extended. The term 'Internet' is scarcely used, given concerns at the time over its potential impacts on young people. Instead the fears then prevalent in the community are referenced in a discussion over the 'limitations of the internet at school' and the importance of 'the guidance of teachers' (7).

Another benefit broadband provides is an opportunity for parental surveillance of teachers and schools, dressed up as 'parental involvement':

> Broadband also enables greater parental involvement in a child's education. There will be more feedback on their child's progress, and greater awareness of curriculum content, teaching methods and what homework is being set for their children. (7)

The existing initiative of online curriculum content provided by the Le@rning Federation is commended. Commitment is promised to continue the development of such resources, again with the view that the provision of access to this content equates with learning:

> Rich, interactive curriculum content across schools, irrespective of their location, can overcome the disadvantages faced by schools and teachers in rural and remote locations. (7)

A Digital Education Revolution was the foundational document which expressed the ALP's intentions should it be elected but it also embodied political imperatives and judgements as to what was electorally attractive and achievable. However, there were significant silences in the policy. One was the question of equity across schools and schooling systems. While the policy noted that some schools did not have sufficient, or indeed any, access to computers, there was no discussion of the contentious issue of resourcing schools or the differential outcomes between and within school systems.

Education as a deliverable

In *A Digital Education Revolution*, education is envisioned as preparation for work, as only work affords future opportunities. This work is of a particular kind: well-paid professional and technical. To enable students to gain these jobs and to achieve success against competition for those same jobs from other countries, the skills they require in the future should be taught in schools. Computing technologies which were already embedded within workplaces are central to this education. The skills required in the sophisticated workplaces described in the policy are transposed to computer applications deemed useful for classroom learning and assumed to be relevant in future years. Students are conceptualised as individuals whose personalised learning will be delivered through a computer connected to the Internet. The computer is envisioned as the teacher and the student as the passive recipient of knowledge, a transmission mode of education where the teacher has been replaced by a machine. Learning is reduced to preparation for work. This conception of learning excludes all others, including the social and relational nature of teaching and learning, and education for citizenship.

As in earlier policies, teachers by inference are positioned as lacking computer skills. Teachers' work and their workplaces are pictured as unsophisticated technologically, hindering their ability to prepare students for their future. The computers to be provided under an ALP Government will redress this situation. The computer will become the medium for communication, for 'e-education. It will change the way teachers teach, and the way students learn' (Rudd, Smith and Conroy 2007, 1). Teaching and learning are thus constructed as deficient. Teachers require training, particularly with broadband which they will employ for the 'enrichment' of students' learning (9). It is only when the term 'Internet' is used, consistent with the prevailing fears of the threat to children's well-being posed by the Internet, that teachers are deemed to have some expertise: 'it is important that students learn internet skills, and the limitations of the internet at school under the guidance of teachers' (7). However, rather than educational experts, teachers are represented as the proxy for parents and guardians.

A Digital Education Revolution acknowledged that many students had access to computers in schools, but argued that greater numbers of computers were necessary to enable students to use computers in ways which were more advanced. The conception of a computer for every individual between Years 9 and 12 is fundamental to the policy. It emanates from the technologically determinist views of the computer as a device to engender change and as the medium of learning. The notion of a computer per student also evokes the manufacturing process. It aligns with the human capital perspective of the individual as the product of a process which can be enhanced by the application of technology. While the policy is premised on the importance of education to the individual student, a particular view of education is imagined, one that is delivered to an individualised senior secondary student by computing technologies. The passive student is to be trained for the world of work which teachers are unable to understand. This is the kind of education deemed valuable for the nation and for the individual.

These assumptions powerfully framed the policy, its focus, the funding allocated to it and the future directions it mapped, which in turn directly influenced its implementation. The bulk of the AU$1 billion allocated in the policy was for the purchase of computers and computing equipment, with AU$100 million of this funding directed to enhancing schools' access to fibre broadband connections. The vision and the plan had been elaborated. The task ahead was to put it into action.

Coming to power

On 24 November 2007, the ALP, led by Kevin Rudd, was elected, ending 11 years of Coalition Government. Former Prime Minister John Howard became only the second prime minister to lose his seat at a federal election. The new government was eager to deliver on its election promises, one of which was the Digital Education Revolution. Following the swearing in of the new government on 3 December 2007, Julia Gillard became Deputy Prime Minister and Minister for the newly created Department of Education, Employment and Workplace Relations (DEEWR). As in the Hawke ALP Government of 1987, Education and Employment, discrete departments under the later years of the Howard Government, were brought together. The title of the new Ministry is an expression of the government's priorities. 'Education' preceded 'employment', the reverse of that under the Hawke Government, demonstrating the new government's focus on education at a time of nearly full employment.

In education, the ALP Government's priority under its proposed Digital Education Revolution was the provision of computers. A timeline was set. Applications for funding were to be received at the end of the government's first 100 days in power (Auditor-General 2011). In a sign of the importance of the policy to the incoming government, the Digital Education Revolution was placed on the agenda for the first Cabinet meeting on 4 December 2007 (Auditor-General 2011). A committee was established to provide advice and support for the Digital Education Revolution. Comprising representatives from key departments, including Treasury and the Department of Prime Minister and Cabinet (DPMC) as well as the Department of Broadband, Communications and the Digital Economy (DBCDE), the committee met for the first time on 7 December 2007 (Auditor-General 2011).

Once in government, the task to put a computer on every school student's desk across the nation proved formidable. Not least, as a national initiative, this promise could not be delivered without consultation and collaboration with the states and territories, responsible constitutionally for the provision of education. The processes through which the policy was developed were complex. There were a number of steps: political decision-making at the level of heads of government, which was prosecuted through the Council of Australian Governments (COAG), and at the ministerial level through MCEETYA; coordination and implementation by DEEWR and state/territory education authorities, and those of the non-government sector; and advice on implementation provided by specific bodies such as AICTEC, which reported to MCEETYA. Translating the policy conception of computers and their role in education to computers on school desks involved a series of difficult questions. What is a computer? How and where is it to be used? For what purposes? What costs are entailed? What are the intended outcomes? Will these be measured, and if so, how? Who will make these and the many other related decisions? Whose priorities will prevail?

Negotiating the revolution

Shortly after the election, a COAG meeting brought together the new Prime Minister and the Chief Ministers of the states and territories. Unusually, all heads of government were from the ALP. At this first meeting, changes to the machinery of the COAG process were agreed to and seven working groups instituted to pursue the federal reform agenda in areas which crossed state boundaries. One of these groups was responsible for 'the productivity agenda – including education, skills, training and early childhood' (COAG 2007, n.p.) and designated the Productivity Agenda Working Group (PAWG). The goal of the Productivity Agenda was two-fold: to ensure the maintenance or enhancement of living standards as the population aged;

and to address disadvantage suffered by low income groups, a focus that had received scant attention during the election campaign (KPMG Econtech 2010). Discussion over the reform of the financial arrangements between the federal government and the states and territories also commenced. The influence of the federal government can be clearly seen in the *Communique* that resulted from the COAG meeting of 20 December. The seven working groups were to be chaired by a federal minister and were to 'provide COAG with its Commonwealth-State implementation plans for the major Commonwealth election commitments' (COAG 2007). PAWG was chaired by Julia Gillard, Deputy Prime Minister and DEEWR Minister.

At the COAG meeting, the states and territories agreed to a survey of their schools to determine the numbers of computers each school had available for student use. Slated for completion in the middle of February 2008, the aim of the survey was to determine which schools had the greatest need. 'Need' was construed in terms of the computer to student ratio. Those schools with the greatest number of students per computer were to be designated the neediest and therefore the first considered in the determination of grants (COAG 2007). However, the capacity of individual schools to put computers to use effectively was also to be assessed. The federal government expected the states and territories to meet any additional costs associated with the delivery and installation of computers provided under the NSSCF. At the December COAG meeting, agreement as to liability for these substantial costs could not be reached (Auditor-General 2011). Costs not budgeted for by the federal government included those for software, data centres, network connectivity, support, and administration. A significant extra cost was the upgrading of power supply to numerous schools to enable them to run extra computers (DEEWR 2008d).

Nevertheless, the commitment to implementation was made by DEEWR Minister Gillard in January 2008. Work began on a strategic plan to formulate the means of implementation, with consultation between DEEWR and the Cabinet Implementation Unit, resulting in a preliminary plan in February 2008 (Auditor-General 2011). Political considerations influenced the initial processes which were developed in ways that had a bearing on the future success of the program. Because of the government's commitment that the first applications would be accepted within 100 days of it taking office, the audit of computers in schools was conducted within the school holidays. The impact of this timeline meant limited consultation between DEEWR and other relevant groups, particularly in relation to the form and content of guidelines for applications from schools to the fund (Auditor-General 2011). Further time for discussion of on-costs was similarly limited.

DEEWR's survey of government and non-government schools saw participation from 2905 of the 2956 secondary schools in Australia. Computers counted in the survey were required to be no older than four years. Considerable variation was revealed in the existing provision of computers in schools across the country. In 946 schools, the ratio of students to computers was eight to one. Not all schools had computers. In total, there were around 210,000 computers under four years old for approximately 990,000 students in Years 9 to 12 in the country, with an estimated requirement for another 789,000 computers (DEEWR 2008d). In February 2008, funding guidelines for the first round of grants were released (DEEWR 2008c). Schools which had a computer to student ratio of one to nine or greater were designated the neediest (Auditor-General 2011). The DEEWR recommended these schools apply for grants in the first round opening in March 2008 (DEEWR 2008c, 5).

Two annual grant payments were to be made to the states and territories or to the designated funding authorities for non-government schools, subject to the states and territories signing a funding agreement with the federal government (DEEWR 2008c). The federal government proposed a maximum grant of AU$1000 which would apply only to the cost of the computer. Accordingly, DEEWR advised schools applying for grants that funding for any costs associated with installing computers must be negotiated with the appropriate state or territory body (DEEWR 2008c). At the next COAG meeting in March 2008, agreement was reached on the principles to govern new funding arrangements between the federal and state and territory governments, the *Intergovernmental Agreement on Federal Financial Arrangements*. Heads of government also agreed that the computer roll-out could begin, although the question as to who was responsible for the additional costs associated with the program was not resolved (Auditor-General 2011).

MCEETYA supported the plan to provide schools with funding for computers. At their April 2008 meeting, ministers 'affirmed their shared goal of building a world-class education and training system in Australia' and 'strongly supported the Digital Education Revolution as a key strategic tool in achieving a revolutionary improvement in Australia's education and training to world class standards' (MCEETYA 2008a, 1). The key terms of 'world-class education' and the 'Digital Education Revolution' from the policy document of 2007 displayed the influence of the federal government. This support was reaffirmed in the June 2008 Joint Ministerial Statement which committed to ensuring that 'Australia will have technology enriched learning environments that enable students to achieve high quality learning outcomes and productively contribute to our society and economy' (MCEETYA. MCVTE 2008). In August 2008 AICTEC published the strategic plan developed to guide the implementation of the Digital Education Revolution. It shared some continuity with 'Learning in an online world' and the commitment to a 'national vision' as well as designating areas to be targeted for change. These were leadership, infrastructure, learning resources and teacher capability, similar to those of 'Learning in an online world' (AICTEC 2008). In this way, earlier policy frameworks retained some influence in the development of the new. As in 'Learning in an online world', a commitment to collaboration and consultation between the different levels of government was stressed as vital to the achievement of success, glossing the dominance of the federal government agenda.

In the first round of funding for the program, announced in June 2008, 116,820 computers were provided to 896 schools around the country (DEEWR 2008a). New South Wales refused to allow its schools to participate in the second round of funding for the program, although agreements between the other states and territories were undertaken through April and May of 2009 (Auditor-General 2011). Shortly afterwards, simmering tensions between the states and territories and the federal government over the on-costs associated with the computer program emerged in the media. The ALP, both in opposition and in government, underestimated the costs associated with the provision of computers for the states and territories. Nor did it anticipate their reactions to the additional costs imposed on them in order to comply with federal government election promises.

New South Wales, which had received 64 per cent of the total funding allocated to the computer program in the first round (DEEWR 2008d), demanded another AU$245 million for the extra costs associated with providing computers to schools (ABC 2008). Victoria too pressed at MCEETYA for extra funding (Auditor-General 2011). New South Wales and Victoria were soon followed by the other states in a potential revolt which threatened the viability of the program. Shortly afterwards, the Prime Minister, Kevin Rudd, appointed a panel to review the extra costs to the states and territories associated with the delivery of the Digital Education Revolution program. The COAG (2008a, 4) meeting on 3 July 2008 noted that 'Commonwealth election commitments have legitimate and additional financial implications for the States and Territories' and that work to consider these more broadly in the context of financial reform was underway.

The review was conducted by senior federal government public servants and it incorporated consultations with state and territory counterparts as well as representatives of the non-government sector. Its report (DEEWR 2008d), published in September 2008, suggested that a ratio of one computer to two students, rather than a computer to every student, would be effective. It estimated the total cost of a single computer, when the additional costs were calculated, including installation, support and electricity remediation, at AU$2500 over a lifespan the report set at four years. While the report noted that extra costs to the states and territories were entailed by the ALP's election promise, it also stressed that states and territories, which strongly agreed with the goal of improving student access to computing technologies, had their own funding responsibilities and that federal funding should not replace state and territory investment. The report also recommended a national partnership agreement to provide security of programs and funding into the future as a new approach to funding models (DEEWR 2008d).

At the November 2008 COAG meeting, far-reaching changes to funding arrangements were instituted which included 'objectives, outcomes, outputs and performance indicators' and a 'new performance reporting framework' which was to apply to each jurisdiction (COAG 2008b, 2). The same meeting saw further funding of AU$807 million allocated to meet the additional costs associated with the implementation of the computers in schools program. The federal government, faced with the prospect that the computer roll-out could not proceed if the states and territories chose not to meet the extra costs, capitulated.

The National Education Agreement which came into force in 2009 detailed the extra funding for computers in schools as a one-time payment to the states and territories. As the review into the additional costs had proposed, an amount of AU$2500 was allocated for each computer: AU$1000 for a computer and AU$1500 to cover the additional costs incurred by states and territories and by individual schools. Some schools had been deterred from applying for computers because they could not meet the extra costs associated with installation and maintenance. An additional round of funding applications was opened to ensure that these schools were able to apply for grants. An interim target of a computer to student ratio of one to two was set to be achieved by 30 June 2010 (Auditor-General 2011). This additional funding to states and territories, however, came with a cost: six monthly reporting by state and territory governments to DEEWR on their progress towards a one to one ratio and an explanation of how they intended to meet the four key elements of change laid down in AICTEC's (2008) Strategic Plan (COAG 2009).

The early steps in the implementation of the computer roll-out reveal the contested terrain of federal and state and territory relations, particularly in areas which are the responsibility of the states and territories. The federal government was reliant on the states and territories to deliver one of its signature election policies. Yet the states and territories were able to resist the federal government's directives fiercely even when all jurisdictions shared the same party political allegiance as they did in 2008. On this occasion, the states and territories were able to win concessions as their resistance threatened the success of the federal government's election promise. The federal government was vulnerable because it had provided a benchmark of the success of its program: the number of computers delivered to schools. Federal government failure to achieve the desired number could be measured easily and remarked on with all the potential for political judgements which could be made. However, the control of funding vested in the federal government gave it other tools, such as the monitoring and accountability processes inscribed in the National Education Agreement, through which it could gain new control while at the same time making the concessions necessary to ensure its priorities were delivered by the states and territories.

The November 2008 COAG meeting was held in the teeth of the unfolding global financial crisis. By the following COAG meeting in February 2009, the dangers to the world economy had become clearer, with deep recessions underway in advanced economies and economic stimulus packages instituted around the world. The federal government undertook a series of measures to stimulate the Australian economy in order to avoid a steep recession. In February 2009, it allocated nearly AU$15 billion to build new infrastructure in primary and secondary schools around the nation in a program known as the Building the Education Revolution (BER), the administration of which was devolved to the states. The states and territories strongly supported the stimulus at the COAG meeting (COAG 2009). The scale and cost of this program as well as the long lead times before individual projects were finished have tended to overshadow the Digital Education Revolution and the delivery of computers to individual schools. An unplanned program, in contrast to the Digital Education Revolution which was announced during the 2007 election campaign, the BER was a response to unforeseen events. It was designed to stimulate the construction industry in ways which would also mesh with the government's focus on education. Often fiercely criticised by opponents, the BER deflected the attention that may otherwise have been directed at the computer program. Questions as to the merits of the computer program and the conceptualisations on which it was built were seldom raised in its earlier stages.

From decision-making to implementation

As COAG, through a process of contestation, determined the parameters of the Digital Education Revolution, MCEETYA elaborated its directions. In 2008 MCEETYA released a set of revised and extended national goals for education, the *Melbourne Declaration on Educational Goals for Young Australians* (MCEETYA 2008b). It reaffirmed a commitment to educational computing, linking it by association with literacy and numeracy: 'Successful learners... have the essential skills in literacy and numeracy and are creative and productive users of technology, especially ICT, as a foundation for success in all learning areas' (8). MCEETYA committees, particularly AICTEC, further expanded on the directions set by MCEETYA. In *Success through Partnership* (AICTEC 2008), the strategic plan designed to form the basis of an implementation plan, AICTEC identified an existing baseline of computing skills in the school population and estimated the shortfall between this baseline and the level targeted by MCEETYA's revised goals. To achieve the goals of the *Melbourne Declaration*, AICTEC identified four elements as critical to effecting change – leadership, infrastructure, learning resources and teacher capability. Strategies to achieve desired change in these four areas were developed and intended outcomes proposed in the implementation plan released early in 2009 (AICTEC 2009). Within this, 'indicative outcomes' to measure achievement towards the goals were outlined (AICTEC 2009, 13). This process mapped the terrain, clarified the lines of responsibility and set targets going forward with the aim of embedding information technologies in all schools. The pathway to achieving the agreed-on 'national vision' was predicated on the view that personalised access to digital technologies and content would improve student learning.

The policy process was top down. Political direction flowed from COAG through PAWG to MCEETYA then AICTEC. That consultations were held with stakeholders such as teachers associations is evident from an Open Day Program held by PAWG and addressed by Julia Gillard, Deputy Prime Minister, DEEWR Minister and Chair of PAWG (Early Childhood Teachers Association 2008). The work of PAWG was explained and a policy framework, which had been endorsed by MCEETYA in April 2008, was presented (MCEETYA 2008a). The degree to which these consultations may have influenced policy positions is unclear. The decision-making processes of MCEETYA, for instance, embodied joint efforts from each level of government to achieve agreed goals. Yet policy processes in education were driven by the federal government's imperative to deliver on its election promises. To this end, the states and territories were progressively tied into performance management and reporting frameworks set by the federal government. The processes which elaborated COAG and MCEETYA decisions and directions were developed through groups drawn from the upper levels of federal, state and territory education bureaucracies as well as representatives from peak bodies in the non-government and higher education sectors, but the federal government retained control of key appointments. The chair of AICTEC, for instance, was a senior public servant from DEEWR. Consultation with other groups, if conducted, was held after political decisions had been made (Durbridge 2009). Little documentary evidence attests to the process of contestation which necessarily accompanies the formulation of policy.

A special purpose funding vehicle, a *National Partnership Agreement on the Digital Education Revolution*, was signed between the federal and the state and territory governments in May 2009 (DEEWR 2009). It formalised the agreement reached across jurisdictions to implement the federal government's Digital Education Revolution and provided AU$2.2 billion for that purpose with an end date of June 2013 for the program. The partnership agreement specified the 'objectives, outcomes and outputs' to be achieved in line with the National Education Agreement (DEEWR 2009, 5). Areas within education were targeted for change to ensure effective implementation of the Digital Education Revolution. These areas were drawn from AICTEC's strategic vision – leadership, infrastructure, learning resources and teacher capability. The primary outcome of the partnership agreement was determined as the achievement of a one to one computer to student ratio by the end of 2011. Following achievement of this ratio, further funding was to be provided for new computers.

Other intended outcomes of the partnership agreement included changes to teaching and learning to ensure access to computing technologies for all students in the senior secondary years, provision of online resources and the establishment of technology competencies for teachers. The outputs required included the provision of high-speed broadband to schools and interoperability of the different technology systems across the nation. As part of accountability requirements, the states and territories were obliged to provide the federal government, through DEEWR, with data on the way funds were spent every six months. This included the number of computers installed. Each state and territory government was also required to provide an implementation plan on a template drawn up by the federal government. As with other partnership agreements, the progress of the states and territories towards achievement of the benchmarks was to be monitored by the COAG Reform Council (Anderson 2010). However, the focus of the outputs on the numbers of computers installed aligned with the belief that more computers would result in better learning. With the numbers of computers delivered set as the benchmark, inevitably the focus was on rolling out computers rather than on mapping any change in teaching and learning (JCPAA 2011).

The first funding rounds conducted by DEEWR had aimed for a one to two computer to student ratio for all schools with considerable flexibility for schools to determine the hardware and software on which funds were to be expended. When this target was achieved in the majority of schools in June 2010 (Auditor-General 2011), further funding rounds were conducted by state and territory governments as set out in their implementation plans. These implementation plans standardised the types of computing devices which could be provided to public schools through specifying block purchasing arrangements as had been required by the federal government. For Victoria and New South Wales, this meant that the Netbook, a small portable device with a value set at a maximum of AU$600, was the computer recommended to shift remaining schools from a one to two computer to student ratio to a one to one ratio. The choice of device was dictated in part by the need to meet the required deadline of a one to one computer ratio at the end of 2011 (DEECD 2009). The price of conforming to federal government accountability measures was written into state implementation plans which thus reflected a greater concern over tight timelines, administrative processes, and 'value for money' rather than the potential suitability of the particular device as an educational technology.

A shift in direction

On the 24th June 2010, Kevin Rudd lost the support of the ALP as leader and was replaced as Prime Minister by Julia Gillard, formerly Deputy Prime Minister and DEEWR Minister. At the federal election on the 21st August 2010, the ALP Government, led by Julia Gillard, failed to win a majority and relied on a handful of independent members to form a government. As the DEEWR Minister, Gillard had shown strong support for the Digital Education Revolution but the direction of policy in school education began to shift following her elevation to the prime ministership. Progressing the

Australian Curriculum, furthering accountability measures and reforming school funding were the new priorities.

The agreement of all Education Ministers to the new Australian Curriculum was announced shortly afterwards in December 2010 (Garrett 2010), completing the moves toward a national curriculum begun at the COAG meeting in December 2007. New and much smaller programs related to digital technologies were publicised as building on the Digital Education Revolution in anticipation of the one to one student to computer ratio which would soon be achieved (DEEWR 2010a). Funding allocations were made for these initiatives, including AU$40 million allocated in 2010 for the *Digital Strategy for Teachers and School Leaders* to provide professional development in information technology for teachers. The Information and Communications Technology Innovation Fund made available AU$16 million to intensify use of digital technologies in classrooms, in particular, through focusing on improving teachers' skills in using computing technologies in the classroom (Gillard 2010). In 2011, AU$41 million was set aside to develop and improve access to online curriculum materials for the Australian Curriculum. An Online Diagnostic Tools Initiative was granted AU$54.3 million (ACARA 2011).

The original policy presented by Kevin Rudd during the election campaign of 2007 had envisaged that 'individual secondary schools would be able to reapply for capital grants every three years to update and upgrade their technology' (Rudd, Smith and Conroy 2007, 9). The 2010 federal budget suggested that further funding of AU$200 million could be allocated in 2013–2014 for the Digital Education Revolution, although it noted that the program was due to expire in June 2013 (Swan and Tanner 2010). However, by 2012, the objectives of the Digital Education Revolution were deemed to have been achieved. The National Partnership funding was to end on 30 June 2013. In the 2013 Budget, only residual funding was allocated to the Digital Education Revolution for the following year (DEEWR 2013a). Despite earlier suggestions that computers would be renewed, the Digital Education Revolution was no longer considered worth funding. Emblematic of this shift was the retention of the rubric, 'education revolution' in administrative documents, although the preface 'digital' had been dropped. Instead, the 'education revolution' was focused on students' schooling outcomes (DEEWR 2013b, 1).

Funding reform was considered key to effecting further change in educational outcomes. The National Plan for School Improvement, or Better Schools, based on the so-called Gonski review of school funding, conducted by David Gonski, was the focus of government effort (Gonski 2011). The key concepts underpinning the National Plan for School Improvement were 'transparency', 'accountability' and 'monitoring', as were 'quality' and 'need' (DEEWR 2013b, 2). Within the document outlining the National Plan for School Improvement is the pledge of 'No Student Left Behind' which vividly evokes 'No Child Left Behind', the contentious American plan for schooling reform introduced under President George W Bush in 2001 (Treasury 2013, 3). In the 2013 Budget, funding was allocated to the Australian Curriculum, Assessment and Reporting Authority (ACARA) to further tools for online assessment and to incorporate ways within the NAPLAN testing to compare results against international benchmarks (Swan and Wong 2013).

The impact of the Digital Education Revolution

The funding provided for the federal initiative of the Digital Education Revolution necessitated collaboration with the states but also involved contestation. The funding arrangements contributed to circumscribing the meaning of the computer as an educational technology as the states and territories sought to fulfil federal imperatives at the same time as integrating these into their existing technology landscape in schools. That this was more complex than the simple vision of 'putting a computer on the desk of every upper secondary student' (Rudd, Smith and Conroy 2007, 2) was attested to by inference in the DEEWR *Better Practice Guide* (2008b) which provided advice on a diverse set of topics related to information and communications technologies, from upgrading schools' bandwidth, the maintenance of cybersafety, software licensing, data protection and server controls, amongst others.

Commercial interests were necessarily involved in supplying computers and related equipment and services. For instance, the New South Wales Department of Education and Training (DET) entered into a contract worth AU$20 million with Adobe Systems Incorporated to license software for the computers to be provided under the Digital Education Revolution (*Education Business Weekly* 2009). Some companies used their involvement with various governments to promote their businesses. In *Australia Experiences A Digital Education Revolution*, the global corporation, Intel, advertised its involvement in the Digital Education Revolution as a supplier of services (Intel Corporation 2010). On its website, Microsoft Corporation promoted a case study explaining how it assisted the DET as it implemented the Digital Education Revolution, thus ensuring the provision of 83,000 computers within six months (Microsoft Corporation 2010). More broadly, the Digital Education Revolution program was an important source of support for sales of imported computers in the Australian market. The growth in the numbers of computers purchased in Australia under the program was estimated to be approximately seven per cent in 2011 (BMI 2012). Ironically, however, the netbook computers purchased for use in many schools were already declining in popularity (BMI 2012).

Internet connections in schools also saw improvement, despite the very small number of schools which were able to connect to the NBN. Between 2008 and 2010, the percentage of schools with broadband connections rose from 92.7 per cent in 2008 to 99.3 per cent in 2010. Growth in fibre connections grew rapidly, from 47 per cent in 2008 to 63.4 per cent in 2010, with a corresponding decline in copper and satellite connections. The number of schools with no access to broadband declined from three per cent in 2008 to 0.1 per cent in 2010. At the same time, download speeds for the majority of schools increased (DEEWR 2010b). In the first part of 2012, the number of computers which had been provided to Australian secondary schools through the NSSCF was over 957,000 with the objective of a one to one student to computer ratio at the nominated year levels deemed to be achieved (DEEWR 2012). On how this ratio, which was claimed to be so important as to demand a national program, could be maintained over time as students progressed to upper secondary school levels, there was only silence.

The limitations of the vision

The policy statement of 2007, *A Digital Education Revolution*, is built on an individualised view of computers and schooling which was later embedded within the one to one computer ratio set as the target of the program in government. It conceptualised the computer connected to the Internet via broadband as the agent of a student's learning, and the goal of such learning as attaining a future well-paying professional career. This representation drew on conceptions of learning with computers which were prevalent in the 1990s and popularised in the slogan of 'anytime, anywhere' learning that accompanied the laptop computer and was implicated with commercial interests and elite independent schools. It also reached far back to the early days of experimentation with educational computing and the depiction of the computer as a tutor which offered individualised instruction (Suppes 1966), a comparison which was again made in 2013 (eg, *Economist* 2013).

The notion of a computer per student was one significant factor framing the meanings on which decision-making about strategy and implementation were built, and expressed in the commitment to a one to one ratio.

The emphasis on the computer rather than students, teachers and schools and the relational practices of teaching and learning was embedded within the directions established by the government in its meetings with COAG and MCEETYA and evident in their *Communiques* of 2007 and 2008. This same emphasis then underpinned the processes for the computer roll-out which were developed by the DEEWR. For instance, to meet the performance outcomes of the National Partnership Agreement, state and territory governments' accountability requirements were based on the numbers of computers delivered to schools. At the same time, promoting individual ownership of a computer as necessary for learning served to further the already popular view of the computer as educationally beneficial (Bigum 2002; Sweeney and McIsaac 2012). The focus in the media and by government on the numbers of computers delivered to schools bolstered the belief that more computers would make for better schooling.

Two other factors were influential in framing meanings of computers. One was the establishment of short timelines to meet politically expedient objectives. The other was the desire to control costs, demonstrated in the insistence that state and territories prioritise value for money. In terms of timelines, the DEEWR, the department responsible for the administration of the Digital Education Revolution, opened the initial funding round in the school holidays in January of 2008, limiting the time for consultation. When funds were distributed, the department required that at least 40 per cent of the funds for computer purchase which were distributed in Round One be expended within six months of receipt. These two conditions meant that political priorities were served: the first meant that the federal government could claim disbursement of the first funds by the completion of its first 100 days in office and the second, that computers would appear in schools within as short a timeframe as possible. In relation to costs, the determination that the effective life of a computer was to be considered as four years rather than the three which was standard in industry meant that a computer could be regarded as accompanying a student through their four years of upper secondary school, thus reducing the numbers of computers required. Setting the cost of a computer at AU$1000 reduced the choice of computer for many schools to what was affordable within that range rather than what was educationally beneficial. These two factors worked to constrain options for state and territory education authorities, the non-government sector and for individual schools as well.

Prioritising 'value for money' through block purchasing arrangements in the later stages of the program had a differential impact (Auditor-General 2011). Schools which had more choice over the way they could utilise funds, for instance, some non-government schools, were able to consider the nature of their school environment and its needs. When decisions were made by state or territory education authorities, different priorities were in play, in particular, equity between students, uniformity and standardisation which contributed to economies of scale (Sweeney and McIsaac 2012). The purchase, as a result, of netbooks with a projected life of four years meant that they were often unable to run effectively within a short period as the software was quickly outmoded (Sweeney and McIsaac 2012). Far from opening new doors, for some students, the performance of the machines was so frustratingly slow that they ended up as 'expensive paperweights' (Braue 2011). Students who were issued with a computer in Year 9 to accompany them through their schooling would find it unable to perform effectively four years later, with the lifespan of the computer effectively exceeded (Sweeney and McIsaac 2012). Some non-government schools, with more flexibility, in some cases chose higher value devices to retain their status as market leaders in technology, with an eye to maintaining their enrolment levels (Sweeney and McIsaac 2012). At the same time, the application process was onerous for schools. It required a technology Strategic Plan which was used to assess the school's capacity to house, maintain and support computers, as well as the level of internet accessibility and the teaching staff's ability to use computers in their teaching. In practice, these constraints meant that consultation was limited by tight deadlines; costs to the states and territories were underestimated; and education authorities and schools had limited planning time over how to house computers and incorporate them into their teaching and learning.

The meanings of the computer for school students were framed by multiple actors at different levels of the policy development and implementation processes. The meanings which were inscribed in the foundational text, *A Digital Education Revolution*, dominated. These were the conceptions which posited the computer as an agent to deliver individualised instruction to senior secondary students, modelled on professional workplace practices and therefore necessitating an individual computer. Political imperatives, assumptions about the purposes and outcomes of school education and the nature of technological change underlay the meanings wrapped around the computer. These meanings took shape in the one to one computer ratio for upper secondary school students. Other models for imagining educational computing existed, particularly in the education community and amongst scholars working in the field, models which may have prioritised junior year levels over those of senior secondary students. More collaborative practices and more expansive purposes of educational computing have been envisioned over many years by those with professional and research-based expertise. These models remain relevant but they were excluded from initial conceptions. Instead, the achievement of the projected vision led to a focus on meeting the numbers targeted and constraining costs.

Accordingly, the computer delivered to many students was less able to perform the tasks required of it and its life was shorter. Status differentials between schools and school systems were not challenged but may have been reinforced. The model of the professional workplace embodied in the text was undermined by the failure to adopt the industry standard of a three year life for a computer, instead, for the sake of convenience and cost, the adoption of a four year lifespan compromised the usefulness of the device in its later years (Sweeney and McIsaac 2012). Above all, setting the measurement of the achievement of the aims of the Digital Education Revolution as the one to one computer to student ratio meant that the program could be regarded as complete, despite the continual entry of new students into these levels each year. It is possible to imagine that a computer to student ratio of one to two or three aimed at junior secondary students could have opened a more productive space and enabled the purchase of fewer but better quality technologies. New and sustainable practices with computing technologies could have flourished in an environment in which professional expertise was allowed scope to pursue more liberal purposes of education than those envisioned in *A Digital Education Revolution*.

Conclusion

A Digital Education Revolution promised that the ALP under Kevin Rudd would transform school education through the provision of technology. The policy was distinguished from earlier ones by its substantial allocation of funding: AU$2.2 billion over four years. Its stated purpose was to address declining productivity as a result of underinvestment in education during the years of the Howard Government. The way to achieve this outcome, argued Rudd in 2007, was through education, as 'education is the platform on which our future economic prosperity will rest' (Rudd and Smith 2007, 27). The designation of education as the solution to a national problem is a familiar one, central to the earlier policies examined in this book. So too is the instrument of reforming education to bring about change: the computer. What set this policy apart from the previous three examined was the substantial funding allocated.

The policy statement of 2007 is silent on questions of need and equity within schools, in the context of a schooling system where the outcomes have been shown to be inequitable and strongly correlated with socio-economic status. Those in lower socio-economic groups have poorer educational attainments and reduced access to higher status careers than those in higher socio-economic groups (Teese and Polesol 2003). Greater access to computing technologies and more advanced levels of proficiency with these is also strongly correlated with students from higher socio-economic backgrounds, a finding that was evident in 2007 (MCEETYA 2007; OECD 2005). In an election campaign, a focus on equity may not have been construed as possessing wide appeal for the swinging voters who typically determine Australian electoral outcomes. Yet from the first days of the ALP Government, it is clear that in terms of computers and schools, its focus was on 'need', which was construed as schools with high student to computer ratios. This focus represents a significant disconnect between the policy statement in opposition and the process of implementation in government.

In government, this definition of 'need' became the determining principle for the disbursement of funds for the purchase of computers for schools. The aim was to improve equity by lifting 'schools from a variable base to a situation where there is equitable access to digital resources and tools' (AICTEC 2008, 10). Because computing technologies were conceived of as central to teaching and learning, the provision of computers was regarded as tackling need and therefore alleviating disadvantage, as opposed to tackling the conditions which created disadvantage. Other partnership agreements were entered into at the same time as that for the Digital Education Revolution and these more directly addressed disadvantage. These were the Low Socio-economic Status School Communities National Partnership and the Literacy and Numeracy National Partnership, which together were allocated AU$1.64 billion of funding, less than the AU$2.2 billion allocated at the same time to the Digital Education Revolution (COAG 2008b). It is open to question as to whether these priorities were justified.

Implementation of the policy when in government was a protracted process. It involved contestation around funding in particular but it was also limited by the original vision of a computer for every student which posed an individualised model of learning delivered through a computer linked to the Internet. Political decisions determined the directions of policy and strategies for implementation were devised largely by senior bureaucrats from the federal government and the states and territories. While there may have been informal consultation with educators or their representatives, their lack of inclusion in formal policy processes meant that their expertise was not valued. Nor was consideration given to introducing greater numbers of computers into schools in ways which would maximise the learning undertaken through integrating these into the distinctive environments in individual schools throughout the country (Sweeney and McIsaac 2012). Putting the computer first militated against a focus on the environment within which the computer was to be used.

When Julia Gillard assumed the prime ministership from Kevin Rudd, the shift in educational priorities to the Australian Curriculum and the National Plan for School Improvement saw the Digital Education Revolution downgraded, with a potential loss of value from the funds that had already been expended (Murphy 2011). When a one to one ratio of computers to students had been achieved, the program was ended, the result of a focus on the object and its delivery. The fact that each year students would be entering the designated year for a computer, Year 9, without being provided with one meant that that ratio, as problematic as it is, faces speedy decline.

The impact of the Digital Education Revolution is difficult to judge. Few evaluations of the program have been published at the time of writing (but see Auditor-General 2011; Sweeney and McIsaac 2012). No doubt there have been many positive experiences for students, teachers and schools as well as negative ones which tend to attract more press attention (eg, Braue 2011). Data collected under NAPLAN testing of ICT literacy skills show that between 2005 and 2011, the proportions of students using computing technologies within schools increased, particularly at Year 10 level, with 51 per cent of these students using computers at school compared to 18 per cent in 2005 (ACARA 2012). Computers delivered under the Digital Education Revolution program are likely to have contributed to greater use amongst students at Year 10 level. The nature of such use, its measurement and its connection with student performance remains an open question, but the investment of government funds further authorised computers as an educational technology. Whether students' and schools' experiences have the potential to disrupt the meanings applied to computers under this program remains to be seen.

However, the Digital Education Revolution had other impacts. It reinforced the influence of the federal government in education in the pursuit of specific purposes and through its disbursement of significant funds in order to achieve its objectives. The power of state and territory governments to resist federal government authority, even when from the same political party, was demonstrated by the New South Wales Government's demand for more funds from the federal government to cover the extra costs associated with the computer roll-out. The refusal in 2013 of some states and territories to agree to the National Plan for School Improvement proposed by the federal government signals their determination to gain the best possible outcomes in terms of funding but also to maintain a degree of independence from federal government imperatives, which can be politically driven and which may not accord with the priorities of state and territory governments. At the same time, it also reflects awareness amongst the states and territories that federal government interventions in education are not always sustained. One-off programs, as the Digital Education Revolution has proved to be, can leave the states and territories with additional funding burdens for programs which have raised expectations within the community about their educational value. At the same time, the intricate funding mechanisms which support such programs are little understood by the public. In this way, the states and territories may bear the odium of the federal government's retreat.

In an effort to bind state and territory governments more firmly to federally determined priorities, new performance and reporting frameworks, already evolving under the Howard Coalition government, were imposed to ensure federally determined standards in education were met. The contested terrain of federal-state relations and responsibilities was redefined. The Abbott Coalition Government, elected in September 2013, promised during the campaign to maintain the funding allocated under the ALP's National Plan for School Improvement, or Better Schools, but to remove 'any parts that allow the Federal Government to dictate what states and territories must do in their schools' (LNP 2013, 6). It remains to be seen how performance and reporting systems applied to the states and territories will be reshaped by the Abbott Government. Few federal governments in the recent past have resisted intervention into state or territory jurisdictions, particularly when confronted with state and territory governments which seek outcomes different from those of the federal government of the day.

Above all, a lack of understanding of the complexity of the issues surrounding computing in schools is a common feature of all the policies examined. Over time, the politicisation of the issue, even more evident in the ALP's election policy text, has resulted in an uncritical acceptance of computers as both a means and a symbol of progress in school education. The task of bringing change in these difficult and contentious areas is delegated to the computer as an apparently neutral and popularly approved technology (Bigum 1997). Issues such as socio-economic status and its impact on student performance, the resourcing of schools and the significant inequities within the existing system, amongst many others, are removed from the public political agenda, appearing instead in arcane funding formulae. Yet with the authority of governments now invested in the computer, the image of one which is aging and not replaced may become a more potent symbol of perceived neglect.

Chapter Seven

The Persistence of Economics

Stability and Change

In 1972, Australian advisers were tasked by the federal government with determining the potential of computers for school education. Their 1976 report expressed polarised views. Some thought that computers were 'education's greatest hope'. Others believed that 'computers will destroy whatever is of value in education' (Wearing et al. 1976, 55). In 1983, policymakers at arms' length from the federal government embraced educational computing with an enthusiasm which was not matched by that of politicians. By 2007, however, politicians were not only passionate proponents of educational computing but actively sought to position the computer as central to modern senior school education. In 1976, only a handful of Australian schools used a computer at all. In 2013, computers have become commonplace in our classrooms.

Federal government policy texts projected that computer use in schools would lead to better education and thereby benefit the nation. The collection of policy texts from 1983 to 2007 examined in this book shows how the federal government and its changing policy communities grappled with the issues raised by new technologies as well as the prism through which they viewed education. At the same time, the texts also illuminate the changing environment within which these policies were produced, the process of their development and the circumstances which were influential in placing the issue of computers and education on the political agenda.

Analysis of the texts demonstrates that several factors were crucial to explain why the federal government promoted the computer as essential for school education at that moment and not at others. The first was the emergence and commercialisation of new computing technologies. The second was the use of these new technologies in Australian workplaces. The third was the perceived economic benefit of such technology for Australia's competitiveness in the international economy, as other countries adopted and deployed such technologies with commercial success. These factors contended also with the arc of the political cycle and the legacy of past decisions and practices which worked to limit or to expand available options for policymakers.

Proposed courses of action and desired outcomes were developed within institutional frameworks which changed significantly over time and gave voice to specific groups and not to others (Fairclough 2003). Thus each text was constructed within a set of frameworks, detailed in this book, which left an imprint in the language of the policy, connecting them to particular sets of values and beliefs. At the same time, each text contributed to new ways of speaking about computers and education as well as authorising actions which directly affected schooling. 'Learning in an online world' in 2000, for instance, led directly to a number of policy statements and guided action based on the framework elaborated within the policy. *A Digital Education Revolution* in 2007, in contrast, was articulated from opposition, and in government was the foundation for new discursive regimes and the development of new frameworks with a range of outcomes.

Policies, however, vary considerably in purpose, affecting their impact. The Wearing report of 1976 exemplifies policy as exploratory. The review was commissioned to determine whether federal government funding should be provided to educational institutions to introduce computers. The decision to recommend no action reveals other aspects that impinge on policy: a new government with other priorities; an extended time frame between the commissioning of the report and its release, by which time it was redundant because the technology it considered had become obsolete; and a political and economic climate which was markedly different from that when the inquiry had begun.

By contrast, in 1983, when *Teaching, Learning and Computers* was produced, a confluence of circumstances prevailed that made it a 'material' policy, one that authorised and directed change (Taylor et al. 1997, 33). Political and economic conditions and an election campaign made action desirable. An institutional framework with the expertise and commitment to produce such a policy already existed, which had not been the case in 1972 when the Wearing report was commissioned. The political will to allocate some funding and to implement its recommendations, no matter how much it fell short of the aspirations of the NACCS, was a crucial determinant of the impact of the policy.

1983: New computers, new government, new policy

In *Teaching, Learning and Computers*, the metaphor of the power of the computer underpinned the claims of the dominant discourses of the report, which were the social democratic, the economic and the technologically determinist. These discourses embodied different visions of the purposes of education associated with divergent world views (Fairclough 2003). The inclusion of diverse interests within the framework of the Commonwealth Schools Commission and its committees meant discursive strategies to achieve consensus were necessary. The new discourse of educational computing that was propounded in *Teaching, Learning and Computers*, contradictory as it often was, retains evidence of conflict over meanings among the members of the committee as they made a case for computers in schools. The strategies employed in the construction of the report involved justifying computers by the following means: invoking the national interest; claiming the enhancement of equality for the disadvantaged; projecting an improvement in the quality of schooling; and the preparation of young people for a future world dominated by computers, particularly in the world of work.

While these discursive strategies draw together the disparate views of the committee into a coherent report, an inherent paradox exists between the competing values and beliefs embedded in the different discourses. The ostensible focus on equality in *Teaching, Learning and Computers*, as indicated by the social democratic discourse employed, is compromised by its conjunction with a technologically determinist discourse which views the computer as the all-powerful agent creating new social and economic conditions. Central to social democratic discourse was the goal of equality of outcomes, based on the belief that society is unequal and that this inequality is reflected and reproduced in education. Government action to improve educational opportunities for the disadvantaged and to work towards the achievement of greater equality is critical. However, the technologically determinist proposition that the computer is the agent of change in fact shifts the attention of government away from the inequalities that exist in society. Providing computers becomes the answer to ameliorating disadvantage, a utopian view which is often associated with new technologies (Light 2001).

The determinist personification of the computer as agent and thus anthropomorphised, both constructive and potentially destructive, confers on it the human-like properties of both good and evil (Sussman 1997). The evocation of threat against an external force justifies the computer's use in education to train the young to gain control over it, thus fulfilling a socially valuable purpose. The use of the computer in schools is further legitimised by emphasising the need for students to acquire computer literacy. Already in widespread use in educational discourse, and the subject of much debate in the late 1970s and early 1980s, the phrase 'computer literacy' suggested that the natural place for learning about the new technology was in schools, where imparting literacy is a key task. Allying the two 'allows mappings of meanings from both domains' (Bigum and Green 1993, 9).

The use of metaphor evokes other discourses through the 'mapping of meanings' that Bigum and Green describe, one of which is the incorporation of a covert human capital discourse. In the report, metaphors of the computer as both a tool and a medium which will improve the productivity of education draw on early developments in human capital theory which emerged in Australia in the 1960s (Marginson 1997a). The image of the computer in the classroom and the functions for which it can be employed ally it closely with its uses in the industrial and business world. The computer is depicted as enabling greater efficiency in education, necessarily positioning schools as backward in relation to both industry and business. Such an appeal connects with contemporary dissatisfaction over the perceived failure of schools to equip students with workplace skills (Beare 1982).

However, it is not just schools which are portrayed as lacking through the human capital discourse of computers in education. Teachers, in particular, are singled out as deficient. Co-located with the computer, teachers are by contrast unskilled, less able to motivate students or to teach them effectively and out of touch with the world outside the school. They need professional development. Paradoxically, *Teachers, Learning and Computers* also recognises that the support provided within schools for teachers will be very limited and that schools will need to rely on the resources and dedication of individual teachers to provide that support.

The computer as a solution

An assumption of national decline underlines *Teaching, Learning and Computers*. The promotion of national economic benefit proposes education as the solution, but only education which incorporates the computer. The computer and its many attributes is the architect of change. It is powerful, complex, potentially able to manipulate the young. At the same time, it is valuable because it is associated with wealth and greater well-being and therefore inevitably desirable. It is creative, intellectual, able to solve problems, but also to provide recreation. It is infinitely patient and dependable, as well as stimulating and motivating for students who find learning difficult or tedious. It is scientific and speeds up the routine business of education. It is pervasive, changing society utterly.

While in *Teaching, Learning and Computers*, unease is expressed over the impact of this powerful device on society, particularly on the young, it is allied with a belief that education will empower young people to take control of the computer. The computer is framed as an instrument of control and a store of value in an uncertain world. At a time when people were fearful of the impact of new technologies, this is a persuasive device. However, high levels of teenage unemployment were the more immediate concern of parents, politicians and educators. A central consideration in the adoption of the initial policy by the ALP in 1982 was the apparent linkage between technological change in the workplace and the new skills which would be needed for it. Computer education in schools would give young people 'access to jobs' (Tate 1982, n.p.). Yet the report is silent on the significant issue of teenage unemployment.

Instead, the report embraces the computer as the way of the future, as imparting necessary skills for both working and living, through implying inadequacies in schools and teachers. It locates the causes of youth unemployment in the education that young people receive, rather than in the political and economic conditions that prevailed or the decisions that were undertaken by government and businesses, particularly in relation to automation and job loss. Advocating the provision of greater numbers of computers to overcome disadvantage focused on the technology as both the problem and the solution, helping to engender the 'pig principle' which held that higher numbers of computers reflected a better school (Bigum 2002, 134). The computer was thus legitimised for education by government intervention. Equipping schools with small numbers of computers was a more achievable target than redressing disadvantage.

1996: New computing technologies and the new economy

The 13 years that elapsed between the publication of *Teaching, Learning and Computers* and *Education and Technology Convergence* saw an environment that was markedly different despite both policies emanating from within the same ALP government. One striking similarity was that the two reports were commissioned at a time of dramatic changes in the technology and policy landscape. In 1996, the personal computers that had focused the attention of politicians and policymakers in 1983 had long since become obsolete, replaced by evermore powerful computers with growing numbers of applications. These had been considerably extended by rapid changes in communications technologies with the introduction of mobile telephones and the Internet.

In 1983, the program to put computers into schools had been a separate stand-alone program which was financed as a discrete, quasi-experimental program. By 1996, the attitude to computers had completely altered. Computers themselves were conceived of differently. A proliferation of new technologies and new applications was reflected in the variety of terms employed to encompass a wide range of computing technologies, such as information technology or more commonly in education, information and communications technologies (ICT). A shift in terminology in the policy texts demonstrates the change in perceptions of computing technologies. The word 'computer', so prominent in *Teaching, Learning and Computers*, in 1996 signified merely the physical object, with terms such as 'information and communications technologies' used to designate the assemblage of applications, equipment and uses of computing technologies. Whereas the 'computer' of 1983 had referred to the physical object, the use of expanded terms in 1996 expressed the embedding of the computer in a web of social and technological relations, with new practices that were no longer captured in the word 'computer'.

In *Education and Technology Convergence*, an attempt is made to construct education as operating on an old industrial economy model and to suggest an intensified use of computing technologies as the solution to bring education into a more modern world. *Educational Technology and Convergence* is characterised by the near homogeneity of the discourses employed. The authors adopt and recontextualise the government's dominant economic discourse, blending it with those of the knowledge economy and globalisation to propose a transformation of education through the use of information technology. Pervading *Education and Technology Convergence* is a totalising discourse that renders people, both teachers and learners, cogs in a vast machine. It attempts to naturalise change as both inevitable and necessary and to enculture particular attitudes towards work, education and technologies. The term 'convergence' is a device to imply a teleological process of change, one brought about by new technologies.

The imagined future world is presented as the result of historical process and therefore inevitable, rather than the outcome of human choices that privilege some interests over others. Despite being constructions, such forecasts have power: their explanation of change includes a plausible plan for the future which promises beneficial outcomes at times of uncertainty.

These forecasts work to foster acceptance of prescriptions for action (Fairclough 2003). The prospective transformation of education is positioned as a function of unavoidable changes in the outside environment, imposing imperatives which must be met, rather than as the result of political choices and actions (Fairclough 2000b). In *Education and Technology Convergence*, the new world which is presented as fact is one in which society is reduced to the economy and the purpose of education is to serve that economy. In *Education and Technology Convergence*, the social democratic discourse of 1983 has disappeared.

As in 1983, education is proposed as both the problem and the solution. Education is cast as failing to equip the workforce with new skills because teachers resist using new technologies. The solution is to apply coercion to bring about more intensive use of computing technologies. Their use will result in changes to the learning process as the technologies themselves become the medium for learning. The benefits will accrue to the nation through the expansion of an existing market, that for international students. This market of students will impose new demands on education and force change on a previously unresponsive sector.

In 1983, placing computers in schools was asserted to be essential. In 1996, the policy rests on this assumption which no longer needs to be stated (Fairclough 2003). Educational discourses are entwined with management discourses in ways which construct computing technologies as the means to reorient education away from the teacher and towards the self-directed learner. The skills that the learner needs to learn more effectively are those skills that are required of workers, such as team work and interpersonal skills (Gee, Hull and Lankshear 1996). Computing technologies are represented as more able to deliver these than people, because information is a property that is attributed to the computer, rather than the product of human-computer interaction. The computer is represented as the engine of change and the tool for transformation of the educational system.

In this vision of education, the educational institution has become a vendor in the global marketplace, selling customised courses to 'educational consumers' (Tinkler et al. 1996, 70). The repetition of such terms reflects a discourse that privileges market-based transactions, consistent with a policy approach that was focused on achieving micro-economic reform in education. While this vision is antithetical to many educators, the contestation of views that is evident in the text of 1983 is scarcely visible in the text of 1996, reflecting the institutional subservience of the NBEET, the body which commissioned the report.

Unlike the policy of 1983 which recommended a course of action and allocated funding to achieve it, *Education and Technology Convergence* attempted to reframe understandings, particularly in education, of the purposes for which computing technologies could and should be used, that is, to inculcate new values (Taylor et al. 1997, 10). These values, consistent with the institutional context within which the report was produced, are economic rationalist ones rather than primarily educational. The authors draw on discourses from other government reports and policies which were influential in education over the preceding years, particularly the Mayer (1992) and Candy (1994) reports. In doing so, they both reproduce and extend the government's economic discourse and attempt to infuse those values and an economistic view of a future dominated by technology into education.

However, *Education and Technology Convergence* as a policy text also reveals the inherent complexities of the policy process. While it bears the authority of the initiating body within its institutional framework, that same framework meant that power was not an automatic property. The report was one of several policy texts, intended to inform others, and in the more comprehensive report, *Converging Technology, Work and Learning* (1995b), different views are advanced on the importance of computing technologies in education that contest some of those put forward in *Education and Technology Convergence*. The latter was only one part of the process of policy development. Some of its recommendations were adopted in *Converging Technology, Work and Learning*. Others were allowed to lapse. The timing of the report, however, released publicly just before the federal election, ensured its demise. However, the ideas within it retain influence in policy circles and echoes of these, particularly with regard to the knowledge economy, recur in later texts.

2000: Action plans for business

The Howard Government's first policy text on computing technologies in education was part of a whole-of-government approach to intensifying the use of computing technologies within society. 'Learning in an online world', the policy for schools, is contained in *Learning for the Knowledge Society: An Education and Training Action Plan for the Information Economy*, which comprised policies for each educational sector. These texts represented the outcome of negotiations within sections of the educational sector, through the EdNA process, with the representation of the states and territories. As noted, it was not a transparent process, but was contested, some echoes of which linger. Nevertheless, ministers from the states and territories and the federal government endorsed the policy despite differences in their views on education, reaching a settlement (Taylor et al. 1997).

Key values and assumptions, which derive from principles enunciated early in the Howard Government's term, were brought to the table from this policy development process and are embedded within the discourses of 'Learning in an online world'. So too are conceptions of computing technologies, their purposes and preferred practices in schooling, some of which have their origin in the National Goals of Schooling revised by MCEETYA in 1999. These values are expressed in the technologically determinist discourse which views the Internet and the World Wide Web as neutral forces changing the world. Managerial discourse is also an important strand which is linked to the technologically determinist through the construct of the 'information economy'.

As in 1983 and 1996, in 'Learning in an online world' changes in society are depicted as occurring independent of people. Computing and communications technologies, especially the Internet, are the agents actively reshaping business and industry, in particular, and through them, national economies (Alston 1999). Computing technologies are envisaged as driving the information economy. The notion of 'convergence' so central to *Education and Technology Convergence* has disappeared and the 'knowledge economy' of 1996 has been overtaken by the 'information economy'. Despite the flaws of the knowledge economy discourse, the replacement of 'knowledge' with 'information' works to construe education as merely a support for other more valued sectors. Education is portrayed as a 'producer, consumer and export earner' (DETYA 2000b, 17), in particular, for 'high quality, locally produced online content' (Commonwealth of Australia 1998, 11). This role is instrumental: education must 'play its enabling role in supporting Australia's transition to the information economy and maintain its place as one of Australia's major export earning industries' (DETYA 2000b, 10).

The phrase 'information economy' is a linguistic device which sanctions government action for some purposes that are then rendered legitimate. The task of managing the national economy is one such sphere for a government committed ideologically to a smaller role for government. While the Howard Government acted to bring about the creation of the information economy, it designated business as the owner of information, as investor, as the provider of services and therefore the information economy as a private business venture. In this way it obscured government actions which shifted regulatory regimes to favour commercial interests. Instead, the government portrayed itself as assisting and 'enabling' business through establishing the architecture which would best enable firms to take advantage of opportunities for profit. Government actions to effect change were explained as the removal of barriers which might hinder the growth of the information economy. The characterisation of education as one such impediment provided a justification for the federal government to target change at the sector as a whole.

Consistent with the Howard Government's promotion of a number of strategies designed to usher in the 'information economy', 'Learning in an online world' depicts embedding the Internet as the primary challenge for the future of schooling. The text envisions computing technologies as a means to achieve necessary change in education and at the same time to equip the public with skills that will enable them to function in a world that is dominated by computing technologies. On the one hand, this is a determinist view of the transformative power of new technologies, specifically the Internet, as an agent of change to both reorganise schooling and to allow greater learning for all. On the other, it is a managerial perspective that embodies a belief in the capacity of the technology to force efficiencies on a schooling sector that is a recipient of substantial government funds.

'Learning in an online world' is an example of a new genre. Unlike the policy documents of 1983 and 1996, it does not include a rationale for and exposition of the purposes of computing technologies in schools. The assumption of the transformative powers of computing technologies has made this type of exposition redundant, as has the agreement between the two levels of government. The policy expresses the negotiated redefinition of governmental boundaries and displays the imprint of power, expressed discursively through the delineation of boundaries and actions contained within it (Fairclough 2003). The policy demarcates responsibilities for the different levels of government and establishes future directions for action by each level of government. Embodied within the policy are beliefs about the roles for each jurisdiction. The federal government is to lead the two levels of government in a national approach. Delivering education within schools is the responsibility of the states and territories.

The proposed national approach is shaped by a fundamental belief that the role of government should be minimised and that business should play a greater role in education, reflecting the influence of the federal government in setting and shaping the agenda. In *Learning for the Knowledge Society*, Minister David Kemp suggests the policy furthers a new approach to dealing with education which will meet the demands of the new technology of the Internet which was 'transforming the way we live and work' (DETYA 2000b, 3). Computing technologies will usher in the 'information economy'. Education is merely the handmaiden.

2007: Computers and an election campaign

Unlike the three earlier policies examined, *A Digital Education Revolution* was constructed in opposition and released during an election campaign. As such, it is an overtly political document designed to showcase an initiative which was presumed to have wide electoral appeal. At a time when economic prosperity was assumed to be widespread, its appeals to the national interest are muted. Instead, its focus is on the individual school student and how he or she can secure a competitive edge in the race for the well-paid high-status jobs of the future. The reappearance of the term 'computer' which had almost disappeared in 'Learning in an online world' draws attention to the physical object and its relationship to the ALP's signature broadband policy. At the same time, it is also an appeal to the hip pockets of parents, who make up a sizable portion of the electorate.

The title of the policy, *A Digital Education Revolution*, is an instance of 'mediatization' in which policy is constructed as a media presentation to the public (Rizvi and Lingard 2010, 19). So the title is hyperbole, designed to capture attention. The term 'revolution' and its reference to the industrial revolution summon up the profound change which computers and computing technologies will bring but it also encapsulates the enduring technological determinism which is also evident in the earlier three policies. Importantly, it is broadband that is depicted as the revolutionary technology rather than the computer. The personal computers which were so threatening in 1983 to the public, to jobs, potentially to the fabric of social life, have become commonplace, one of several portals to the Internet. People have mastered computers and their use in the workplace is both routine and vital.

The evocation of the workplace is omnipresent in the policy. Workplace uses of computers are mapped onto applications which can be used in education. These examples infer a white collar professional field despite lip-service reference to the trades. The computers which will be provided under the program will equip students with the computing skills that will secure their future jobs against competition from individuals abroad. At a time of high skilled migration, this was a strategy to play on concerns over future job prospects for students following graduation. A human capital discourse justifies the proposed spending on technology as a benefit to the workforce of the future. Government spending is thus legitimised in an attempt to counter a potential critique of wasteful extravagance. The computer is portrayed as essential to the creation of a 'world class' education system and buttressed by selective references to the OECD's PISA testing regime to suggest deficiencies within the education system which the proposed computer program will overcome.

The policy is silent on the question of disadvantage. In each of the other three policies, disadvantage is considered, although construed differently, and the computer is posed as a potential benefit to the disadvantaged. In 1983, the disadvantaged included the poor, girls, the disabled, and Indigenous citizens. In 1996, the disadvantaged had been redefined as women, Indigenous citizens, disabled people, people from language backgrounds other than English and those living in remote areas. The authors also identified a new category of disadvantage, the 'information poor' who lacked access to computing technologies (Tinkler et al. 1996, 126). In 2000, those living in rural and remote areas and the Indigenous were regarded as disadvantaged. In *A Digital Education Revolution*, disadvantage is no longer a property associated with people, but rather with place, where it is construed as merely a set of obstacles which the provision of specific resources will ameliorate. That in government the focus was on schools in need, established by a survey of available and functioning computers, suggests the failure to focus on disadvantage was strategic. Cast as an investment, the computer program could be justified on economic grounds. Defining disadvantage involved complex questions and contested categorisations which could be met with a charge that the policy was essentially redistributive and therefore open to political rebuttal.

In government, the translation of the policy into implementation was accompanied by discursive regimes which drew directly from *A Digital Education Revolution*. Thus 'revolution', 'digital' and 'world class' are repeated again and again in COAG and MCEETYA *Communiques*, in administrative guidelines, in strategic and implementation plans. They signify the influence of the federal government and its agenda in its negotiations with the states and territories but also signal the belief that computers and broadband were essential for learning, a belief which had become so entrenched that the expensive plan to give computers to students was barely contested. Nor was there a widespread debate over whether the significant funding for the program could have been allocated for different purposes.

In 1983, AU$18 million was allocated over three years to provide a small number of computers to each secondary school in the country, with a focus on Year 9. In 2007, the initial sum of AU$1 billion over four years was allocated, with AU$100 million of this amount set aside for schools' connection to broadband. Adjusted for inflation, the Digital Education Revolution's proposed funding was nearly thirty times larger than the National Computer Education Program of 1983. In government, the funding which applied to the Digital Education Revolution program was increased by AU$807 million, marking a very substantial expenditure of AU$2.2 billion in total. The stimulus measures which were undertaken by the Rudd Government during the global financial crisis, particularly the Home Insulation Program and the schools' extensions under the BER received wide coverage and trenchant criticism. Scrutiny of the Digital Education Revolution was more limited in the public arena, particularly in relation to its outcomes, and to date few evaluations have been published (but see Auditor-General 2011; Sweeney and McIsaac 2012). This limited scrutiny can be attributed in part to the widespread belief that sees computers, unlike school halls, as crucial for learning with outcomes that can only be positive.

Economic or economical?

The policy texts examined in this book propounded a construction of the future world in which the computer is represented as an instrument for improving Australia's position in a competitive global economy and providing future employment skills for young people. Linked with an economic discourse is a technologically determinist discourse that posits computers as causal elements in social change, one to which policymakers must respond. Technological determinism is a discourse with a long history, with similar claims for educational benefit being made for earlier technologies and technologies of different kinds (Cuban 1986). When combined, economic and technologically determinist discourses about computers within schools place both computers and schools within a framework where education serves the interests of the economy in two primary ways: as a producer of skilled workers, but also as a consumer of industrial manufactures. These discourses themselves and the actions authorised within them contribute to creating that world.

However, the promotion of the computer as an educational technology conflicts with another of the federal government's central preoccupations: how to control expenditure on education, a tension that is evident, in different ways, in the four policy documents examined. The recurrent theme which runs through the policies is that of the benefits of computing technologies for the national economy. This is entwined with the aim of achieving these benefits at the lowest possible cost to the federal government. While this is a reflection of contested federal-state relations, particularly over funding, central to it is a view of education as a consumer of resources. This orientation is evident from the first federal government report into the use of computers in education, the Wearing report of 1976, which suggests that of several possible policy alternatives, a preferred one 'should enable marketplace forces to operate on current activity to ensure eventual cost-beneficial applications at no extra cost to the Australian government' (57).

In 1983, in *Teaching, Learning and Computers*, the committee recognises with regret that funding allocated by the minister to the proposed National Computer Education Program is limited and will not 'enable all schools to make dramatic improvements in use of information and technology in general and computing in particular' (CSC. NACCS 1983, 34). In 1996, Tinkler et al. comment that 'the purchase of appropriate software, maintenance and upgrading of equipment has been given a low priority', although they note the role of the federal government in providing grants (Tinkler et al. 1996, 16). In 2000, the policy text recommends internet 'access at an affordable price' (DETYA 2000b, 10) and notes that quality online materials are 'expensive', justifying collaboration amongst states and territories as 'there are major savings to be made', an echo of *Teaching, Learning and Computers* in 1983 (CSC. NACCS 1983, 55). In *A Digital Education Revolution*, the provision of computers must 'maximise value for money' (Rudd, Smith and Conroy 2007, 9). The future of learning with computers that is extolled in the policies is not matched by the resources which would enable that future to be realised.

Conclusion

There are a number of themes that are common over time in the four policy documents: the commercialisation of new technologies attracting political interest and their use internationally; the significance of the electoral cycle; the privileging of economic values over others; the assertion of the link between computing technologies and the national interest; the view of the schooling sector in particular as providing a platform for the development of local industry; and the desire of federal governments over this period to achieve their aims at the same time as minimising expenditure.

There are also telling differences. In particular, in 1983, computers could still be considered peripheral in education despite rhetoric to the contrary. Computers were important in many workplaces but not yet pervasive. Governmental attention was focused on high unemployment, inflation and government debt. In the early 1990s, computers were more widely diffused through society, particularly in business. As new technologies were commercialised and exploited by large corporations, creating conflict with existing institutional regimes, the stakes for government, and the pressures for government to act to resolve such conflicts, became very high (Brock 2003). In the period between 1993 and 1996, the Keating Government grappled with this conflict. In *Education and Technology Convergence* in 1996, it is evident that fundamental questions were not yet resolved. While newly available, the institutions and regulatory architecture that would support the Internet and World Wide Web in their present form were not then in place. Indeed, the parameters of these institutions and architecture remained in doubt, the subject of much contestation, inquiry and lobbying. *Education and Technology Convergence* is a part of a governmental process of exploring options and considering the shape of potentially new practices at a time of change.

By 2000, when *Learning for the Knowledge Society* was released, the nature of that political interest had changed, as had that of the technology itself. Assisted in the first place by changes in regulation in the US, the home of the largest technology corporations, and supra-national organisations such as the OECD, a global institutional model was asserted, one which led to the dominance of the Internet and the World Wide Web (Galperin 2004b). This model was itself promoted heavily by the lobbying of these large technology companies and required deregulation of telecommunications monopolies where they existed, the establishment of property rights over digital data, and favourable pricing regimes (Brock 2003). The promotion of business interests was at the core of the Howard Government's values. The action plans instituted by the government, following *A Strategic Framework for the Information Economy* (Commonwealth of Australia 1998), including in education, are focused on creating the institutions and regulatory architecture which will most advantage business. This focus is apparent in 'Learning in an online world' which emphasises telecommunications regulations, costs and an appropriate legal framework, particularly in relation to copyright, as the primary tasks of the federal government in relation to technology use within the school sector.

By 2007, the advent of DSL broadband meant rapid adoption of the Internet by householders but particularly businesses and governments, for whom DSL was more attractive given the higher speeds when compared to dial-up services. Computers were used in nearly 90 per cent of businesses in Australia, with 77 per cent using the Internet (ABS 2007c). Governments and businesses used the technology of the Internet to communicate with the public, to deliver services, to gain new markets and to extend existing ones during a time of economic expansion. The economic benefits to Australia from this expansion meant that from opposition, a more significant role was envisioned for the federal government in the provision of computing technologies to all senior secondary school students. *A Digital Education Revolution*, announced during an election campaign, projected the computers it would provide as an educational benefit. The same computers would ensure additional customers for the NBN and continuing growth into the future of the 'digital economy' (BMI 2012). The new policy built on the decisions and regulatory framework established under the previous Howard Government and guaranteed a role for the federal government in the direction of the state and territory responsibility of education. A political document, *A Digital Education Revolution* served unaltered as the foundation for implementation following the ALP's election. The pledge to deliver computers was fulfilled even as the new computing technologies of tablets and smart phones were altering cost structures and offering new possibilities.

Over the same period of 24 years, the power of the educational community at large to project other meanings of computing technologies declined. The growth of political control over the institutional frameworks of policy development limited the access of those in the educational community so that only a small number of voices from the educational sector could be heard. These voices generally accorded with those of the government of the day. The voices of teachers, those who had to implement programs, those who were constantly exhorted to use computing technologies in their teaching, were not represented. More often than not, teachers in each of the policy texts were regarded as lacking essential knowledge and skills in computing technologies, as well as the will to use them. Principals, too, were depicted as having insufficient awareness of the benefits of computing technologies. Students, in each of the texts, were framed in contradictory ways, as natural partners of technologies, but also as captive and passive subjects of the educational process. The attention is always on the computer, and later, on computing technologies: powerful, magical, transformative. If only teachers would use them!

Chapter Eight

The Disappearing Computer

Over time, multiple strands of meaning have built up around the computer, beginning with its origins within the US military establishment which invested it with power and authority as it was developed and deployed by governments and businesses in that country and in others, including Australia. The foundational discourse which attached to the computer represented it through the ascription of the human faculties of intelligence and memory. Its enmeshment in workplace practices for automation and information processing purposes gave rise to new discourses which highlighted the tirelessness and comparative cheapness of the computer, conferring superiority on it over the humans it was employed to displace. When communications were enabled via the computer, new depictions portrayed it as the engine which would drive another industrial revolution along the superhighway of the Internet. Still later it was envisaged as the portal to a new world of interconnectivity between people dispersed around the globe. At each stage the embedding of the computer into new practices in government, institutions, businesses, workplaces, homes, amplified some meanings over others even as the influence of earlier ones persisted. Strands of these meanings and the roles imagined for computers in schools can be discerned in the competing discourses within the collection of texts examined in this book.

It was by no means inevitable that computers would be used in Australian schools. Indeed, computers were first promoted for educational use by the US federal government nearly 20 years before the Australian federal government took action and then in a different form: instituting a national computer education program. The first national policy vision, *Teaching, Learning and Computers* of 1983, established the foundations for the program and was pivotal to the casting of the computer as an essential educational technology for Australian schools. It marked the appearance of the federal government as a crucial actor. Since that moment in 1983, the federal government's promotion of the computer and its allocation of funds towards schools' computing initiatives have conferred authority on the technology.

At intervals over the following years, Australian federal government politicians and policymakers claimed that computers were an essential educational technology for secondary school students. In diverse policy texts, computer skills were depicted as vital to raise national economic competitiveness and to ensure young people's career prospects. Schools were envisaged as providing Australian businesses and governments with a substantial and unexploited base which could expand economic opportunities for both private and public benefit. Computer use at school was portrayed as enriching learning through motivating students and improving teachers' effectiveness. Computers, it was argued, would also transform the business of schooling, to make it more equitable, efficient and effective.

Such projections of a future world worked to mobilise support for government intervention to introduce and extend the use of computing technologies in schools. The basis of these projections shifted over time according to the state of the national economy. Perceptions of Australian decline provided impetus to government policymakers in 1983 and 1996. The computer, as a symbol of potential wealth, of scientific progress, of business success, and as a means of overcoming the barriers of time and distance, intersected with fears that Australia's international competitors would use computing technologies to gain competitive advantage. Anxiety over Australia's possible irrelevance in a new world was intensified by fears that the educational system was failing. Paradoxically, education was positioned as the answer to improving Australia's national performance, but only education of a particular kind – education with computers. Computers could thus be presented as the tool to reposition Australia in a globalising world in order to enhance national wealth and competitiveness.

In the more prosperous economic conditions which prevailed in 2000 and 2007, the computer project was reoriented to prioritise the development of skills perceived to be in demand in a tightening labour market and to effect reform of a schooling system which was deemed backward. In 2007, individual access to a computer was portrayed as the means to raise educational standards systemically and thereby catapult Australian students to the top of the league ladder of international educational performance, assuring them of success in the high-skill high-wage workforce. The claim that the computer was an instrument of power which would transform schooling remained the same in each of the policies, but the nature of the promised transformation shifted over time as new computing and communications technologies were diffused through the workplace.

The economic trajectory of educational computing

Faith in technology to effect educational change is a belief with a long lineage. Larry Cuban (1986) documented a cycle in the US in which new technological developments from radio and film to television have been appropriated by educational reformers and repurposed for schools in a bid to make education more productive. Each of these technologies in turn was lauded for its potential to transform education but taken together, they failed to live up to the visions outlined for them by their promoters. To policymakers in the US and later in Australia, computing technologies appeared to offer greater chances of success than the earlier technologies of radio, film and television. Technological advances in computing and communications and their applications in workplaces in ways which achieved greater efficiencies provided plausible grounds for policymakers to believe that the use of computing technologies could be similarly effective in education. The expanded range of uses for computing and communications technologies offered new opportunities for communication and interactivity as well as automation and information processing in a cycle of innovation which continues to gather speed.

As each technological development broke new ground, it was accompanied by the hyperbole which often attends the diffusion of new technologies, as was demonstrated with the personal computer in the early 1980s. Such public amplification of the potential of new technologies and fears in the electorate over their likely impact on society are important spurs which contribute to the momentum for the adoption of new technologies in schools (Cuban 1986). The most vivid example of such a phenomenon is the internet technology bubble of the late 1990s. Following the commercialisation of the Internet, new technology stocks soared in the US, accompanied by inflated claims which circulated globally through the media. Predictions that 'the Internet was the most revolutionary development since the electric dynamo, the printing press, or the wheel' became commonplace (Cassidy 2002, 1). At the same time, in both the US and in Australia, as in other countries, policymakers responded to change and to the perceptions of change, launching initiative after initiative directed at intensifying the use of computers for educational purposes.

Yet while significant, the advent of a new technology will not necessarily impel policymakers to promote its use in schools. In 1976, the suitability of the relatively new technology of the computer for school education was considered in the Wearing report but not endorsed by the committee. Nor is a new technology in itself a sufficient condition for policy to emerge. Policy which promotes computers for schools may be adopted for other reasons. In 2007, when the ALP under Kevin Rudd proposed to provide all senior secondary students with individual computers, these were scarcely new technologies. The advances in communications technologies represented by broadband which underlay the policy were not accompanied by the same fervour and public excitement of the earlier technology boom, despite the appeal of faster broadband communication for some sectors of the community.

Two other factors were decisive and worked in different ways to place the issue of schools computing on the political agenda of the day for Australian policymakers. One was the use of computing and communications technologies in school education internationally. The second was the perception of political and economic gains or losses which would accrue to Australian society and to particular political interests. Of the policies examined in this book, only two proposed significant funding for the provision of computers to schools, those of 1983 and 2007. That computers were promised for schools during election campaigns denotes the importance of political considerations. In 2007, the pledge of individual computers was a central policy pitch. But computers also featured in the economic calculations of policymakers. In 1983, schools were envisioned as providing a market for a local computing industry. In 1996, computers were projected as a means of earning export income through international education. In 2000, computers in schools would advance the nascent internet economy through opening a new market, that of schools, to private business. In 2007, the central concern was the development of workplace skills at a time of skills shortages. In each case, through the projections in these texts of future worlds dominated by technology and the actions authorised within them, policymakers contributed to shaping the future in ways that accorded with these visions (Fairclough 1992).

This is not to deny that there are benefits in using computing technologies educationally but, instead, to argue that the claims made for computers and the attributes ascribed to them are often generated from places other than schools. The visions of computing technologies in the service of education are more often animated by simplistic notions of the educational process. The discourses which contend within the policy texts from 1983 to 2007 reveal purposes imagined for the schools computing project which bore little relationship to the enhancement of teaching and learning. Over time, these federal government policies on computers in education mapped a trajectory for educational computing that valorised economic purposes over others. As political voices increasingly dominated policymaking, computers were recast as learning technologies, obscuring the essentially economic purposes which lay behind their promotion.

Government and policy

The policies considered here were influenced by, and are the product of, differing institutional frameworks for educational policy development in the federal sphere. Successive federal governments reconstructed administrative and advisory structures in education in order to achieve their priorities. These frameworks structured and authorised, or excluded, representation from a range of interests and perspectives. At the same time, these new structures were expressions of governmental priorities that shaped the nature of the problems to be considered and targeted action towards or away from particular sectors (Galperin 2004a). For instance, the creation of the Department of Employment, Education and Training in 1987 prioritised employment and positioned education as central to the development of workforce skills. In 2007, the creation of the Department of Education, Employment and Workplace Relations expressed the prioritisation of education, but within a framework which retained connections to the workplace. These linkages between education and employment also enabled the inclusion of particular interests, for instance, trade unions, within policy development.

Increasingly over time, the texts contain discourses which originate with the federal government, demonstrating its greater involvement in the state and territory responsibility of education and an increased desire to influence its direction. This desire took shape in frameworks, such as COAG and the successive ministerial councils, over which politicians, and particularly federal government politicians, asserted greater control. The exercise of federal power, while mediated by the states and territories, is sedimented into the language of the texts, a feature which is particularly evident from 2000 onwards. The targets for action identified in 'Learning in an online world' in 2000 recur again and again in successive texts produced by MCEETYA to guide the implementation of computing and communications technology plans in schools. The disruption of these terms and their replacement by new terms following the election of the Rudd ALP Government in 2007 can be traced across a number of texts (eg, AICTEC 2008).

The texts also display changing structures within the Australian economy and reference the governmental actions which brought these about while at the same time obscuring the government's role in altering the rules which permit both public and private profit. The juxtaposition of the transformative discourse of the powerful computer with the economic discourse of deregulation, evident in the texts from 1996, suggests that these actions have been instituted by the technologies themselves rather than government (Sussman 1997). Broader governmental actions that attempt to manage change in an ever more complex and diverse nation, at both the macro and the micro level are visible in the intersecting discourses of technology, communications and regulatory reform. First evident in 1996, these are particularly striking in the policy of 2000 and evoke the complexities of deregulation and privatisation through which successive governments have altered regulatory frameworks. The struggles of policymakers in an uncertain environment are made visible but the questions as to who profits, by how much, and who loses when the ground rules are altered, are not posed. An important objective of each of the policies is that the education sector, particularly the large school sector, acts as a support to Australian businesses to develop new industries or to expand existing ones. However, there is a significant silence in all the texts on the profits which will accrue to businesses as a result of policy changes. That commercial relationships existed is apparent in the first three policies but elided. In the fourth, where these relationships had not yet been brought into being, the necessity to do so is glossed.

These policies were issued at times of differing economic conditions and political realities: at times of economic weakness, as in 1983 and 1996; at a time of challenge, as in 2000; during an election campaign in an economically robust period in 2007. That the timing of the electoral cycle is significant is shown in the close coupling of 'computers and broadband' in *A Digital Education Revolution* and its references to productivity which tie this text to others produced for campaigning purposes. The nature of the problem which each policy was designed to address was different. In 1983, the social impact of computers was posed as the problem. In 1996, the problem was considered to be the lack of competitiveness that resulted from insufficient use of computers in the Australian education system as a whole. In 2000, the coordination of government activities to achieve greater use of computers in education is the focus of problem solving. In 2007, the problem was conceived as inadequate access to computers and high-speed broadband which hindered the development of future workplace skills. In each case, the computer is presented as the solution, although the purposes depicted for its use vary. In 1983, the projected purpose for the educational use of computers was the acculturation of students. In 1996, the purpose was to extend students' skills in order to enhance Australia's economic competitiveness. In 2000, computers would permit the delivery of online curricula to students, thereby creating a market for content. In 2007, computers would deliver the skills and knowledge to school students that would enable them to compete globally for the secure well-paid jobs of the future.

Discourses which dominate government policies have impact. They are adopted and recirculated in text after text, embedded in the language of curricula, funding applications and more recently, standards and assessment protocols at the national level, thus exerting influence over education (Lankshear et al. 2000). Whose discourses dominate is therefore crucial in determining the values and beliefs which are given expression in the directions mapped for education. These texts show that over this period, in respect of computing and communications technologies, educational discourses have diminished. This is evidence of declining representation at a formal level from those involved in the daily delivery of education at the classroom level. While institutional frameworks had a decisive impact on the policy texts that resulted and how policy was implemented, they also demonstrate the capacity of politicians to remake these structures in order to achieve their aims. Increasingly, educational voices are subservient to political ones.

A modernisation project

The discourses that tie together the computer and education do not emanate from a vacuum, but from the broader social, political and economic context within which they are formed (Apple 1993) and which political voices both reflect and shape. Federal government control over the content of educational policies has increased and reoriented education to economic purposes. The four policy texts have been dominated by variants of an economic discourse which has shifted over time according to the economic values and priorities of the government of the day. In 1983, an older economic discourse prioritised the national interest. The texts of 1996 and 2000 are pervaded by economic rationalism. In 2007, human capital discourse is most prominent. While the dominance of these economic discourses in *A Digital Education Revolution* has received considerable attention (eg, Moyle 2010; Murphy 2011), their constancy in policies which advocate computers in schools demonstrates that economic values have been fundamental to the advocacy of computers by the federal government since that first policy in 1983. These economic discourses are built on the technologically determinist belief that computing technologies, rather than people, are changing the world.

Importantly, each of the policy texts focused on computing technologies rather than on education. The computer was framed as an object which could be inserted into an existing system, but it was represented as a particular kind of object, one which was the apogee of a modern, sophisticated and scientifically based society. The framing of the computer as a modern technology ironically draws on discourses that have surrounded the computer from its beginnings and which position it as an agent transforming societies, a protean device, with powers that transcend those of people. This framing demonstrates a central concern of Australian policymakers across this span of years. The computer was a symbol of a developed, wealthy nation, bringing into sharp focus Australia's continuing anxiety over its status as a developed economy. For policymakers, the contrast was with the imagined other, the third world country that Australia might become, were it not to keep up with other countries which used computers throughout society. Allied to the national interest, the computer had the potential to transform industries, education and the nation's economic performance.

Powerful discourses connect the computer to education, but they have different origins and are associated with different value systems that reveal ideological underpinnings: those of technological determinism, globalisation, the knowledge economy and information society, human capital, and in 1983, a social democratic discourse. The depiction of the computer within these discourses between the policies of 1983 and 2007 reveals not just changing technologies but a shifting sense of Australia's position in the world economy. Australian anxiety over its place in that world was forcibly expressed in 1983. The government project to restructure the Australian economy and therefore, society, was begun by the Hawke–Keating ALP Government and its echoes are found in the policy of 1996. The Howard Coalition Government continued this project and further oriented it to the neoliberal Information Revolution Agenda (Galperin 2004b). In 2007, the term 'world class education' expresses a more ambitious aspiration, that Australia should aim to be amongst the top countries in a globally competitive world, a signal of greater economic prosperity than in earlier times (Rudd, Smith and Conroy 2007). Across these differing times and conditions, the computer as a symbol of progress, of modernisation, of Australia's enmeshment in a globalising world, of capital expenditure, is ready-made to persuade the electorate of the government's political commitment to education: an education of the individual for a market society. By 2007, this adjustment seems complete.

Central to the construction of the computer as the emblem of modernity is the depiction of school education as unchanged and unchanging: computers are conceived as the epitome of the modern and schools as bastions of backwardness. The government venture to introduce and extend computer use in schools is a modernisation project which aims to produce economic benefit for the nation as a whole. Julia Gillard, then Prime Minister, described it as such in 2012 when she referred to her role in the 'big modernisations: computers in school, Building the Education Revolution, national curriculum' (House of Representatives 2012, 13640). That the link between computers and education often occurred at times of technological change and economic uncertainty is suggestive of an instrumental outlook on the place of computing in education that is fundamentally driven by the desire to instil vocational skills in Australian school students and to allow the school system to provide a supportive base for Australian business. Increasingly, policymakers have come to view education as the servant of the economy.

Other ways of conceptualising education existed, as they do today. An important purpose of education was the social justice agenda in the 1970s and into the early 1980s, traces of which were still evident in *Teaching, Learning and Computers* of 1983. However imperfectly in this text, education was viewed as playing a part in improving the plight of the disadvantaged. Government action was deemed vital to redress disadvantage. The struggles evident in *Teaching, Learning and Computers* to ensure that the disadvantaged in society, broadly defined, are given particular consideration, are less evident later. In the policy of 1996, attention is directed to those lacking in information, the 'information poor' (Tinkler et al. 1996, 126). In 2000, they are redefined as Australians in rural and remote areas and Indigenous Australians. In 2007, contrary to the later translation of the policy when in office, the disadvantaged were invisible.

In 1996, 2000 and particularly in 2007, there is a much greater emphasis on the vocational aspects of educational computing. Through using computers in schools, students will be equipped for the workforce, responsible for their own careers and retraining, flexible and adaptable in the face of job loss, and better able to manage change as well as to compete with other individuals from abroad for well-paid jobs. Governments will provide the tools, such as computers and access to broadband and telecommunications. It becomes the role of the school and the family to determine how students should best take advantage of what is on offer. The role of government is limited to setting the stage, rather than ameliorating social inequalities which stem from structural elements within society. Instead, social inequalities are renamed as failures, of teachers, of students, of schools.

As the texts show, beliefs amongst policymakers, particularly politicians, rest on an assumption that the use of computers in schools will improve teachers' effectiveness and productivity and develop vocational skills in students which will lead to their employment. This is no small matter. The projection of the computer as the architect of change has led to the expenditure of billions of dollars to equip schools with technologies intended to bring about improved outcomes for students. Yet the underlying assumption of the powerful computer and its ability to engender change betrays a misunderstanding of education which privileges only one purpose of education: the vocational. Other purposes of education and other means by which change may have been achieved have been foreclosed.

New purposes for computers in schools

Change as it is envisioned in the policy texts is projected as a smooth transition to a new world, even though the projections themselves have resulted from struggle, negotiation and resistance (Cormack 2003). Traces of those struggles remain in the texts themselves, revealing differing visions of future worlds, silencing yet others. The world of my classroom was not one I found in the policy texts. The voices of the teachers, of the students, who every day were to use computers in their work, are not represented. Professional expertise is routinely denied and teachers are denigrated as obstacles, reluctant to change. Policymakers' views of what that change should entail and how quickly it should proceed underestimate the complexity of the schooling environment and the multiplicity of tasks which face teachers in their everyday working lives in schools.

For teachers, the imperatives of daily classroom instruction interact each day with curricular regimes, differing institutional settings and boundaries, professional norms, parental expectations and diverse student populations, all built on long-standing procedures and practices (Cuban 1986). The translation of governmental visions for educational computing to the more pragmatic space of the classroom is inevitably protracted. Nor is it linear. Contrary to the representations made of schools by politicians who tend to portray schools as unchanging backwaters, change is proceeding within schools although it may not accord with the imagined worlds depicted by policymakers. In 1983, scarcely any schools possessed computers for student use. In 2011, computers were commonplace. Indeed, students' use of computers in schools had increased since 2005 (ACARA 2012). Teachers and school systems change slowly over time, yet change they do (Cuban 1986).

Many teachers use computing technologies in their teaching, in their professional activities outside the classroom and in their lives outside the school. The same technologies promoted by policymakers for student learning contribute also to the possibilities for teachers to redefine their use in education. Teachers share their ideas and professional expertise in online communities, blogs and forums. They undertake professional development online and stimulate their students' interest in the use of new technological applications in their learning. They adopt and repurpose existing technologies for classroom use in a way that is consistent with their educational values. They generate new visions of what can be achieved with computers and how computers can be incorporated into educational practice.

This circulation of ideas within the profession, the resistance to instrumental views and the generation of new discourses is important, but it is not sufficient. Teachers' voices are not heard in the policy debate. While there may be influential informal conduits between teachers and policymakers, these are invisible. The lack of prominence of educational discourses within the policy texts examined suggests that teachers lack institutional power, which is vital to enable other views of education and its purposes to be represented in policy visions. Promoting their discourses of education, and the place of the computer within them, is a task for the profession, one which is growing in urgency.

The continuing production of policies to advance the adoption of computing technologies in schools, particularly evident in *A Digital Education Revolution* of 2007, is evidence that the transformation of schooling which computers were intended to effect has not yet occurred. Policymakers across the texts have shown continuing concern with outcomes from schooling that continue to be differentiated according to student background and location. The texts show that they believed that placing computers in schools would work to achieve more equitable outcomes. To date, expressions of disappointment from policymakers in diverse locations have become more common (Bakia et al. 2011). As earlier investigations suggested, more recent data confirm that there are significant differences in computing between school populations and that these are correlated with socioeconomic status, Indigeneity and location (ACARA 2012). Rather than question the assumption that computing technologies would effect better teaching and learning, politicians in particular point the finger at those within the educational system who present resistance.

This political frustration with the apparent failure of computers to effect the required change in education is beginning to take shape. An emerging discourse within the federal government sphere in 2012 and 2013 is that of school improvement which builds on assessment data from national testing via the NAPLAN and draws its inspiration in part from the US. The expressed intention of the federal government is to use the computing technologies now in schools to conduct online assessments which will 'benchmark students… across the country and internationally, to make sure we're not falling behind' (Treasury 2013, 10). The commitment to deliver NAPLAN testing online was maintained by the Coalition parties in the lead up to the September 2013 election (LNP 2013). In the weeks after the election, Minister for Education Christopher Pyne hoped that the move to online delivery could take place as soon as was practicable. The only difficulty he foresaw was 'trying to get the states and territories to agree that they have the hardware necessary' (*Sydney Morning Herald* 2013), a view at once simplistic and dismissive.

Ironically, the technologies promoted as enhancing student learning will be used in the future to collect data for monitoring and accountability purposes on individual schools and their performance relative to others, presenting new challenges to school communities: students, teachers, leaders and parents. In a standards-based environment, data may be used to stigmatise these disparities as failures of teachers, of schools and most importantly, of students, rather than as a reflection of societal inequities. The potential for teachers and schools to be caught in the crossfire is high. For individual students, particularly the most disadvantaged, at a time of increasing political focus on schooling and when life chances are more critically impacted than ever by educational achievement or failure, the voices of educators are vital. They can draw attention to the social inequities which condition and contribute to academic success or failure and the way existing constructions of the computer may well have served to entrench more deeply existing disadvantage.

Time to seize the moment

The specific moments that the texts open to view paint a portrait of a changing world. In 1982, only 30 per cent of students in government schools undertook Year 12 (Productivity Commission 1995). By 2007, more than 70 per cent did so (ABS 2013). In 1983, few schools possessed even one computer for student use. In 2007, computers were commonplace in the majority of schools. In 1983, policymakers believed that government action to institute a computer education program was justified and could be accepted as legitimate on a number of grounds. In 2007, such intervention could only be justified on an economic basis. In 1983, following recession, policymakers expressed anxiety over Australia's apparent decline compared to other countries. In 2007, the ambition was to be amongst the global leaders from a position which was already close to it. The considerable changes in computing and communications technologies are also showcased, from the stand-alone personal computer of 1983 to the multiple devices and the broadband infrastructure of 2007. Yet views of education remain remarkably static.

Trajectories of use were mapped for technologies while they were evolving and visions were constructed which placed these technologies as central within classrooms despite their fluidity. The advent of new devices, such as smart phones and tablets, and new ways of interacting through these again reprise the cycle of technological development, workplace use and public concern, leading to calls for their use in education for a range of purposes and from different interests. Yet as of writing, political interest in computers in schools, which is vital to the production of policy, has once more waned at the federal level. With new fiscal constraints and in an environment where the Abbott Coalition Government has signalled a retreat from funding new educational programs, it is unlikely that further policies to implement new programs for schools computing will be introduced unless they are associated with the collection of school data. This very haphazardness of federal government attention to computing technologies in schools over 24 years and its withdrawal once again in 2012 opens a space in which the instrumental meanings applied to computing technologies by policymakers can be contested and reimagined by those with professional expertise.

As the process of implementation of the Digital Education Revolution program demonstrated, the fashioning of meanings for computing technologies and their uses in schools is refracted through many steps. Meanings can be expanded or circumscribed in this process. The sense of mastery over the computer which was palpable in *A Digital Education Revolution* in 2007 must be challenged. Reconsideration of the computer in its polymorphous forms is now urgent. The computer itself is disappearing, but the discourses in which it has been enmeshed will remain potent, transferring to other devices and technologies. In time, the computer may be an almost forgotten artefact, overtaken by the newer devices of tablets and smart phones, and others not yet on the market. This moment of disjuncture must be seized. Smaller and cheaper devices are more flexible for many classroom uses and offer new opportunities for teachers and students to experiment and to fashion new meanings. They can create new uses which suit their students, their purposes, in ways that expand, rather than diminish, educational opportunities for all. Together, teachers and students can dislodge policy projections of the computer as central to teaching and learning and instead craft new discourses which position the relationship between teachers and students, however enabled, as at the core of school education.

References

ABC (Australian Broadcasting Commission). 2007. 'ALP Education Revolution in the spotlight'. *7.30 Report*. Accessed 22 May 2013. Available from: http://www.abc.net. au/7.30/content/2007/s2109329.htm.

ABC (Australian Broadcasting Commission). 2008. 'Costa "demands an extra $245m" for school computers'. Accessed 22 May 2013. Available from: http://www.abc.net.au/ news/2008-06-29/costa-demands-an-extra-245m-for-school-computers/2488254.

ABC (Australian Broadcasting Commission). 2013. *Capital Hill*. Friday 19 April.

ABS (Australian Bureau of Statistics). 1994a. *Business Use of Information Technology*. ABS Catalogue no. 8129.0. Canberra: ABS.

ABS (Australian Bureau of Statistics). 1994b. *Household Use of Information Technology*. ABS Catalogue no. 8128.0. Canberra: ABS.

ABS (Australian Bureau of Statistics). 1997a. *Business Use of Information Technology*. ABS Catalogue no. 8129.0. Canberra: ABS.

ABS (Australian Bureau of Statistics). 1997b. *Take-up Rate for Modem and Internet Use Low. Household Use of Information Technology, Australia, 1996*. Media Release. ABS Catalogue no. 8146.0. Canberra: ABS.

ABS (Australian Bureau of Statistics). 1999a. *Business Use of Information Technology, Preliminary, 1997–1998*. ABS Catalogue no. 8133.0. Canberra: ABS.

ABS (Australian Bureau of Statistics). 1999b. *Commercial Business Use of Internet Technology Low. Business Use of Information Technology, 1997–1998*. Media Release. ABS Catalogue no. 8129.0. Canberra: ABS.

ABS (Australian Bureau of Statistics). 2000a. *Increasing Use of the Internet and Home Computers. Use of the Internet by Householders*. Media Release. ABS Catalogue no. 8147.0. Canberra: ABS.

ABS (Australian Bureau of Statistics). 2000b. *New ABS Data Says Business Use of Information Technology Growing Rapidly. Business Use of Information Technology, 1999–2000*. Media Release. ABS Catalogue no. 8129.0. Canberra: ABS.

ABS (Australian Bureau of Statistics). 2003. *Household Use of Information Technology, Australia, 2001–2002*. ABS Catalogue no. 8146.0. Canberra: ABS.

ABS (Australian Bureau of Statistics). 2006. *Business Use of Information Technology, 2005–2006*. ABS Catalogue no. 8129.0. Canberra: ABS.

ABS (Australian Bureau of Statistics). 2007a. *Business Use of Information Technology, Australia, 2005–2006*. ABS Catalogue no. 8129.0. Canberra: ABS.

ABS (Australian Bureau of Statistics). 2007b. *Household Use of Information Technology, Australia, 2006–2007*. ABS Catalogue no. 8146.0. Canberra: ABS.

ABS (Australian Bureau of Statistics). 2007c. *Yearbook Australia 2007*. Canberra: ABS.

ABS (Australian Bureau of Statistics). 2011a. *Australian Social Trends June 2011. Online @ Home*. ABS Catalogue no. 4102.0. Canberra: ABS.

ABS (Australian Bureau of Statistics). 2011b. *Business Use of Information Technology, 2009–2010*. ABS Catalogue no. 8129.0. Canberra: ABS.

ABS (Australian Bureau of Statistics). 2013. *Internet Activity, Australia, June 2013*. ABS Catalogue no. 8153.0. Canberra: ABS.

ACARA (Australian Curriculum, Assessment and Reporting Authority). 2011. *National Report on Schooling in Australia 2011*. Sydney: ACARA. Accessed 15 November 2013. Available from: http://www.acara.edu.au/reporting/national_report_on_schooling_ 2011/national_report_on_schooling_2_1.

ACARA (Australian Curriculum, Assessment and Reporting Authority). 2012. *National Assessment Program – ICT Literacy Years 6 and 10 Report 2011*. Sydney: ACARA. Accessed 15 November 2013. Available from: http://www.nap.edu.au/verve/_ resources/NAP_ICTL_2011_Public_Report_Final.pdf.

ACMA (Australian Communications and Media Authority). 2013. *Like, Post, Share: Young Australians' Experience of Social Media*. Melbourne: ACMA. Accessed 4 November 2013. Available from: http://www.acma.gov.au/theACMA/Library/ researchacma/Digital-society-research/young-australians-and-social-media.

AICTEC (Australian Information and Communications Technology in Education Committee). 2006. *Broadband Connect and Clever Networks: Supporting Investment in Sustainable Broadband Infrastructure*. Accessed 15 April 2008. Available from: http://www.aictec.edu.au/aictec/go/home/about/pid/95.

AICTEC (Australian Information and Communications Technology in Education Committee). 2008. *Success through Partnership. Achieving a National Vision for ICT in Schools. Strategic Plan to Guide the Implementation of the Digital Education Revolution Initiative and Related Initiatives*. Canberra: DEEWR. Accessed 30 November 2013. Available from: http://aictec.edu.au/priorities/digital-education-revolution-der/der-strategic-plan-and-implementation-roadmap-advice/.

AICTEC (Australian Information and Communications Technology in Education Committee). 2009. *Digital Education Revolution Implementation Roadmap*. Canberra: DEEWR. Accessed 30 November 2013. Available from: http://aictec. edu.au/wp-content/uploads/AICTEC-DER-Roadmap-Advice.pdf.

Allard, K. 2008. 'The new investment cycle in Internet commerce: Web 2.0 goes mainstream'. *Information Today* 25 (4): 20.

Alston, R. 1999. 'Australia – the information economy'. *Business/Higher Education Round Table* 5: 1–2.

Anderson, G. 2010. 'Whither the Federation? Federalism under Rudd'. *Public Policy* 5 (1): 1–22.

Anderson, R; Klassen, D; Johnson, D. 1981. 'In defense of a comprehensive view of computer literacy – a reply to Luehrmann'. *The Mathematics Teacher* 74: 687–690.

Apple, M. 1993. 'Thinking "right" in the USA: Ideological transformations in an age of conservatism'. In *Schooling Reform in Hard Times*, edited by Lingard, B; Knight, J; Porter, P. London: The Falmer Press: 49–62.

Arnold, M; Gilding, A. 1994. 'Schools, laptop computers and post-fordism'. *Discourse* 15 (2): 34–47.

Aspray, W. 1991. *An Interview with Andrew Molnar*. Minneapolis: Charles Babbage Institute, Center for the History of Information Processing, University of Minnesota. Accessed 19 October 2005. Available from: http://www.cbi.umn.edu/ oh/display.phtml?id=151.

ASX (Australian Stock Exchange). 2013. *Historical Market Statistics*. Webpage. Accessed 15 November 2013. Available from: http://www.asx.com.au/about/historical-market-statistics.htm#End_of_month_values.

Auditor-General. 2011. *Digital Education Revolution Program – National Secondary Schools Computer Fund. Department of Education, Employment and Workplace Relations. Audit Report No. 30 2010–2011. Performance Audit*. Canberra: Australian National Audit Office.

Aulich, C; O'Flynn, J. 2007. 'John Howard: The great privatiser?' *Australian Journal of Political Science* 42 (2): 365–381.

Baker, F. 1971. 'Computer-based instructional management systems: A first look'. *Review of Educational Research* 41 (1): 51–70.

Baker, J. 1978. 'Corporate involvement in CAI'. *Educational Technology* April 1978: 12–16.

Baker, R. 2000. 'Mighty erudite'. *Sydney Morning Herald.* Accessed 12 May 2013.
Available from: http://newsstore.fairfax.com.au/apps/viewDocument.ac?page=1
&sy=nstore&kw=online+and+education&pb=sag&pb=age&pb=smh&dt=enter
Range&dr=1month&sd=01%2F01%2F2000&ed=31%2F12%2F2000&so=relev
ance&sf=text&sf=headline&rc=100&rm=200&sp=adv&clsPage=1&docID=ne
ws000315_0089_6074.

Bakia, M; Murphy, R; Anderson, K; Trinidad, G. 2011. *International Experiences with
Technology in Education: Final Report.* Washington DC: US Department of
Education. Accessed 15 November 2013. Available from: http://www.unesco.org/
new/en/unesco/themes/icts/single-view/news/international_experiences_with_
technology_in_education/#.Uqk8-9IW18E.

Baldwin, P. 1990. *A Clever Country? Australian Education and Training in Perspective.*
NBEET, Conference Proceedings, 1–3 November, Coffs Harbour: 24–30. Accessed
8 April 2008. Available from: http://www.dest.gov.au/sectors/training_skills/
publications_resources/indexes.

Ball, S. 1997. *Education Reform.* Buckingham: Open University Press.

Beale, D. 2009. 'The construction of educational computing: The computer in Australian
government policy texts 1983–2000'. Unpublished PhD thesis. Melbourne: Monash
University.

Beare, H. 1982. 'Education's corporate image'. *Unicorn* 8 (1): 12–28.

Becker, H. 1984. 'Computers in schools today: Some basic considerations'. *American
Journal of Education* 93 (1): 22–39.

Bell, L; Stevenson, H. 2006. *Education Policy: Process, Themes and Impact.* London:
Routledge.

Berkeley, E. 1949. *Giant Brains; or, Machines That Think.* New York: Wiley.

Berkman. 2010. *Next Generation Connectivity: A Review of Broadband Internet Transitions
and Policy from around the World.* Cambridge Mass: The Berkman Center for
Internet and Society at Harvard University. Accessed 5 May 2013. Available from:
http://cyber.law.harvard.edu/sites/cyber.law.harvard.edu/files/Berkman_Center_
Broadband_Final_Report_15Feb2010.pdf.

Bigum, C. 1987. 'Architects or bees? Understanding the new technologies'. In *Coming
to Terms with Computers in Schools,* edited by Bigum, C; Bonser, S; Evans, P;
Groundwater-Smith, S; Grundy, S; Kemmis, S; McKenzie, D; McKinnon, D;
O'Connor, M; Straton, R; Willis, S. Geelong Vic: Deakin Institute for Studies in
Education: 9–26.

Bigum, C. 1992. 'Computing schools from the "clever country": The prospects for virtual
schooling'. In *Computing the Clever Country?* ACEC 92 Proceedings, Tenth Annual
Australian Computing in Education Conference, 5–8 July, Melbourne. Richmond
North Vic: Computing in Education Group of Victoria: 59–64.

Bigum, C. 1997. 'Teachers and computers: In control or being controlled?' *Australian
Journal of Education* 41 (3): 247–261.

Bigum, C. 2002. 'Design sensibilities, schools and the new computing and
communication technologies'. In *Silicon Literacies: Communication, Innovation and
Education in the Electronic Age,* edited by Snyder, I. London: Routledge: 130–140.

Bigum, C; Green, B. 1993. 'Technologizing literacy: Or, interrupting the dream of
reason'. In *Literacy in Contexts: Australian Perspectives and Issues,* edited by Luke. A;
Gilbert, P. St Leonards NSW: Allen and Unwin: 4–27.

Birman, B; Ginsburg, A. 1983. 'A federal role for computers in the schools'. *Theory into
Practice* 22 (4): 281–290.

Blackmore, J. 2000. 'Warning signals or dangerous opportunities? Globalization, gender and educational policy shifts'. *Educational Theory* 50: 467–486.

BMI (Business Monitor International). 2012. *Australia Information Technology Report Q3 2012*. London: Business Monitor International.

BMI (Business Monitor International). 2013a. *Australia Information Technology Report Q2 2013*. London: Business Monitor International.

BMI (Business Monitor International). 2013b. *United States Information Technology Report Q3 2013*. London: Business Monitor International.

Boslaugh, D. 1999. *When Computers Went to Sea: The Digitization of the US Navy*. Los Alamitos Calif: IEEE Computer Society.

Braue, D. 2011. 'Rudd giveaway gripes: Students slam "slow" laptops'. *Age*. Accessed 4 April 2013. Available from: http://www.theage.com.au/digital-life/computers/rudd-giveaway-gripes-students-slam-slow-laptops-20110812-1iq3w.html#ixzz26bKjeefp.

Brock, G. 2003. *The Second Information Revolution*. Cambridge Mass: Harvard University Press.

Bryan, D. 1991. 'Australian economic nationalism: Old and new'. *Australian Economic Papers* 30 (57): 290–309.

Bulletin. 1983a. 'Hewlett-Packard on personal computing'. March 1, n.p.

Bulletin. 1983b. 'Just when the others think they've caught up, Wang goes ahead and develops The Professional Computer'. March 22, n.p.

Bulletin. 1983c. 'Personally... it has to be NEC'. January 18, n.p.

Bulletin. 1983d. 'There's no telling how far you can go with Toshiba's T100'. March 1, n.p.

Burt, E. 1982. 'Computer education in Victorian state secondary schools: Analysis and interpretation of the 1981 secondary computer education committee survey'. Unpublished Master of Educational Studies project. Melbourne: Monash University.

Butler, S. ed. 2013. *Macquarie Dictionary*. Sixth edition. Sydney: Macquarie Dictionary Publishers.

Campbell-Kelly, M; Aspray, W. 1996. *Computer. A History of the Information Machine*. New York: Basic Books.

Candy, P, chair. 1994. *Developing Lifelong Learning through Undergraduate Education*. Commissioned Report No. 28. Canberra: AGPS.

Capling, A; Considine, M; Crozier, M. 1998. *Australian Politics in the Global Era*. South Melbourne: Longman Australia.

Cassidy, J. 2002. *Dot.con. The Greatest Story Ever Sold*. New York: Harper Collins Publishers.

Castells, M. 2000. *The Rise of the Network Society*. Second edition. Oxford: Blackwell.

CBMS (Conference Board of the Mathematical Sciences). 1972. *Recommendations Regarding Computers in High School Education*. ERIC Document ED064136.

Ceruzzi, P. 2003. *A History of Modern Computing*. Second edition. Cambridge Mass: The MIT Press.

Chaney, M. 2007. *Growing Social Prosperity in a Growth Economy*. Speech. Sydney: Business Council of Australia. Accessed 9 July 2013. Available from: http://www.bca.com.au/Content.aspx? ContentID=101212.

COAG (Council of Australian Governments). 2007. *Communique. 20 December 2007*. Canberra: Commonwealth of Australia. Accessed 15 May 2013. Available from: http://www.coag.gov.au.

COAG (Council of Australian Governments). 2008a. *Communique. 3 July 2008*. Canberra: Commonwealth of Australia. Accessed 15 May 2013. Available from: http://www.coag.gov.au.

COAG (Council of Australian Governments). 2008b. *Communique. 29 November 2008*. Canberra: Commonwealth of Australia. Accessed 15 May 2013. Available from: http://www.coag.gov.au.

COAG (Council of Australian Governments). 2009. *Communique. 5 February 2009*. Canberra: Commonwealth of Australia. Accessed 15 May 2013. Available from: http://www.coag.gov.au.

Commonwealth of Australia. 1997. *Investing for Growth. The Howard Government's Plan for Australian Industry*. Canberra: Commonwealth of Australia. Accessed 14 April 2008. Available from: http://backingaus.innovation.gov.au/docs/statement/invest_growth.pdf.

Commonwealth of Australia. 1998. *A Strategic Framework for the Information Economy*. Canberra: AGPS.

Commonwealth of Australia. 2001. *Backing Australia's Ability – An Innovation Action Plan for the Future*. Canberra: Commonwealth of Australia. Accessed 15 June 2009. Available from: http://www.dest.gov.au/sectors/science_innovation/publications_resources/profiles/backing_australias_ability_innovation_action_plan.htm.

Commonwealth of Australia. 2003. *Australia's Broadband Connectivity. The Broadband Advisory Group's Report to Government*. Canberra: Commonwealth of Australia. Accessed 15 April 2008. Available from: http://www.dbcde.gov.au/__data/assets/pdf_file/0003/21288/BAG_report.pdf.

Commonwealth of Australia. Commonwealth Numbered Acts. 1983. *States Grants (Education Assistance – Participation and Equity) Act*. Canberra: Commonwealth of Australia. Accessed 9 May 2009. Available from: http://www.austlii.edu.au/au/legis/cth/num_act.

Commonwealth of Australia. Commonwealth Numbered Acts. 1996. *States Grants (Primary and Secondary Education Assistance) Act No 70 – Section 12*. Canberra: Commonwealth of Australia. Accessed 12 April 2008. Available from: http://www.austlii.edu.au/au/legis/cth/num_act.

Commonwealth of Australia. Commonwealth Numbered Acts. 2000. *States Grants (Primary and Secondary Education Assistance) Act No 70 – Section 12*. Canberra: Commonwealth of Australia. Accessed 12 April 2008. Available from: http://www.austlii.edu.au/au/legis/cth/num_act.

Cormack, P. 2003. *Adolescence, Schooling and English/Literacy: Formation of a Problem in Early Twentieth Century South Australia*. PhD thesis, University of South Australia. Accessed 30 May 2009. Available from: http://www.unisa.edu.au/hawkeinstitute/cslplc/publications/default.asp#Cormack.

CSC (Commonwealth Schools Commission). 1981. *Report for the Triennium 1982–84*. Canberra: Commonwealth Schools Commission.

CSC (Commonwealth Schools Commission). 1982. *Recommendations for 1983*. Canberra: Commonwealth Schools Commission.

CSC (Commonwealth Schools Commission). 1983. *Recommendations for 1984*. Canberra: Commonwealth Schools Commission.

CSC. NACCS (Commonwealth Schools Commission. National Advisory Committee on Computers in Schools). 1983. *Teaching, Learning and Computers*. Report of the National Advisory Committee on Computers in Schools. Canberra: Commonwealth Schools Commission.

CSIRO (Commonwealth Scientific and Industrial Research Organisation). 2011. *CSIRAC: Australia's First Computer*. Webpage. Accessed 4 September 2013. Available from: http://www.csiro.au/Outcomes/ICT-and-Services/National-Challenges/CSIRAC.aspx.

CSTB (Computer Science and Telecommunications Board). 1999. *Funding a Revolution: Government Support for Computing Research*. Committee on Innovations in Computing and Communications: Lessons from History. Washington DC: National Research Council, National Academy Press. Accessed 24 March 2009. Available from: http://books.nap.edu/openbook.php?record_ict-6323&page=R1.

Cuban, L. 1986. *Teachers and Machines. The Classroom Use of Technology Since 1920*. New York: Teachers College Press.

Culp, K; Honey, M; Mandinach, E. 2005. 'A retrospective on twenty years of education technology policy'. *Journal of Educational Computing Research* 32 (3): 279–307.

Curriculum Corporation. 1999. *Strategy for Generating On Line Curriculum Content for Australian Schools*. Accessed 12 April 2008. Available from: http://www.thelearningfederation.edu.au/tlfz/sitefiles/assets/docs/brochures_reports/research/strategy_generating.pdf.

Davis, M. 2007. 'Rudd vows tax break to step up education'. *Sydney Morning Herald*. Accessed 5 May 2013. Available from: http://newstore.fairfax.com.au/apps/viewDocument.ac?page=1&sy=nstore&kw=Rudd+&pb=age&pb=smh&dt=enterRange&dr=1month&sd=01%2F09%2F2007&ed=01%2F11%2F2007&so=relevance&sf=text&sf=headline&rc=100&rm=200&sp=adv&clsPage=1&docID=SMH071020FK57M7ST69U.

Dawkins, J. 1988. *Strengthening Australia's Schools: A Consideration of the Focus and Content of Schooling*. Canberra: AGPS.

Dawkins, J. 1990. 'Keynote address'. *A Clever Country? Australian Education and Training in Perspective*. NBEET, Conference Proceedings, 1–3 November, Coffs Harbour: 5–23. Accessed 8 April 2008. Available from: http://www.dest.gov.au/sectors/training_skills/publications_resources/indexes.

Dedrick, J; Kraemer, K. 1993. *Caught in the Middle: Australia's Information Technology Policy*. Center for Research on Information Technology and Organizations (CRITO). California: University of California, Irvine. Accessed 22 November 2003. Available from: http://www.crito.uci.edu/git/publications/pdf/pac-004.pdf.

DEECD (Department of Education and Early Childhood Development). 2009. *Digital Education Revolution. Implementation Plan*. Melbourne: DEECD. Accessed 14 May 2013. Available from: http://www.federalfinancialrelations.gov.au/content/npa/education/digital_education_revolution/VIC_IP.pdf.

DEET (Department of Employment, Education and Training). 1988. *Annual Report 1987–1988*. Canberra: AGPS. Accessed 15 April 2008. Available from: http://www.dest.gov.au.

DEEWR (Department of Education, Employment and Workplace Relations). 2008a. *Annual Report*. Canberra: DEEWR.

DEEWR (Department of Education, Employment and Workplace Relations). 2008b. *Better Practice Guide: ICT in Schools. June 2009 Update*. Canberra: DEEWR. Accessed 15 May 2013. Available from: http://www.deewr.gov.au.

DEEWR (Department of Education, Employment and Workplace Relations). 2008c. *National Secondary School Computer Fund. Round One Guidelines 2008–2011*. Canberra: DEEWR. Accessed 15 May 2013. Available from: http://www.deewr.gov.au.

DEEWR (Department of Education, Employment and Workplace Relations). 2008d. *Review of Legitimate and Additional Financial Implications of the National Secondary School Computer Fund*. Canberra: DEEWR. Accessed 15 May 2013. Available from: http://www.deewr.gov.au.

DEEWR (Department of Education, Employment and Workplace Relations). 2009. *National Partnership Agreement on the Digital Education Revolution*. Canberra: DEEWR. Accessed 15 May 2013. Available from: http://foi.deewr.gov.au/node/266.

DEEWR (Department of Education, Employment and Workplace Relations). 2010a. *ICT Innovation Fund Guidelines 2010–2012*. Canberra: DEEWR. Accessed 13 May 2013. Available from: http://deewr.gov.au/ict-innovation-fund.

DEEWR (Department of Education, Employment and Workplace Relations). 2010b. *School Broadband Connectivity Survey 2010*. Canberra: DEEWR. Accessed 13 May 2013. Available from: http://docs.education.gov.au/node/703.

DEEWR (Department of Education, Employment and Workplace Relations). 2012. *Annual Report 2011–2012*. Canberra: DEEWR.

DEEWR (Department of Education, Employment and Workplace Relations). 2013a. *Budget. Agency Budget Statements 2013–2014. Outcomes and Performance. Outcome 2*. Canberra: DEEWR. Accessed 17 June 2013. Available from: http://deewr.gov.au/portfolio-budget-statements-2013–14.

DEEWR (Department of Education, Employment and Workplace Relations). 2013b. *Schools Assistance Act 2008. Administrative Guidelines*. Canberra: DEEWR. Accessed 21 June 2013. Available from: http://foi.deewr.gov.au/system/files/doc/other/saa_administrative-guidelines-2013-update.docx.

Department of Education. Community Information Service. 1998. *Learning Technologies in Victorian Schools: 1998–2001*. Melbourne: Department of Education.

DEST (Department of Education, Science and Training). 2007. *Australian Government Programmes for Schools, Quadrennial Administrative Guidelines 2005–2008, 2007 Update*. Canberra: DEST. Accessed 1 June 2009. Available from: http://www.dest.gov.au.

DETYA (Department of Employment, Education, Training and Youth Affairs). 2000a. *Annual Report 1999–2000*. Canberra: DETYA. Accessed 15 April 2008. Available from: http://www.dest.gov.au.

DETYA (Department of Employment, Education, Training and Youth Affairs). 2000b. *Learning for the Knowledge Society: An Education and Training Action Plan for the Information Economy*. Canberra: DETYA. Accessed 15 April 2008. Available from: http://www.dest.gov.au.

Diebold, J. 1962. 'The application of information technology'. *Annals of the American Academy of Political and Social Science* 340: 38–45.

Dieterich, D. 1972. 'The magical, mystical, mechanical schoolmaster, or, the computer in the English classroom'. *The English Journal* 61 (9): 1388–1395.

Directorate of School Education. 1994. *Technologies for Enhanced Learning. Current and Future Use of Technologies in School Education*. Report of the Victorian Government Working Party on the Use of Technology as an Education and Communications Facility in Schools. Melbourne: Directorate of School Education.

Drury, B. 1999. 'Magical markets'. *Sydney Morning Herald*. Accessed 5 May 2013. Available from: http://newstore.fairfax.com.au/apps/viewDocument.ac?page=1&sy=nstore&kw=new+economy&pb=sag&pb=age&pb=smh&dt=enterRange&dr=1month&sd=06%2F06%2F1999&ed=03%2F03%2F2000&so=relevance&sf=text&sf=headline&rc=100&rm=200&sp=adv&clsPage=1&docID=news991208_0560_2344.

Dudley, J; Vidovich, L. 1995. *The Politics of Education. Commonwealth Schools Policy 1973–1995*. Camberwell: ACER.

Durbridge, R. 2009. 'National School Curriculum: The Politics of Curriculum in Gillard's "Education Revolution"'. *Arena* 103: 6–7.

Early Childhood Teachers Association. 2008. *COAG Working Group on the Productivity Agenda. Education, Skills, Training and Early Childhood Development. 12 June 2008. Open Day Program*. Accessed 16 April 2013. Available from: http://www.ecta.org.au/_dbase_upl/08_COAG_12%20June.pdf.

Economist. 2013. 'New technology is poised to disrupt America's schools, and then the world's'. Accessed 2 July 2013. Available from: http://www.economist.com/news/briefing/21580136-new-technology-poised-disrupt-americas-schools-and-then-worlds-catching-last.

Education Business Weekly. 2009. 'New South Wales Department of Education and Training selects Adobe for Digital Education Revolution Initiative'. May 6: 5.

Emmery, M. 1999. *Industry Policy in Australia*. Research Paper No. 3, Parliamentary Library. Canberra: Parliament of Australia. Accessed 6 September 2013. Available from: http://www.aph.gov.au/About_Parliament/Parliamentary_Departments/Parliamentary_Library/pubs/rp/rp9900/2000RP03.

Fahrer, J. 2006. 'Broadband in Australia: Present and future'. *The Melbourne Review* 2 (2): 37–43.

Fairclough, N. 1992. *Discourse and Social Change*. Cambridge: Polity Press.

Fairclough, N. 2000a. 'Discourse, social theory, and social research: The discourse of welfare reform'. *Journal of Sociolinguistics* 4 (2): 163–195.

Fairclough, N. 2000b. *New Labour, New Language*. London: Routledge.

Fairclough, N. 2001. 'The dialectics of discourse'. *Textus* 14 (2): 231–242. Accessed 6 July 2005. Available from: http://www.ling.lancs.ac.uk/staff/norman/2001a.

Fairclough, N. 2003. *Analysing Discourse*. London: Routledge.

Fairclough, N; Wodak, R. 1997. 'Critical discourse analysis'. In *Discourse as Social Interaction*, edited by van Dijk, T. London: Sage Publications: 259–284.

Falk, H. 1981. 'The small computer stands tall'. *Nation's Business* 69 (11): 77–81.

Fletcher, J; Atkinson, R. 1972. 'Evaluation of the Stanford CAI program in initial reading'. *Journal of Educational Psychology* 63 (6): 597–602.

Galperin, H. 2004a. 'Beyond interests, ideas and technology: An institutional approach to communication and information policy'. *The Information Society* 20 (3): 159–168.

Galperin, H. 2004b. *New Television, Old Politics. The Transition to Digital TV in the United States and Britain*. Cambridge: Cambridge University Press.

Gans, J; King, S. 2010. '"Big Bang" Telecommunications Reform'. *The Australian Economic Review* 43 (2): 179–186.

Garrett, P. 2010. *Education Ministers Endorse Australian Curriculum*. Media Release. 8 December 2010. Accessed 30 May 2013. Available from: http://ministers.deewr.gov.au/garrett/education-ministers-endorse-australian-curriculum.

Gatty, B. 1983. 'Personal computers are coming of age'. *Nation's Business* 71 (9): 46–49.

Gee, J; Hull, G; Lankshear, C. 1996. *The New Work Order: Behind the Language of the New Capitalism*. St Leonards NSW: Allen and Unwin.

Gillard, J. 2010. *$40m for Teachers' Professional Development in ICT*. Media release. Accessed 13 June 2013. Available from: http://ministers.deewr.gov.au/gillard/40m-teachers%E2%80%99-professional-development-ict.

Glennan, T Jr. 1997. *Surplus Federal Computers for Schools. An Assessment of the Early Implementation of EO 12999*. Santa Monica CA: Rand Corporation. ED 409 887.

Goatly, A. 1997. *The Language of Metaphor*. Harlow England: Longman.

Goatly, A. 2007. *Washing the Brain – Metaphor and Hidden Ideology*. Amsterdam: John Benjamins Publishing Company.

Goldsworthy, A, ed. 1980. *Technological Change – Impact of Information Technology 1980*. Canberra: Information Technology Council.

Gonski, D, chair. 2011. *Review of Funding for Schooling – Final Report*. Canberra: DEEWR. Accessed 10 December 2013. Available from: http://www.appa.asn.au/content/gonski-report/Review-of-Funding-for-Schooling-Final-Report-Dec-2011.pdf.

Gore, A. 1994. *Remarks Prepared for Delivery by Vice President Al Gore*. California: Royce Hall, UCLA Los Angeles. Accessed 1 June 2009. Available from: http://www. ibiblio.org/icky/speech2.html.

Grattan, M. 2007. 'A modestly priced digital revolution'. *Age*. Accessed 5 May 2013. Available from: http://newsstore.fairfax.com.au/apps/viewDocument.ac?page=1&sy=nstore&kw=digital+and+revolution&pb=age&pb=smh&dt=enterRange&dr=1month&sd=01%2F09%2F2007&ed=01%2F12%2F2007&so=relevance&sf=text&sf=headline&rc=100&rm=200&sp=adv&clsPage=1&docID=AGE071127BK1UM5FSDAI.

Grattan, M; Murphy, K. 2007. 'Howard splurges another $9bn'. *Age*. Accessed 5 May 2013. Available from: http://newsstore.fairfax.com.au/apps/viewDocument.ac?page=1&sy=nstore&kw=howard+and+splurges&pb=age&pb=smh&dt=enterRange&dr=1month&sd=01%2F09%2F2007&ed=01%2F12%2F2007&so=relevance&sf=text&sf=headline&rc=100&rm=200&sp=adv&clsPage=1&docID=AGE071113RB27A653VOA.

Grayson, L. 1971. 'The US Office of Education and computer activities: A summary of support'. *Educational Technology* November: 51–54.

Gregory, R; Stricker, P. 1981. 'Youth employment: The Australian experience of the 1970s. An overview paper'. In *Youth Employment, Education and Training*, edited by Baird, C; Gregory, R; Gruen, F. Canberra: CEPR, Australian National University: 1.1–1.50.

Griffey, J. 2012. 'The rise of the tablet'. *Library Technology Reports* April: 7–13.

Groen, M. 2012. 'NCLB – The educational accountability paradigm in historical perspective'. *American Educational History Journal* 39 (1): 1–14.

Grover, P. 1980. 'Computer usage in education'. Unpublished Master of Educational Studies project. Melbourne: Monash University.

Grundy, S; Bigum, C; Evans, P; McKenzie, D. 1987. 'Teaching teachers – Educational computing and the professional development of teachers'. In *Coming to Terms with Computers in Schools*, edited by Bigum, C; Bonser, S; Evans, P; Groundwater-Smith, S; Grundy, S; Kemmis, S; McKenzie, D; McKinnon, D; O'Connor, M; Straton, R; Willis, S. Geelong Vic: Deakin Institute for Studies in Education: 42–61.

Gude, P. 1998. *Blueprint for Learning Technologies*. Media release. Melbourne: Office of the Minister for Education. Accessed 2 July 2007. Available from: http://www.legislation.vic.gov.au.

Hawke, B. 1983. *ALP Election Policy Speech*. Accessed 20 June 2013. Available from: http://electionspeeches.moadoph.gov.au/speeches/1983-bob-hawke.

Held, D; McGrew, A; Goldblatt, D; Perraton, J. 1999. *Global Transformations: Politics, Economics and Culture*. Oxford: Polity Press.

Herszberg, N. 1986. 'Computers in schools: The administration of the Commonwealth and State Education Departments' policies on computers in education as they affect primary schools'. Unpublished Master of Educational Studies project. Melbourne: Monash University.

Hoos, I. 1960. 'The sociological impact of automation in the office'. *Management Technology* 1 (2): 10–19.

Hosie, R. 1965. 'The quiet nightmare revolution part 1'. *The Educational Magazine* 22 (1): 147–153.

House of Representatives. 2012. *Australian Education Bill 2012. Second Reading Speech*. 13639–13644. Canberra: Parliament of Australia. Accessed 5 May 2013. Available from: http://parlinfo.aph.gov.au/parlInfo/genpdf/chamber/hansardr/50ef4858-02bd-437b-a64f-599769ecfec6/0005/hansard_frag.pdf;fileType=application%2Fpdf.

IBM. n.d. *A Snapshot of IBM Milestones in Australia*. Accessed 30 July 2013. Available from: http://www-03.ibm.com/press/au/en/presskit/34675.wss.

Industry Commission. 1995. *Computer Hardware Software and Related Service Industries.* Report No. 46. Canberra: AGPS. Accessed 16 April 2009. Available from: http://www.pc.gov.au/_data/assets/pdf_file/0009/6993/46compha.pdf.

Intel Corporation. 2010. *Australia Experiences a Digital Education Revolution.* Accessed 13 May 2013. Available from: http://download.intel.com/education/transformation/Ed_Transformation_CS_Australia_LoRes.pdf.

James, M. 1994. *Broadband Convergence on the Digital Information Superhighway.* Parliamentary Research Service, Background Paper No. 24. Canberra: Parliament of Australia. Accessed 30 May 2013. Available from: http://www.aph.gov.au/binaries/library/pubs/bp/1994-95/95bp24.pdf.

JCPAA (Joint Committee of Public Accounts and Audit). 2011. *Report 428. Review of Auditor-General's Reports Nos 16 to 46 2010–2011.* Canberra: Parliament of Australia. Accessed 30 May 2013. Available from: http://www.aph.gov.au/Parliamentary_Business/Committees/House_of_Representatives_Committees?url=info/npschedule.htm.

Johnson, P. 1983. *Modern Times. The World from the Twenties to the Eighties.* New York: Harper and Row.

Johnston, K. 1983. 'A discourse for all seasons? An ideological analysis of the Schools Commission Reports, 1973 to 1981'. *The Australian Journal of Education* 27 (1): 17–32.

Jones, B. 1983. *Sleepers, Wake!* New edition. Melbourne: Oxford University Press.

Joseph, R. 1996. 'The redefinition of Australian telecommunications policy: An historical overview'. *Telecommunications Journal of Australia* 46 (2): 51–63.

Kahn, R; Leiner, B; Cerf, V; Clark, D; Kleinrock, L; Lynch, D; Postel, J; Roberts, L; Wolff, S. 1997. 'The evolution of the Internet as a global information system'. *International Information and Library Review* 29: 129–151.

Karmel, P, chair. 1973. *Schools in Australia: Report of the Interim Committee for the Australian Schools Commission.* Canberra: AGPS.

Karmel, P; Brunt, M. 1963. *The Structure of the Australian Economy.* Melbourne: F W Cheshire.

Kearns, P; Grant, J. 2002. *The Enabling Pillars. Learning, Technology, Community, Partnership.* A Report on Australian Policies for Information and Communication Technologies in Education and Training. Kambah ACT: Global Learning Services. Accessed 1 October 2007. Available from: http://www.ictpolicy.edna.au/sibling/publications.

Keating, P. 1995. *A National Strategy for Information and Communications Services and Technologies.* Statement by the Prime Minister, Hon. P J Keating MP. Canberra. Accessed 19 December 2007. Available from: http://www.nla.gov.au/oz/gov/press/pm0495.html.

Kennedy, K. 1988. 'The policy context of curriculum reform in Australia in the 1980s'. *Australian Journal of Education* 32 (3): 357–374.

Kennedy, T. 1946. 'Electronic computer flashes answers, may speed engineering'. *New York Times* 15 February: 1–3.

Knight, J. 1992. 'The political economy of industrial relations in the Australian education industry, 1987 – 1991'. *Unicorn* 18 (4): 27–38.

Korporaal, G. 1995. 'PM backs acceleration to "Superhighway"'. *Sydney Morning Herald.* Accessed 5 May 2013. Available from: http://newsstore.fairfax.com.au/apps/viewDocument.ac?page=1&sy=nstore&kw=information+superhighway&pb=shd&pb=sag&pb=age&pb=smh&dt=enterRange&dr=1month&sd=01%2F01%2F1995&ed=30%2F01%2F1996&so=relevance&sf=text&sf=headline&rc=100&rm=200&sp=adv&clsPage=1&docID=news950302_0064_1524.

Kozma, R. 2011. 'A framework for ICT policies to transform education'. In *Transforming Education: The Power of ICT Policies*. Paris: UNESCO: 19–36.

KPMG Econtech. 2010. *Measuring the Impact of the Productivity Agenda*. Canberra: DEEWR. Accessed 18 July 2013. Available from: http://apo.org.au/node/21456.

Lankshear, C; Snyder, I; Green, B. 2000. *Teachers and Techno-literacy*. Crows Nest NSW: Allen and Unwin.

Levin, H; Rumberger, R. 1987. 'Educational requirements for new technologies: Visions, possibilities, and current realities'. *Educational Policy* 1 (3): 333–54.

Light, J. 2001. 'Rethinking the digital divide'. *Harvard Educational Review* 71 (4): 709–33.

Lingard, B. 1993. 'Corporate federalism: The emerging approach to policy-making for Australian schools'. In *Schooling Reform in Hard Times*, edited by Lingard, B; Knight, J; Porter, P. London: The Falmer Press: 24–35.

Lingard, B. 2000. 'Federalism in schooling since the Karmel Report (1973), *Schools in Australia*: from modernist hope to postmodernist performativity'. *Australian Educational Researcher* 27 (2): 25–61.

LNP (Liberal–National Party). 2013. *The Coalition's Policy for Schools: Students First*. Canberra: Liberal Party. Accessed 15 September 2013. Available from: http://www. liberal.org.au/our-policies.

Lowe, S. 1995. 'Blessed are the digitally deprived'. *Sydney Morning Herald*. Accessed 5 May 2013. Available from: http://newsstore.fairfax.com.au/apps/viewDocument.ac ?page=1&sy=nstore&kw=information+superhighway&pb=shd&pb=sag&pb=age&p b=smh&dt=enterRange&dr=1month&sd=01%2F01%2F1995&ed=30%2F01%2F1 996&so=relevance&sf=text&sf=headline&rc=100&rm=200&sp=adv&clsPage=1&d ocID=news950613_0098_1974.

Lowe, S. 1999. 'School's in for online HSC classes'. *Sydney Morning Herald*. Accessed 8 March 2013. Available from: http://newsstore.fairfax.com.au/apps/viewDocument. ac?page=1&sy=nstore&kw=school+and+online+and+HSC&pb=age&pb=smh&dt =enterRange&dr=1month&sd=01%2F01%2F1999&ed=31%2F12%2F1999&so=r elevance&sf=text&sf=headline&rc=100&rm=200&sp=adv&clsPage=1&docID=ne ws990729_0516_0604.

Lucarelli, B. 2003. 'Deindustrialisation under Labor 1983–1996'. *Journal of Australian Political Economy* 51: 77–102.

Luehrmann, A. 1981. 'Computer literacy – what should it be?' *The Mathematics Teacher* 74: 682–690.

Luke, A. 1995. 'Text and discourse in education: An introduction to critical discourse analysis'. *Review of Research in Education* 21: 3–48.

Luke, A. 1997. 'New narratives of human capital: Recent redirections in Australian educational policy'. *Australian Educational Researcher* 24 (2): 1–21.

Madden, M; Lenhart, A; Duggan, M; Cortesi, S; Gasser, U. 2013. *Teens and Technology 2013*. Washington DC: Pew Research Center. Accessed 20 October 2013. Available from: http://www.pewinternet.org/Reports/2013/Teens-and-Tech.aspx.

Magidson, E. 1978. 'Issue overview: Trends in computer-assisted instruction'. *Educational Technology* April: 5–8.

Manyika, J; Chui, M; Bughin, J; Dobbs, R; Bisson, P; Marrs, A. 2013. *Disruptive Technologies: Advances That Will Transform Life, Business and the Global Economy*. McKinsey Global Institute. Accessed 4 November 2013. Available from: http:// www.mckinsey.com/insights/business_technology/disruptive_technologies.

Marginson, S. 1997a. *Educating Australia. Government, Economy and Citizen Since 1960*. Cambridge: Cambridge University Press.

Marginson, S. 1997b. *Markets in Education*. St Leonards NSW: Allen and Unwin.

Martin, S. 1999. *Labor and Financial Deregulation. The Hawke/Keating Governments, Banking and New Labor*. PhD thesis. University of Wollongong. Accessed 31 May 2009. Available from: http://www.library.uow.edu.au/adt-nwu/public/adt-NWU20030720.114507.

Mason, J. 2000. 'EdNA. An historical snapshot'. *Post-Script* 2 (1): 110–119. Accessed 25 May 2009. Available from: http://www.edufac.unimelb.edu.au/insight/pscript.shtml.

Mayer, E, chair. 1992. *Key Competencies*. Report of the Committee to Advise the Australian Education Council and Ministers of Vocational Education, Employment and Training on Employment-related Key Competencies for Post-compulsory Education and Training. Melbourne: AEC. MOVEET.

McCann, D; Thorne, P. 2000. *The Last of the First. CSIRAC: Australia's First Computer*. Melbourne: University of Melbourne.

McDonnell, L. 2005. 'No Child Left Behind and the federal role in education: Evolution or revolution?' *Peabody Journal of Education* 80 (2): 19–38.

McDougall, A. 1980. *Computers and Post-primary Education in Victoria. A Study of Needs*. Report to the Computer Policy Committee. Melbourne: Monash University.

MCEETYA (Ministerial Council on Education, Employment, Training and Youth Affairs). 1989. *The Hobart Declaration on Schooling*. Hobart: MCEETYA. Accessed 15 June 2009. Available from: http://www.mceetya.edu.au/mceetya/hobart_declaration,11577.html.

MCEETYA (Ministerial Council on Education, Employment, Training and Youth Affairs). 1999. *The Adelaide Declaration on National Goals for Schooling in the Twenty-first Century*. Adelaide: MCEETYA. Accessed 12 April 2008. Available from: http://www.mceetya.edu.au/mceetya/nationalgoals/natgoals.htm#nat.

MCEETYA (Ministerial Council on Education, Employment, Training and Youth Affairs). 2003. *Draft Report of the MCEETYA ICT in Schools Taskforce*. Carlton South Vic: MCEETYA. Accessed 24 May 2009. Available from: http://www.myceetya.edu.au.

MCEETYA (Ministerial Council on Education, Employment, Training and Youth Affairs). 2004. *Bandwidth Implementation Plan 2004–2005*. Carlton South Vic: MCEETYA. Accessed 24 May 2009. Available from: http://www.myceetya.edu.au.

MCEETYA (Ministerial Council on Education, Employment, Training and Youth Affairs). 2005a. *Building a Knowledge Culture. An Education and Training Action Plan for the Information Economy 2005–2007*. Carlton South Vic: MCEETYA. Accessed 15 April 2008. Available from: http://www.myceetya.edu.au.

MCEETYA (Ministerial Council on Education, Employment, Training and Youth Affairs). 2005b. *MCEETYA Joint Statement on Education and Training in the Information Economy*. Carlton South Vic: MCEETYA. Accessed 15 April 2008. Available from: http://www.mceetya.edu.au/verve/_resources/infoeconomy2005_file.pdf.

MCEETYA (Ministerial Council on Education, Employment, Training and Youth Affairs). 2005c. *The ICT Literacy Report Years 6 and 10*. Carlton South Vic: Curriculum Corporation. Accessed 24 May 2009. Available from: http://www.myceetya.edu.au.

MCEETYA (Ministerial Council on Education, Employment, Training and Youth Affairs). 2006. *Report of the MCEETYA ICT in Schools Taskforce*. Carlton South Vic: MCEETYA. Accessed 24 May 2009. Available from: http://www.myceetya.edu.au.

MCEETYA (Ministerial Council on Education, Employment, Training and Youth Affairs). 2007. *National Assessment Program – ICT Literacy*. Carlton South Vic: MCEETYA. Accessed 24 May 2013. Available from: http://www.nap.edu.au/results-and-reports/national-reports.html.

MCEETYA (Ministerial Council on Education, Employment, Training and Youth Affairs). 2008a. *Communique, 17–18th April 2008*. Carlton South Vic: MCEETYA. Accessed 15 May 2013. Available from: http://www.mceecdya.edu.au/mceecdya/meetings,11402.html.

MCEETYA (Ministerial Council on Education, Employment, Training and Youth Affairs). 2008b. *Melbourne Declaration on Educational Goals for Young Australians*. Carlton South Vic: MCEETYA. Accessed 15 November 2013. Available from: http://www.mceecdya.edu.au/mceecdya/publications,11582.html.

MCEETYA (Ministerial Council on Education, Employment, Training and Youth Affairs). 2009. *National Assessment Program: Information and Communication Technology Literacy*. Carlton South Vic: MCEETYA. Accessed 12 May 2009. Available from: http://www.myceetya.edu.au.

MCEETYA ICT in Schools Taskforce. 2005. *Learning in an Online World Progress Report 2005*. Carlton South Vic: MCEETYA. Accessed 12 May 2008. Available from: http://www.myceetya.edu.au.

MCEETYA. MCVTE (Ministerial Council on Education, Employment, Training and Youth Affairs. Ministerial Council for Vocational and Technical Education). 2008. *Joint Ministerial Statement on Information and Communications Technologies in Australian Education and Training: 2008–2011*. Carlton South: MCEETYA. Accessed 15 May 2013. Available from: http://www.mceecdya.edu.au/mceecdya/publications,11582.html.

McMahon, W. 1968. 'The current state of the economy'. *Narration* 7 (5): 15–19.

McMorrow, J. 2003. 'Education policy'. In *The Hawke Government. A Critical Retrospective*, edited by Ryan, S; Bramston, T. North Melbourne: Pluto Press Australia: 184–201.

Meredyth, D; Russell, N; Blackwood, L; Thomas, J; Wise, P. 1999. *Real Time. Computers, Change and Schooling*. Canberra: DETYA.

Metiri Group. 2009. *National Trends Report: Enhancing Education through Technology (EETT) Round 6, Fiscal Year 2007*. Washington DC: The State Educational Technology Directors Association. Accessed 22 June 2013. Available from: http://www.setda.org.

Microsoft Corporation. 2010. *Australian Schools Deploy 83,000 Netbook Computers in Six Months*. Webpage. Accessed 18 June 2013. Available from: http://www.microsoft.com/casestudies/Microsoft-System-Center-Configuration-Manager-2007/New-South-Wales-Department-of-Education-and-Training/Australian-Schools-Deploy-83-000-Netbook-Computers-in-Six-Months/4000007061.

Molnar, A. 1971. 'Critical issues in computer-based learning'. *Educational Technology* August: 60–64.

Molnar, A. 1978. 'The next great crisis in American education: Computer literacy'. *Journal of Educational Technology Systems* 7 (3): 275–285.

Moont, S. 1984. 'Computer literacy: An anthropological viewpoint'. In *Computers and Education. Dreams and Reality*. Proceedings of the Second Australian Computer Education Conference, September 1984, Sydney, edited by Hughes, J. West Gosford NSW: Computer Education Group of New South Wales: 31–34.

Moore, B. 2004. *The Australian Concise Oxford Dictionary*. Fourth edition. South Melbourne: Oxford University Press.

Moyle, K. 2002. *Digital Technologies in Australian Public Schools: A Narrative Study of Government Policies*. PhD Thesis, Swinburne University. Accessed 27 February 2008. Available from: http://adt.lib.swin.edu.au/public/adt-VSWT20060721.132427.

Moyle, K. 2005. 'Computing technologies in school education: Policies and standards and standard policies'. Conference Proceedings, *The Australian Association for Research in Education*. Parramatta NSW: AARE. Accessed 27 February 2008. Available from: http://www.aare.edu.au/05pap/moy05462.pdf.

Moyle, K. 2010. *Building Innovation: Learning with Technologies*. Camberwell Vic: ACER.

Murphy, I. 2011. 'Educational reform and the enacted curriculum in English – A narrative from the field of the Digital Education Revolution'. *English in Australia* 46 (1): 62–72.

Myers, R, chair. 1980. *Technological Change in Australia*. Report of the Committee of Inquiry into Technological Change in Australia, Vol. 1. Canberra: AGPS.

NAA (National Archives of Australia). 1983a. Economic Policy Committee, Cabinet Minute, Decision No. 124 (EP), Submission No. 16 – 1983–1984 – Economic Policy Considerations. Canberra: National Archives of Australia.

NAA (National Archives of Australia). 1983b. Ryan, S. For Cabinet. Submission No. 114, To Establish a Computer Program, 5 May 1983. Canberra: National Archives of Australia.

NBEET (National Board of Employment, Education and Training). 1990. *A Clever Country? Australian Education and Training in Perspective*. NBEET Conference Proceedings, 1–3 November, Coffs Harbour. Accessed 8 April 2008. Available from: http://www.dest.gov.au/sectors/training_skills/publications_resources/indexes.

NBEET (National Board of Employment, Education and Training). 1992. *Future Directions*. Canberra: AGPS.

NBEET (National Board of Employment, Education and Training). 1995a. *Annual Report 1994–1995*. Canberra: AGPS. Accessed 8 January 2008. Available from: http://www.dest.gov.au/sectors/training_skills/publications_resources/indexes.

NBEET (National Board of Employment, Education and Training). 1995b. *Converging Technology, Work and Learning*. Canberra: AGPS. Accessed 8 January 2008. Available from: http://www.dest.gov.au/sectors/training_skills/publications_resources/indexes.

NBEET (National Board of Employment, Education and Training). 1996. *Annual Report 1995–1996*. Canberra: AGPS. Accessed 8 January 2008. Available from: http://www.dest.gov.au/sectors/training_skills/publications_resources/indexes.

NCA (National Commission of Audit).1996. *Report to the Commonwealth Government*. Canberra: NCA. Accessed 22 May 2009. Available from: http://www.finance.gov.au/publications/archive-of-publications/ncoa/coaintro.htm.

Newhouse, P. 1998. 'The impact of portable computers on classroom learning environments'. *Australian Educational Computing* 13 (1): 5–11.

Noble, D. 1984. *Forces of Production. A Social History of Automation*. New York: Alfred A. Knopf.

Noble, G. 1999. 'Domesticating technology. Learning to live with your computer'. *Australian Journal of Communication* 26 (2): 59–75.

NOIE (National Office for the Information Economy). 2002. *Broadband in Education: Availability, Initiatives and Issues*. Canberra: DCITA. Accessed 15 April 2008. Available from: http://www.archive.dcita.gov.au/__data/assets/pdf_file/0018/20448/NOIE-AusNatBB-23-1.pdf.

NOIE (National Office for the Information Economy). 2004. *Australia's National Broadband Strategy*. Canberra: DCITA. Accessed 15 April 2008. Available from: http://www.archive.dcita.gov.au/2007/12/national_broadband_strategy.

NSF (National Science Foundation). 1971. *National Science Foundation Annual Report.* Washington DC: US Government Printing Office. Accessed 19 October 2005. Available from: http://128.150.4.107/pubs/1970/annualreports.

NTIA (National Telecommunications and Information Administration). 2010. *Exploring the Digital Nation: Home Broadband Internet Adoption in the United States.* Washington DC: NTIA. Accessed 7 November 2013. Available from: http://www. ntia.doc.gov/report/2010/exploring-digital-nation-home-broadband-internet-adoption-united-states.

NTIA (National Telecommunications and Information Administration). 2013. *Exploring the Digital Nation: America's Emerging Online Experience.* Washington DC: NTIA. Accessed 7 November 2013. Available from: http://www.ntia.doc.gov/report/2013/exploring-digital-nation-americas-emerging-online-experience.

OECD (Organisation for Economic Co-operation and Development). 1998a. *A Borderless World: Realising the Potential of Global Electronic Commerce.* Conference Conclusions, 7–9 October 1998, Ottawa, Canada. Paris: OECD. Accessed 7 October 2008. Available from: http://www.ottawaoecdconference.org/english/homepage.html.

OECD (Organisation for Economic Co-operation and Development). 1998b. *A Borderless World: Realising the Potential of Global Electronic Commerce, OECD Action Plan for Electronic Commerce.* Paris: OECD. Accessed 7 October 2008. Available from: http://www.ottawaoecdconference.org/english/homepage.html.

OECD (Organisation for Economic Co-operation and Development). 2005. *Are Students Ready for a Technology-rich World?* Paris: OECD. Accessed 15 November 2013. Available from: http://www.oecd.org/education/school/programmeforinternationalstudentassessmentpisa/35995145.pdf.

OECD. CERI (Organisation for Economic Co-operation and Development. Centre for Educational Research and Innovation). 1998. *New Developments in Educational Software and Multimedia.* Background Paper Prepared for the OECD Ministerial Conference: *A Borderless World: Realising the Potential of Global Electronic Commerce.* 7–9 October 1998 Ottawa, Canada. Accessed 7 April 2008. Available from: http://www.ottawaoecdconference.org/english/homepage.html.

O'Regan, T; Ryan, M. 2004. 'From multimedia to digital content and applications: Remaking policy for the digital content industries'. *Media International Australia incorporating Culture and Policy* 112: 28–49.

Papert, S. 1972. 'Teaching children thinking'. *Mathematics Teaching* 58: 2–7.

Parkin, A; Anderson, G. 2007. 'The Howard Government, regulatory federalism and the transformation of Commonwealth–State relations'. *Australian Journal of Political Science* 42 (2): 295–314.

Parliament of Australia. 1991. *Bounty Legislation Amendment Bill 1991.* Accessed June 5 2009. Available from: http://parlinfo.aph.gov.au.

Pearcey, T. 1988. *A History of Australian Computing.* Caulfield East: Chisholm Institute of Technology.

Penter, K; Sully, J. 1984. 'The coming backlash against computer education'. In *Computers and Education. Dreams and Reality.* Proceedings of the Second Australian Computer Education Conference, September 1984, Sydney, edited by Hughes, J. West Gosford NSW: Computer Education Group of New South Wales: 251–255.

Perkins, D. 1985. 'The fingertip effect: How information-processing technology shapes thinking'. *Educational Researcher* 14 (7): 11–17.

Peters, M. 2001. 'National education policy constructions of the "knowledge economy": Towards a critique'. *Journal of Educational Enquiry* 2 (1): 1–22.

Philipson, M, ed. 1962. *Automation. Implications for the Future*. New York: Vintage Books.

Potter, B. 1995. 'New Optus plan puts schools on Information Superhighway'. *Age*. Accessed 5 May 2013. Available from: http://newsstore.fairfax.com.au/apps/viewDocument.ac?page=1&sy=nstore&kw=information+superhighway&pb=shd&pb=sag&pb=age&pb=smh&dt=enterRange&dr=1month&sd=01%2F01%2F1995&ed=30%2F01%2F1996&so=relevance&sf=text&sf=headline&rc=100&rm=200&sp=adv&clsPage=1&docID=news950628_0227_7049.

Prasser, S. 1997. 'Public management 1996: Once more unto the breach'. *Australian Journal of Public Administration* 56 (1): 110–118.

Productivity Commission. 1995. *Report on Government Service Provision 1995*. Canberra: Productivity Commission. Accessed 15 November 2013. Available from: http://www.pc.gov.au/gsp/rogs/1995.

Pugh, E; Aspray, W. 1996. 'Creating the computer industry'. IEEE *Annals of the History of Computing* 18 (2): 7–17.

Reed, L. 2000. 'Domesticating the personal computer: The mainstreaming of a new technology and the critical management of a widespread technophobia'. *Critical Studies in Media Communication* 17 (2): 159–185.

Reisigl, M; Wodak, R. 2001. *Discourse and Discrimination. Rhetorics of Racism and Antisemitism*. London: Routledge.

Richardson, D. 1997. *Industry Policy: Mortimer, Goldsworthy and The Economist Intelligence Unit*. Current Issues Brief 4 1997–1998. Canberra: Parliament of Australia. Accessed 12 March 2008. Available from: http://www.aph.gov.au/library/pubs/cib/1997-98/98cib04.htm.

Richtmyer, R. 1965. 'The post-war computer development'. *The American Mathematical Monthly* 72 (2): 8–14.

Rizvi, F; Kemmis, S. 1987. *Dilemmas of Reform: An Overview of Issues and Achievements of the Participation and Equity Program in Victorian Schools 1984–1986*. Geelong Vic: Deakin Institute for Studies in Education, Deakin University.

Rizvi, F; Lingard, B. 2010. *Globalizing Education Policy*. Abingdon Oxon and New York: Routledge.

Roberts, L. 1983. 'The computer age comes to our nation's classrooms'. *Theory into Practice* 22 (4): 308–312.

Roberts, L. 1998. *Reaching the President's Technology Literacy Challenge: What's Next?* Proceedings of the Families, Technology, and Education Conference, October 30 – November 1, 1997, Chicago Il, ED 424 991.

Rolley, C. 1995. 'Wired for work'. *Sydney Morning Herald*. Accessed 3 May 2013. Available from: http://newsstore.fairfax.com.au/apps/viewDocument.ac?page=1&sy=nstore&kw=convergence&pb=shd&pb=sag&pb=age&pb=smh&dt=enterRange&dr=1month&sd=01%2F01%2F1995&ed=30%2F01%2F1996&so=relevance&sf=text&sf=headline&rc=100&rm=200&sp=adv&clsPage=1&docID=news950526_0139_7071.

Rose, N. 1999. *Powers of Freedom. Reframing Public Thought*. Cambridge: Cambridge University Press.

Rosenzweig, R. 1998. 'Wizards, bureaucrats, warriors and hackers: Writing the history of the Internet'. *American Historical Review* 103 (5): 1530–1552.

Rudd, K. 2007. *Campaign Launch Speech*. Brisbane: ALP. Accessed 14 November 2013. Available from: http://electionspeeches.moadoph.gov.au/speeches/2007-kevin-rudd.

Rudd, K; Conroy, S; Tanner, L. 2007. *New Directions for Communications. A Broadband Future for Australia – Building a National Broadband Network*. Canberra: ALP. Accessed 11 November 2007. Available from: http://www.kevin07.com.au.

Rudd, K; Smith, S. 2007. *The Australian Economy Needs an Education Revolution*. Canberra: ALP. Accessed 11 November 2007. Available from: http://www.kevin07.com.au.

Rudd, K; Smith, S; Conroy, S. 2007. *A Digital Education Revolution*. Accessed 11 November 2007. Available from: http://www.kevin07.com.au.

Schnaars, S; Carvalho, S. 2004. 'Predicting the market evolution of computers: Was the revolution really unseen?' *Technology and Society* 26: 1–16.

'School Computer Seminar'. 1969. *Education News* 12 (2): April: 17.

Selfe, C. 1999. *Technology and Literacy in the Twenty-first Century: The Importance of Paying Attention*. Carbondale Il: Southern Illinois Press.

Shaul, M; Ganson, H. 2005. 'The No Child Left Behind Act of 2001: The federal government's role in strengthening accountability for student performance'. *Review of Research in Education* 29: 151–165.

Shaw, A. 1966. *The Economic Development of Australia*. Melbourne: Longmans.

Shears, L, ed. 1995. *Computers and Schools*. Camberwell Vic: ACER.

Shears, L; Dale, E. 1983. *Computers in Education*. A Report to the Honourable Robert Fordham MP, Minister of Education. Melbourne: Office of the Coordinator General of Education.

Sherington, G. 1990. 'Organisation and control in Australian schools'. *A Clever Country? Australian Education and Training in Perspective*. NBEET, Conference Proceedings, 1–3 November, Coffs Harbour: 98–99. Accessed 8 April 2008. Available from: http://www.dest.gov.au/sectors/training_skills/publications_resources/indexes.

Smart, D; Dudley, J. 1990. 'Education policy'. In *Hawke and Australian Public Policy*, edited by Jennett, C; Stewart, R. South Melbourne: MacMillan: 204–222.

Smith, B; de Ferranti, B. 1976. *Computers and the Future of Education*. Centre for Continuing Education, Occasional Papers in Continuing Education, No 15. Canberra: The Australian National University.

Smith, M; Levin, J; Cianci, J. 1997. 'Beyond a legislative agenda: Education policy approaches of the Clinton administration'. *Educational Policy* 11 (2): 209–226.

Snyder, I, ed. 2002. *Silicon Literacies. Communication, Innovation and Education in the Electronic Age*. London: Routledge.

Snyder, I. 2008. *The Literacy Wars*. Crows Nest NSW: Allen and Unwin.

Solo, R. 1963. 'Automation: Technique, mystique, critique'. *The Journal of Business* 36 (2): 166–178.

Spender, D. 2007. 'Digi-kids and a new way of learning'. *Sydney Morning Herald*. Accessed 5 May 2013. Available from: http://newsstore.fairfax.com.au/apps/viewDocument.ac?page=1&sy=nstore&kw=internet+and+education&pb=all_ffx&dt=enterRange&dr=1month&sd=1%2F1%2F2007&ed=30%2F12%2F2007&so=relevance&sf=text&sf=headline&rc=200&rm=200&sp=adv&clsPage=1&docID=SMH0705191F7R279IBQN.

Stager, G. 2000. 'Dream bigger'. In *Transforming Learning... an Anthology of Miracles in Technology-rich Classrooms*, edited by Little, J; Dixon, B. Port Melbourne: Kids Technology Foundation: 109–122.

Stahl, W. 1995. 'Venerating the black box: Magic in media discourse on technology'. *Science, Technology, and Human Values* 20 (2): 234–258.

Stedward, G. 2003. 'Education as industrial policy: New Labour's marriage of the social and the economic'. *Policy and Politics* 31 (2): 139–152.

Stewart, B. 1998. 'National Office for the Information Economy'. *Bulletin of Public Administration* 88: 83–86.

Stolarchuk, E; Fisher, D. 2001. 'First years of laptops in science classrooms result in more learning about computers than science'. *Issues in Educational Research* 11: 25–39.

Suppes, P. 1966. 'The uses of computers in education'. *Scientific American* 215: 206–223.

Sussman, G. 1997. *Communication, Technology and Politics in the Information Age.* Thousand Oaks: Sage Publications.

Swan, W; Tanner, L. 2010. *Australia's Federal Relations. Budget Paper No 3.* Canberra: Treasury. Accessed 21 June 2013. Available from: http://www.budget.gov.au/2013-14/content/bp3/html/index.htm.

Swan, W; Wong, P. 2013. *Budget. Budget Measures. Budget Paper No. 2 2013–2014.* Canberra: Treasury. Accessed 21 June 2013. Available from: http://www.budget.gov.au/2013-14/content/bp2/download/BP2_consolidated.pdf.

Sweeney, J; McIsaac, K. 2012. *Student Devices and the Digital Education Revolution: Lessons Learned.* IBRS. Accessed 13 May 2013. Available from: http://i.dell.com/sites/content/business/solutions/whitepapers/en/Documents/student-devices-and-the-digital-education-revolution-lessons-learned-ibrs-australia.pdf.

Sydney Morning Herald 2007. 'Move over Grandpa and let me at the computer'. *Sydney Morning Herald.* Accessed 15 May 2013. Available from: http://newsstore.fairfax.com.au/apps/viewDocument.ac?page=1&sy=nstore&kw=move+and+Grandpa&pb=age&pb=smh&dt=enterRange&dr=1month&sd=01%2F11%2F2007&ed=30%2F11%2F2007&so=relevance&sf=text&sf=headline&rc=10&rm=200&sp=adv&clsPage=1&docID=SMH071115SV6GP5FCBQT.

Sydney Morning Herald. 2013. 'Christopher Pyne floats privatisation of HECS debt'. *Sydney Morning Herald.* Accessed 30 October 2013. Available from: http://www.smh.com.au/federal-politics/political-news/christopher-pyne-floats-privatisation-of-hecs-debt-20131029-2wcic.html.

Tarica, E. 2007. 'Trouble in Cyberia'. *Age.* Accessed 15 May 2013. Available from: http://newsstore.fairfax.com.au/apps/viewDocument.ac?page=1&sy=nstore&kw=internet&pb=all_ffx&dt=enterRange&dr=1month&sd=1%2F1%2F2007&ed=31%2F12%2F2007&so=relevance&sf=text&sf=headline&rc=200&rm=200&sp=adv&clsPage=1&docID=AGE0710222A6N47HDSVD.

Tate, M. 1982. 'Discussion of matter of public importance'. Senate *Hansard*, 2 December: 3065. Canberra: Parliament of Australia. Accessed 27 May 2009. Available from: http://parlinfo.aph.gov.au.

Tatnall, A. 1992. 'Computing and education: The business connection'. In *Computing the Clever Country?* ACEC 92 Proceedings, Tenth Annual Australian Computing in Education Conference, 5–8 July, Melbourne, 1992. Richmond North Vic: Computing in Education Group of Victoria: 523–526.

Tatnall, A. 1993. *A Curriculum History of Business Computing in Victorian Tertiary Institutions from 1960–1985.* MA thesis, Deakin University. Accessed 5 May 2009. Available from: http://tux.lib.deakin.edu.au.

Tatnall, A; Davey, B. 2004. 'Streams in the history of computer education in Australia'. In *History of Computing in Education,* edited by Impagliazzo, J; Lee, J. Boston: Kluwer Academic Publishers, IFIP: 83–90.

Tatnall, A; Davey, B. 2006. 'Early computer awareness courses in Australian secondary schools'. In *History of Computing and Education 2,* edited by Impagliazzo, J. Boston: Springer: 107–116.

Taylor, S. 2004. 'Researching educational policy and change in "new times": Using critical discourse analysis'. *Journal of Education Policy* 19 (4): 433–451.

Taylor, S; Rizvi, F; Lingard, B; Henry, M. 1997. *Educational Policy and the Politics of Change.* London: Routledge.

Teese, R; Polesel, J. 2003. *Undemocratic Schooling. Equity and Quality in Mass Secondary Education in Australia.* Carlton Vic: Melbourne University Press.

The White House. 2013. *ConnectEd: President Obama's Plan for Connecting All Schools to the Digital Age*. Accessed 16 November 2013. Available from: http://www.whitehouse.gov/sites/default/files/docs/connected_fact_sheet.pdf.

Thorneycroft, B. 1967. 'Computer appreciation'. *The Secondary Teacher* June: 30–33.

Thornton, B; Linton-Simpkins, F; Stanley, P; Locksley, G. 1983. *Report on Computers in Australia III*. Sydney: Foundation for Australian Resources.

Time. 1950a. 'Mark III. Can man build a superman?'. Cover. Accessed 1 June 2009. Available from: http://www.time.com/time/covers/0,16641,19500123,00.html.

Time. 1950b. 'The thinking machine'. Accessed 1 June 2009. Available from: http://www.time.com/time/magazine/article/0,9171,858601,00.html.

Time. 1983a. 'The computer, machine of the year'. Cover. Accessed 1 June 2009. Available from: http://www.time.com/time/covers/0,16641,19830103,00.html.

Time. 1983b. 'A new world dawns'. Accessed 1 June 2009. Available from: http://www.time.com/time/magazine/article/0,9171,953631,00.html.

Tinkler, D; Lepani, B; Mitchell, J. 1996. *Education and Technology Convergence*. Canberra: AGPS. Accessed 8 January 2008. http://www.dest.gov.au/sectors/training_skills/publications_resources/indexes.

Toffler, A. 1970. *Future Shock*. London: Pan Books.

Tomazin, F. 2007. 'Howard's technical colleges to counter Rudd's hi-tech hijinks'. *Age*. Accessed 5 May 2013. Available from: http://newsstore.fairfax.com.au/apps/viewDocument.ac?page=1&sy=nstore&kw=hi-tech+and+hijinks&pb=all_ffx&dt=enterRange&dr=1month&sd=15%2F10%2F2007&ed=01%2F11%2F2007&so=relevance&sf=text&sf=headline&rc=10&rm=200&sp=adv&clsPage=1&docID=AGE071030E66TH4T0CN5.

Treasury. 2013. *National Plan for School Improvement*. Canberra: Treasury. Accessed 21 June 2013. Available from: http://www.budget.gov.au/2013-14/content/glossy/gonski_policy/download/NPSI.pdf.

Trinitas. 2000. *Delivering the Promise*. Hobart: Trinitas. Accessed 15 June 2009. Available from: http://www.thelearningfederation.edu.au/verve/_resources/trinitas.pdf.

UN (United Nations). Department of Economic and Social Affairs. Statistical Office. 1971. *Demographic Yearbook*. New York: United Nations. Accessed 30 June 2009. Available from: http://unstats.un.org/unsd/demographic/products/dyd/dyb2.htm.

UNESCO (United Nations Educational, Scientific and Cultural Organization). 2011. *Transforming Education: The Power of ICT Policies*. Paris: UNESCO. Accessed 20 November 2013. Available from: http://www.unescobkk.org/education/ict/online-resources/databases/ict-in-education-database/item/article/transforming-education-the-power-of-ict-policies-1/.

US Congress. 1991. *High-Performance Computing and National Research and Education Network Act of 1991*. Accessed 24 March 2009. Available from: http://thomas.loc.gov/cgibin/query/F?c102:2:./temp/~c102VqWhrw:e736: 25 3 09.

US Congress. House of Representatives. 1992. *Management of NSFNET*. Hearing before the Subcommittee on Science of the Committee on Science, Space, and Technology. One Hundred Second Congress, Second Session. Washington DC: US Government Printing Office. ED 350 986. Accessed 15 June 2009. Available from: http://www.eric.ed.gov/ERICDocs/data/ericdocs2sql/content_storage_01/0000019b/80/12/f1/8d.pdf.

US Congress. OTA (Office of Technology Assessment). 1981. *Computer-based National Information Systems: Technology and Public Policy*. Washington DC: US Government Printing Office. Accessed 24 March 2009. Available from: http://govinfo.library.unt.edu/ota/allota.htm.

US Congress. OTA (Office of Technology Assessment). 1982. *Informational Technology and Its Impact on American Education*. Washington DC: US Government Printing Office. Accessed 24 March 2009. Available from: http://govinfo.library.unt.edu/ota/allota.htm.

US Congress. OTA (Office of Technology Assessment). 1987. *Trends and Status of Computers in Schools: Use in Chapter 1 Programs and Use with Limited English Proficient Students*. Washington DC: US Government Printing Office. Accessed 24 March 2009. Available from: http://govinfo.library.unt.edu/ota/allota.htm.

US Congress. OTA (Office of Technology Assessment). 1988a. *Power On! New Tools for Teaching and Learning*. Washington DC: US Government Printing Office. Accessed 24 March 2009. Available from: http://govinfo.library.unt.edu/ota/allota.htm.

US Congress. OTA (Office of Technology Assessment). 1988b. *Technology and the American Economic Transition*. Washington DC: US Government Printing Office. Accessed 24 March 2009. Available from: http://govinfo.library.unt.edu/ota/allota.htm.

US Congress. OTA (Office of Technology Assessment). 1995. *Teachers and Technology: Making the Connection*. Washington DC: US Government Printing Office. Accessed 24 March 2009. Available from: http://govinfo.library.unt.edu/ota/allota.htm.

US Department of Education. 1981. *Report of the US Department of Education on Learning and Electronic Technology*. Washington DC: Department of Education. ED 211 068.

US Department of Education. 1996. *Getting America's Students Ready for the 21st Century: Meeting the Technology Literacy Challenge. A Report to the Nation on Technology and Education*. Washington DC: US Department of Education. Accessed 13 November 2013. Available from: http://www2.ed.gov/about/offices/list/os/technology/plan/national/index.html.

US Department of Education. 2000. *e-Learning – Putting a World-Class Education at the Fingertips of All Children*. Washington DC: US Department of Education. Accessed 15 November 2013. Available from: http://www2.ed.gov/about/offices/list/os/technology/reports/e-learning.pdf.

US Department of Education. 2009. *Race to the Top Program. Executive Summary*. Washington DC: US Department of Education. Accessed 15 November 2013. Available from: http://www2.ed.gov/programs/racetothetop/executive-summary.pdf.

US Department of Education. 2010. *Transforming American Education. Learning Powered by Technology*. Washington DC: US Department of Education. Accessed 15 November 2013. Available from: http://www.ed.gov/technology/netp-2010.

Usselman, S. 1996. 'Fostering a capacity for compromise: Business, government, and the stages of innovation in American computing'. *IEEE Annals of the History of Computing* 18 (2): 30–39.

Vergari, S. 2012. 'The limits of federal activism in education policy'. *Educational Policy* 26 (1): 15–34.

Victorian Auditor-General. 1999. *Report on Ministerial Portfolios May 1999*. Melbourne: Victorian Auditor-General. Accessed 30 April 2009. Available from: http://www.download.audit.vic.gov.au/old/mp99/mp99doe.htm.

Walker, R. 1991. 'The development of educational computing policy in the Victorian school system, 1976–1985'. *Australian Journal of Education* 35 (3): 292–313.

WCCIPAS (Working Conference on Computing and Information Processing in Australian Schools). 1982. *Report to Australian Education Council: Working Conference on Computing and Information Processing in Australian Schools*, 11–13 October, 1982. Perth: WCCIPAS.

Wearing, A; Carss, B; Fitzgerald, D. 1976. *Computers and Teaching in Australia.* Australian Advisory Committee on Research and Development in Education, AACRDE Report No. 6. Canberra: AGPS.

White, G. 2000. 'Australian education content bundling'. Adelaide: *Education.au* Limited. Accessed 15 April 2008. Available from: http://www.educationau.edu.au/jahia/webdav/site/myjahiasite/shared/papers/berlin.pdf.

White, M. 1986. 'Implications of the technologies for human learning'. *Peabody Journal of Education* 64 (1):155–170.

Williams, M; Bigum, C. 1994. 'Connecting schools to global networks: Curriculum option or national imperative?'. *Australian Educational Computing* September: 9–16.

Willingham, N. 1998. 'When is a policy not a policy? Australia's quest for a national information policy'. *The Australian Library Journal* May: 168–176.

Wodak, R. 2001a. 'The discourse-historical approach'. In *Methods of Critical Discourse Analysis*, edited by Wodak, R; Meyer, M. London: Sage Publications: 63–93.

Wodak, R. 2001b. 'What CDA is about – a summary of its history, important concepts and its developments'. In *Methods of Critical Discourse Analysis*, edited by Wodak, R; Meyer, M. London: Sage Publications: 1–13.

Wyzard, C. 2011. 'National Education Technology Plans: Implications for education'. *National Social Science Technology Journal* 1 (3): n.p. Accessed 15 November 2013. Available from: http://www.nssa.us/tech_journal/volume_1–3/vol1-3_article_10.htm.

Zammit, S. 1989. 'Evolution not revolution. An examination of the uses of computers in Australian education settings'. Unpublished PhD thesis. Melbourne: Monash University.